The Politics of Management Knowledge

The Politics of
Management Knowledge

edited by
Stewart R. Clegg and Gill Palmer

SAGE Publications
London • Thousand Oaks • New Delhi

First published 1996

SAGE Publications Ltd
6 Bonhill Street
London EC2A 4PU

SAGE Publications Inc
2455 Teller Road
Thousand Oaks, California 91320

SAGE Publications India Pvt Ltd
32, M-Block Market
Greater Kailash - I
New Delhi 110 048

British Library Cataloguing in Publication data

A catalogue record for this book is available from the
British Library

ISBN 0 8039 7933-9
ISBN 0 8039 7934-7 (pbk)

Library of Congress catalog card number 96-69550

Typeset by Photoprint, Torquay, Devon
Printed in Great Britain by Redwood Books,
Trowbridge, Wiltshire

Contents

Notes on Contributors

José Luis Alvarez is the Chair of the Organizational Behavior Department in the International Graduate School of Management (IESE) in Barcelona, Spain. He holds a PhD in Organizational Behavior from Harvard University. His research focuses on executive careers and educational methods in management education. He has published chapters in several books, and in journals, on these topics.

Mary Barrett is a Lecturer in the Department of Management at Brisbane's Queensland University of Technology (QUT). She is researching in the areas of both small business and female entrepreneurs and managers.

Gibson Burrell is justly famous for his earlier work with Gareth Morgan on *Sociological Paradigms and Organizational Analysis*, as well as for more recent work on postmodernism and on sex in organization analysis. He holds a Chair at Warwick University Business School. He is co-editor of the journal, *Organization*.

Jean-François Chanlat is a Professor in the École des Hautes Études Commerciales in Montréal. Originally from France, where he still researches and visits frequently, he is one of francophone Canada's leading organization theorists, best known for his work on the intersection of anthropology and organization analysis. He is the president of the International Sociology Association, Committee 17.

John Child is the Guinness Professor of Management Studies at the University of Cambridge. He was previously Dean of the Faculty of Management and Modern Languages at Aston University. He is one of the world's foremost organization theorists and was editor of the journal *Organization Studies* from 1992 to 1996.

Thomas Clarke is the DBM Professor of Corporate Governance at Leeds Business School, where he leads research into corporate governance, intellectual copyright and innovation. He was a key researcher for the Royal Society of Arts Inquiry into 'Tomorrow's Company', and has recently been working closely with the Performing Rights Society. Previously, he was a member of the Management Department at the University of St Andrews.

Stewart R. Clegg is Foundation Professor of Management, and Head of the Department of Management and Marketing, at the University of Western Sydney, Australia, and has previously held Chairs in the Universities of St Andrews and New England. He has contributed a number of books and articles to the literature largely in the fields of the analysis of power and organizations. He is a Fellow in the Academy of Social Sciences in Australia and was a past editor of the journal *Organization Studies*.

Paul du Gay is Lecturer in Sociology and Secretary of the Pavis Centre for

Sociological and Social Anthropological Studies at the Open University. His research work is located at the interface of cultural studies and the sociology of economic life. His most recent publications include *Consumption and Identity at Work* and, with Stuart Hall, *Questions of Cultural Identity*.

Richard Dunford is Professor of Management at the Victoria University of Wellington, New Zealand, having previously worked closely with Ian Palmer at UTS. He was a founder member, with Stewart Clegg, of the Asian Pacific Researchers in Organization Studies (APROS), and has been published in journals such as the *Administrative Science Quarterly*, as well as having written a best-selling book on *Organization Behaviour*.

Larry Dwyer is Associate Professor of Economics in the Faculty of Business and Technology at the University of Western Sydney. Currently he is researching in the areas of the management and economics of innovation, and the management of tourism. He was a member of the research team into 'embryonic industries' for the Karpin Inquiry into Leadership and Management for the Twenty First Century, established by the Australian Federal Government.

John Gray is a Lecturer in Management in the Faculty of Business and Technology at the University of Western Sydney. Currently he is researching in the areas of the service organizations and professional innovation. He was a member of the research team into 'embryonic industries' for the Karpin Inquiry into Leadership and Management for the Twenty First Century, established by the Australian Federal Government.

Klaus P. Hansen is a Professor of American Studies in the Universität Passau in Germany. As part of his research he decided to delve into the canon of management books by chief executives, which is how the contribution to this collection arose.

Eduardo Ibarra-Colado is a Professor at the Universidad Autónoma Metropolitana in Mexico City, where he has been researching Mexican higher education and theoretical issues in the analysis of organizations for a number of years. He is a leading figure in the Asian Pacific Researchers in Organization Studies (APROS) network, and a member of the National System of Researchers (SNI) in Mexico.

Sharon Kemp is an Associate Lecturer in Management in the Faculty of Business and Technology at the University of Western Sydney. Currently she is researching the management of scientific research centres. She was a member of the research team into 'embryonic industries' for the Karpin Inquiry into Leadership and Management for the Twenty First Century, established by the Australian Federal Government.

Jane Marceau is Professor in Public Policy in the Australian National University Research School of Social Sciences in Canberra, Australia, and has previously held the Eleanor Rathbone Chair of Social Policy at Liverpool University and worked 'or the OECD as a researcher in Paris. She has written and researched widely. In the past much of her research was in the area of education, its management and policy, while lately a key interest has been in areas of technological innovation.

Gill Palmer is Professor and Dean of the Faculty of Commerce at the University of

Wollongong, Australia, and was previously Head of the Department of Management and Professor and Foundation Director of the Key Centre in Strategic Management at Queensland University of Technology. She has contributed a number of books and articles to the literature, principally in the industrial relations and human resources areas.

Ian Palmer is an Associate Professor in the University of Technology, Sydney (UTS). He researches widely in the fields of human resource management, the management of cultural organizations and theoretical issues in the use of metaphor in organization analysis.

Harvie Ramsay is Professor of International Human Resource Management in the University of Strathclyde. He is one of the most cited and widely read contributors to the literature of industrial democracy, as author of the ground-breaking 'Cycles of Control' article in the journal *Sociology* in 1977. Since then he has contributed a number of articles and books to the literature, ranging across management, industrial relations, politics and strategy issues. He has researched internationally and has held a number of Visiting Professorships, including one at Griffith University in Brisbane, Australia.

Suzana Rodrigues is one of Brazil's foremost researchers in the organization field, holding a Professorial appointment at the Federal University of Minas Gerais. She holds a Bradford PhD and has been very active in the European Group for Organization Studies (EGOS) and the International Sociology Association (ISA) Research Committee in the Sociology of Organizations. In 1992 she was a Visiting Professor at the University of St Andrews, and is Visiting Fellow of Lucy Cavendish College, Cambridge.

Bengt Sandkull is a Professor in the University of Linköping Institute of Technology, where he has been at the forefront of research in Sweden into the conjuncture of labour process and organization theory, particularly where the use of new technologies is concerned. Recently he has been involved in considerable comparative research between Sweden and countries in Asia, including Australia.

Harry Scarbrough works at Warwick University Business School, where he researches issues in the management of technology and expertise. His latest (edited) book is *The Management of Expertise*.

Introduction: Producing Management Knowledge

Stewart R. Clegg and Gill Palmer

Management: Knowledge and Power

From its early modern form management has been defined through a set of practices that developed following the substantial increase in scale of organizations occurring towards the end of the nineteenth century (Clegg and Dunkerley 1980; Clegg 1990). At that time it was a 'rational' discourse: one that sought to impose specific conceptions of order on organizations. Management was a body of knowledge initially developed to render direct control, and then internal contracting, less essential. Initially, these forms of control were necessary to manage relatively large bodies of people collected together on one site, often in one factory or workshop. However, as scale increased forms of personal or direct control shifted and were supplemented by more rationalized, standardized and formalized bodies of knowledge designed to order organizational behaviour. Early managers operated in a context where the limited scale of productive organizations and their spatial and temporal distribution afforded opportunities for personal control by the owner or an agent of the owner. The basic procedural necessity was that of direct, personal control. Direct control was premised on shared physical proximity between those managed and those managing. In addition, it entailed the establishment of differentiated capacities for mastery, surveillance and 'super-vision' on the part of the managers, as well as a shared occupational or craft knowledge, through 'mastery', of what it was that was being managed.

Early management relied on two conditions. The first was shared knowledge, often derived from a common basis in craft knowledge, between those who were supervising and those being supervised. On this basis less opportunity existed for the latter to 'cheat' the former: that is, to work outside the limits of a rationality bounded by shared assumptions about the nature of the work being undertaken, and the appropriate organization and control of its labour process. The second was spatio-temporal proximity in a space inscribed within a physically limited setting. The vocabulary of early management, focused on 'super-vision', meaning vision from above, vision that is superordinate, and vision that advises, makes this clear. The conditions for supervision were not only a common body of knowledge of the labour process, shared between management and workers, but also opportunities for surveillance of the latter by the former. Frequently, management by supervision would entail simple devices for ensuring the maximization of the visibility of the workers whilst simultaneously minimizing the visibility of the managers. Supervision that took place from an elevated position, a walkway or a raised platform, or from a higher place with greater opportunities for looking out than for looking in, fulfilled these conditions.[1] Hence, in many older factories or workshops, or more contemporary ones that carry the same organizational assumptions, one will frequently find management offices overlook the shop-floor. No accident attached to this design.

The practices of management produce, reproduce and transform organizations. They irremediably involve both 'power' and 'knowledge', as the brief historical excursus suggests. They involve power, because organization everywhere is premised on imperatively coordinated relations, constituted through persuasive or coercive means. They involve knowledge, because these practices include training, drill, habituation, creativity, and above all, discourse: management shapes deeds through words, whether textual, as in best-selling management books, or verbal, in situated actions of managers practically involved in trying to communicate their sense of how things should be organized.

Most of what managers do is discursive: it consists of discussion, ordering, cajoling, pleading, condensing, summarizing, synthesizing, presenting, reporting – all activities that take place through the media of various texts and representations of immediate co-presence. Management mostly concerns words that do things, presented in many various arenas, sometimes personally, sometimes impersonally, sometimes in role, sometimes unscripted and unwarranted by the roles that exist already, the narratives already written. Management, above all, is a performative activity: it does what it says and it says what it does: its utterances and its actions are so frequently fused, so politically meshed.

In an influential formulation, management knowledge functioned as a means of instilling those limits that Herbert Simon (1957) referred to as 'bounded rationality'. Simon saw bounded rationality as referring to human behaviour that intends to be rational but is so only imperfectly. The limits to perfect rationality, according to Williamson (1975: 21) are 'imposed by neuropsychology' and 'language'. The former refers to the incapacity to receive, store, retrieve and process information without error. The latter refers to the intersubjective inability of individuals to articulate their knowledge adequately to others. In essence, bounded rationality occurs where there are reasons for imperfect market signals, in economic parlance.[2]

The development of forms of knowledge that successively reduced the need for unmediated control, proximity, and shared occupational or craft knowledge meant that management could not only conquer space and time

– manage at a physical or geographical distance – but also manage at an
intellectual distance. We know these forms of knowledge well: they are the
stuff of modern management, the currency of those 'writers on organizations' that Pugh and Hickson (1989) encapsulate so concisely, from Taylor
to Mintzberg. A starting point in understanding the effects of management
knowledge is to see one of their results as the creation of 'discipline', a
concern first located by Weber (1978) in the impersonal rule of bureaucracy, rule by rules.[3] Later writers were to build management knowledge
on similar disciplines: Taylor (1947) focused on the detailed prescription of
the division of labour; Fayol (1949) on the administrative structures
necessary to coordinate, communicate with, and control the large and
specialized organizations thus created; Follett (1941) on the communica-
tive competencies that new types of authority relations required; while
Mayo (1947) sought to provide a moral and ethical basis for new practices
of authority that, like Follett's vision, saw persuasion as a better basis for
organization than coercion. Since management first embraced the 'human
relations' focus that Mayo pioneered, the rate of innovation of new
persuasive approaches has increased markedly, as the chapters of this book
elaborate.

Cohen et al. (1972) suggest that different types of managers operate with
disciplinary solutions, ready to define their operating environment as one
in which things can be treated not just as problems but as those problems
that they can deal with. Of course, where there is more than one
disciplinary solution being proffered, power-plays would seem inevitable.
Managers (in the status sense of those with managerial power) do not all
share the same objectives, they do not always work together, and top
management power is not absolute. The sources of managerial power are
varied, distributed in complex ways, and often inconsistent with each
other. What they have in common is one thing: when managers make a
claim for a certain expertise or prerogative they tie themselves irrevocably
to specific knowledges – knowledges that are management theory, as a
result of these claims. Management is a process of social control, in which
power is likely to be distributed unevenly around the networks of all those
with an interest in influencing that control.

Management theory, as a body of knowledge, is thus a political discourse
par excellence. It is not only knowledge pertaining to power in terms of
complex relationships between individuals and corporate agencies,
between one organization and another organization, those relations that
frame the everyday intrigues, disclosures and dramas of working life. It is
also political knowledge in the ways that its theory legitimates some
practices while it marginalizes others, in the ways that its rhetoric provides
not just a legitimation but the *raison d'être* for what it is that some people
are able to do to some other people.[4]

Management, ideally, in so many of its own representations, confers
order, reduces uncertainty: it is the capacity to render the uncertain
manageable, to conquer space and time with strategic discretion, that

marks out the manager. How are such feats performed? What knowledge enables this mastery of the universe? Many of the books already in the marketplace would have it that it is science, and scientific knowledge, that renders the unknown knowable, the unpredictable predictable, the unmalleable malleable. Yet, in this volume, we want the reader to think of management less in terms of dominating or predicting nature and more in terms of wisdom in applying knowledges, knowledges of ingredients that are to be found in the local environment or that have been traded into it. These knowledges focus on blending these elements, shaping them to the custom of local taste and the resources that local markets make available. Sometimes the markets that are local also will be global, because of the important role that local knowledge has in the world economy, as is the case with North America; other times they are strictly local, restricted to specific communities defined by a particular language, by specific writers, and by particular practice.

The globalization of management towards the end of the twentieth century, together with the accelerating rate of technological change, mean new challenges for existing management knowledge. Primarily a North American and English-language phenomenon, it is now confronted by issues of not only technical discontinuity but also cultural fragmentation, as organizations implode national and cultural boundaries. Yet, any knowledge through which culture may be transcended is itself culture bound, tied up in local recipes, local situations. This forms one of the fundamental paradoxes of management.

Management as Recipes of Knowledge

Management is less a science and more like cookbook knowledge: it is knowledge of recipes and their application, we think. Many of the best-selling texts present management as a form of recipe knowledge.[5] The notion of practical understandings as 'recipes' is not new: it goes back at least to Schutz (1962; 1964; 1966; 1967), and has been used widely in comparative analysis of organizations, as for instance in the work of Whitley (1992). This introduction builds on this ground by framing the politics of management knowledge through the metaphor of 'recipes'.

How rationality is bounded, how behaviour is ordered, how individuals are controlled and creative, depend on the recipes in use: just as in cuisine recipes are what unleash and discipline creativity (and different approaches to recipes will stress either end of the continuum), so too in management. Different management recipes will produce different discretionary limits in the way that bounded rationality is constituted. Recipes do not come only from 'cookbooks'. In addition, they derive from the stock of knowledge that is general in a community; tried and trusted ways of doing things, as well as from new and glossy manuals, in management as in the cultural arts.

In this book the contributors dissect management knowledge from several countries, through several perspectives, in several contexts of inquiry. They seek to unpack some of the 'recipe knowledge' that frames modern management. Each chapter in this book elucidates, from different auspices, the way that relations of power intermingle with relations of knowledge, in such a way that we may say that no recipe is 'innocent'. No recipe is disinterested, absolutely technical, without interest and connection to the social fabric that embeds it. Whether we are concerned with the tortuous migration of excellence from entrepreneurial capitalism to bureaucratic status, or the denigration of bureaucracy in favour of the delights of the market, or the translation of lean production from Japan to the world, or the constitution of management fit for the twenty-first century, or whatever, the formation and accumulation of the knowledge that makes such development and translation of recipes possible are always, simultaneously, mechanisms of power (Townley 1995: 5). Power makes knowledge as knowledge makes power: recipes codify differing relations of ingredients, and discourses sustain the generic sensibility within which recipes locate.

In the culinary arts recipes serve up dishes. In the art of management recipes serve up subjects: the enterprising subject; the bureaucratic personality; the lean producer; the joint venturer; the heroic business person, to name but a few of the subjects treated in this text. What management theories produce are differential ways of being reflexive: of seeing oneself in and acting on oneself as a subject of theory that premises action. The radical upshot of this way of viewing management is seeing that it is both nothing and anything; or, rather, that it is no one thing and it may be any thing. The manager may be bureaucrat, entrepreneur, hero: no necessity attaches to the recipes with which one might produce oneself or be produced. The manager 'is continuously constituted and constructed through social relationships, discourses and practices' (1995: 11) so that in teaching management one always constitutes it as that practice that is being taught. In turn, that practice that is being taught always has a tangential relationship to that practice that the subjects of that teaching may do now, in the past, or in the future, as managers. Some will seek to prescribe; others to critique; and yet others to reform. All are admissible; none are *a priori* more practical positions than the others. Recipes produce managers; different recipes produce different appetites of taste, anticipation and discipline.

Producing Managers

Management today is a high-status occupation, its credentials achieved through expensive study in specialist tertiary courses and institutions.[6] Initially, as the chapter by du Gay demonstrates, recipes for management derived not from elite business schools, like INSEAD or Stanford, as they might today, but from the everyday recipes for action derived from the pervasiveness of the bureaucratic form. We might say that early forms of management knowledge, rather than critical reflection on it derived from empirical research and observation of bureaucratic practice, provided the early models. Recently, bureaucracy has suffered widespread denigration as a model for management; whatever role bureaucracy might have played in the past, it is not an appropriate template for the future of modern management, whether for the corporate giants or the small and medium sectors. Yet, formal models of bureaucracy such as Weber's (1978; see the discussion in Clegg 1990) always implied a highly developed liberal ethic of universal rights, impartially applied without fear or favour. Bureaucracy always contained certain classically liberal guarantees, such as the promise of equality before the law. Bureaucracy, for Weber, was always a moral project. It was a way of giving ethical meaning to key areas of governance in the world. In recent times, the agenda of classical political liberalism and that of economic liberalism, with its celebration of rugged individualism, have parted ways, or so du Gay argues. The triumph of economic over political liberalism places rights crucial to the political liberal project on the defensive. The attack on 'bureaucracy', despite the 'liberal' origin of recent critiques in 'market-oriented' perspectives, has diminished rather than augmented or replaced core liberal political values.

Under widespread attack, bureaucracy has ceased to be a positive resource so much as a ritual symbol of abuse, notably from charismatic consultants such as Peters and Waterman (1982), as well as from more 'radical' critics, such as feminists (see the contents of Ferree and Martin 1995 for a systematic sample of the range of contributions). The spread of antagonism is broad. What is lost in the dismissal and critique of bureaucracy? What are the ethical bases of that which replaces it? What are the consequences, particularly for public sector management, of this denigration of bureaucracy? What are the consequences of a de-bureaucratization of the world? These are the questions that du Gay addresses.

Empirically, many people will derive whatever formally framed insight they have into the nature of modern organization life from reading popular accounts of management. Popular management books sell in the millions. Many more people will read and derive their understanding of management from these than will ever be likely to see the inside of a business school or study the formal knowledge of a management curriculum. These popular accounts come largely from the fictionalized experience of successful American business people. We are tempted to think of the genre produced by successful corporate executives, after the classic *karaoke* song, as the ' "I Did It My Way" accounts'. What characterizes these accounts is precisely what characterizes the lyric for Sinatra: an excess of individualism, a laudatory account of 'My Way', a heroic perspective on the struggles of a life seen from the perspective of the autobiographer, as a rugged individualist who strove to be a good team player but whose basic values were highly individualist, nonetheless. Much of popular management knowledge derived from these sources is a reflection and a reinforcement of American individualist values that lionize heroic, male and 'tough' decision-making as 'entrepreneurship'.

Top management experience sells. This much has been clear since Chester Barnard (1948) was able to turn his experience as a major executive into a best-selling US textbook in the 1930s. Since then, particularly in the last decade or so, books by North American top executives on management have become one of the best-selling genres. Yet, they are rarely reflected upon, either as management texts or as texts in their own right. The chapter by Hansen brings the apparatus of sophisticated literary criticism to bear upon notable recent business autobiographies. It is not an edifying spectacle, either in literary terms or in terms of the more mundane accomplishments that constitute the works in question. Popular stereotypes serve to reinforce the very values that other contributors to the volume argue must be abandoned. The translation of these, essentially American, individualist and masculine verities into other cultures poses particular problems, especially where the culture is more collectivist and feminine (such as Thailand: see the discussion in Lawler and Atimiyanandana 1995). For as long as the assumptions of modernization and convergence held sway such questions of cultural translation seemed relatively uninteresting: as the world would become more like the USA we only needed to know it to know the future of anywhere. It is evident now, however, after the emergence of the newly industrialized countries of East Asia (see the chapters collected in Clegg et al. 1986 and Clegg and Redding 1990), that there is more than one organizational route to modernity.

One area of activity, of necessity, demands transcultural management: that of strategic alliance and joint venture management across boundaries. Here, the politics are indeed complex: politics of translation from one culture and language to another; politics of another kind of translation, the translation of the interests of the other parties into those of the agent seeking to enrol. The politics of everyday organizational life overlie these translations. Is the project secure in the politics of the organizations in question? Has the faction that advances the alliance got the numbers and resources to sustain it? When these politics are then overlain by the framework of an alliance across very different political systems, such as Western capitalism and Chinese state socialism, the political complexities compound. These are among the cases investigated by John Child and Suzana Rodrigues in their study of 'The Role of Social Identity in the International Transfer of Knowledge through Joint Ventures'. Where the transfer of knowledge takes place within a politics of distance, vicious cycles tend to characterize the exchange. Thus, although international joint ventures with Chinese firms seem attractive as economic options for Western firms, given the huge market in China and the cheap costs of labour, as well as its compliant and ready supply, if they are considered only in economic terms then the balance sheet will fail to record the all-important politics of the transaction, premised on the distinct identities being allied. This is particularly the case where the knowledge being translated relates to new systems and strategic understanding. Of course, it is much more difficult to produce a recipe where the ingredients and processes are uncertain.

The case of China, destined to be the world's largest economy by about 2010 on current estimates, is a classic example of the twin influences of globalization and cultural specificity coming into collision with each other. It is impossible to do business within China without adapting to local conditions, suggest Child and Rodrigues. How the adaptation is made, the way in which the globalizing organization seeks to manage its business, the ethical dilemmas that internationalization across different systems can entail, provide the crucial knowledge informing joint venture success or failure.

Comparative Cultural Recipes for Management

Popular management recipes in recent times have included *lean production, excellence* and *entrepreneurship*. Each has been chosen for inclusion in this volume because each has been widely disseminated and used by managers in many organizations. To lean production, whether as rationale, rhetoric or ritualistic response to the economic recession of the late 1980s and early 1990s, has been attributed considerable 'downsizing' or 'rightsizing' power, as organizations sought to survive hard times by making themselves lean. Similarly with excellence and entrepreneurship: both have been crucial in the vocabulary of espoused rationales for widespread changes that many firms have made in the recent past. Who would not want to strive for excellence, to be entrepreneurial? To strive for these qualities is to partake of a search for the very essence of thoroughly modern management. Yet, a degree of scepticism may be in order. Sandkull is inclined to regard suggestions that the future of management lies with lean production as a 'myth'. Management have adopted the myth of lean production to try and maintain older models of management control and compliance in technologically routinized production systems that are highly vulnerable to resistance from the workforce, he suggests. Rather than functioning as a wholly new grid for management action, instead lean production functions as a way of achieving more stretch out of existing techniques and methods of production.

In the past the most popular forms of management knowledge and industrial order had their roots in an ideological tradition of domination, and a particular historical situation, the United States. A strong dynamic in the development of the United States industrial order was, and is, 'mechanization'. The transformation of the workplace achieved through technology gradually changed the relationship between capital and labour. Such transformations are never predetermined but, by and large, it has been management thought that has determined the shape of production systems. Despite struggles and contest, at the end of the day it was generally management that succeeded in getting labour's compliance. The success of United States management contained the potential seeds of failure. Management control was won through highly automating production. Yet, highly automated production systems are much more vulnerable to disruption than those less automated. To save the present order, those manufacturers who went furthest with automation have had recourse to the concept of lean production. This is now treated as a magic wand for making Western industry as competitive as the Japanese. Whereas lean production is often presented as a way of involving the employees in a participative way, the evidence from Japanese transplants in the UK and the USA tells another story.

Perhaps the fact that lean production came from Japan, with all the cultural capital that accrues to Japanese management techniques in the modern world, was its biggest selling point? Japan being the source of management recipes is a very recent trend (see Dunphy 1986 for the documentation). The assumption once flourished that American knowledge characterized modernity, much as did other symbols of cultural imperialism such as Coca-Cola or Mickey Mouse. Management recipes from America found common expression, wherever they were to be applied, because they addressed some fundamental truth about the nature of management, and thus could use the same methods and ingredients. The proposition seems increasingly doubtful. All discursive knowledge, even that which is highly formalized and abstract, relates back to the context in which its ideas were embedded. Knowledge never floats free of its embedded context. A case in point is the key idea of post-bureaucratic management – entrepreneurship.

Alvarez discusses the popularization of 'entrepreneurship' ideas in Spain, Britain and Mexico in the 1980s to demonstrate that managerial knowledge can be studied in an analogous way to the development of ideologies. Ideas from the sociology of knowledge and neo-institutional organization theory can be used to create a sociology of business knowledge. He reports significant differences in the promotion of entrepreneurship in the three societies. In Britain a strong and cohesive entrepreneurship movement started in response to government concerns with unemployment. Academics were encouraged to research small businesses and politicians used an enterprise and small-business focus to delegitimize Keynesianism and corporatism. In Mexico the movement was driven by powerful business people who were concerned to legitimize an active social, economic and political role for civil society in opposition to the powerful regime of the Party of Institutionalized Revolution (PRI). They used their influence over prestigious business schools to import US material. Self-employment or micro-firms became the integrated theme. In contrast, in Spain, the entrepreneurship movement was sponsored by a few professors but there was no consistent or powerfully reinforced theme, because no social group from politics, business or academia pursued the ideas with significant organizational or cultural resources. Alvarez's analysis demonstrated that the expression of management knowledge, even where the core idea is ostensibly the same, depends upon the organizational and cultural resources of differing social groups from politics, business and academia, underscoring the social construction of management knowledge and its cultural embeddedness.

Closely related to the theme of entrepreneurship in the recent literature has been that of excellence. As du Gay developed, excellence is frequently seen as an achievable outcome only when bureaucracy is abandoned, charismatic leadership advanced and entrepreneurship embraced. Such recipes have been embraced even in the midst of huge public bureaucracies, such as the national Mexican university system, one of the largest in the world. Newly developing economies, because of the generally 'less developed' or 'under developed' context in which elite management ideas are interpellated, may show extreme features of postmodernism. This is evident in the very rapid introduction and juxtaposition of differing foreign bodies of knowledge, the rapidity of which, in the name of planning, undercuts precisely that which it seeks to plan. An example is provided by the development of government policy in the universities of Mexico across three time periods: from 1970 to 1978; from 1979 to 1988; and from 1989 to 1994. A discourse of excellence has replaced the planning focus of 1979–88 and the equal opportunity focus of the 1970–8 period. State regulation has moved from *laissez-faire*, through planning, to greater surveillance using evaluative and financial techniques. Financing according to student demand has been replaced by a two-tier system of basic funding with the second tier of extra funds linked to the evaluation process, and fed through to some academic salaries by a wage policy that allows wage discrimination based on evaluation.

Ibarra-Colado's analysis suggests, in a review of Mexico, that these most recent approaches to 'excellence' necessarily have negative characteristics. To include, it is necessary to exclude; to grant privilege, it is necessary to degrade; and to reward, it is necessary to punish. Even though the country in question is just over the border from the United States, from where the recipes emanate, this study makes clear also that one cannot assume that a recipe cooked up in the USA will necessarily be recognizable when it is reproduced with local materials elsewhere. Paradoxically, particularly in sites far from their primogenesis, the search for excellence demands the preservation of mediocrity, a finding that the context of a newly developing economy makes more transparent. Foucault's (1977) view about power requiring resistance to justify its strategies would seem to be borne out, once more. Ibarra-Colado's contribution is one of a number that suggest that management recipes composed in the United States do not travel well, not even over the proximate border. Although the Mexican border demarcates a less from a more developed society, the USA's other border, with Canada, assuredly does not. Yet, it seems to matter little whether the border is north or south: in spaces where language frames things differently, then different recipes seem to emerge.

North America is the heartland of modern management theory. Most of it is initially produced there and the implicit assumptions of this society often constitute the audience and context of the sense that these texts make. Yet, even within North America, there is one site of socially organized and politically constituted resistance to the dominant anglophone culture. Chanlat's chapter takes Québec as a case study of the development of a different, autonomous and authentic sphere of management knowledge. It is one constructed out of increasingly dissimilar elements from that of the anglophone world. The embeddedness of management knowledge is apparent in this inability of forms of knowledge to achieve the same transcultural content. Instead, they remain deeply embedded in the specificities of local cultures, resistant to homogenization and serving as repositories for the expression of deeply embedded preferences. French organization theory is distinctly different to its English competition, drawing on quite distinct traditions and styles of work. We might say that the ideas that frame its knowledge are quite different from those of the remainder of the North American context. Québec may be in North America geographically but, in terms of the frames that they use, francophone management academics, and their clients and students in Québec, according to Chanlat, owe far more allegiance to the linguistic context than to the geographical context. Language is thus one of the major limits to the spread of a transcendent set of recipes with which to bound rationality.

The Future for Management

The question of Québec in Canada throws a practical issue into sharp relief. How do management educators respond when they become convinced that management knowledge is socially, culturally and linguistically embedded? In fact, since the popularity of the 'paradigm' concept in business schools (from Burrell and Morgan 1979 onwards), one way of coping with seemingly incommensurable differences has been through the notion of different styles of theory providing different frames for thinking. The significance of this way of thinking is perhaps greater for students than it is for researchers. Researchers are trained to handle ambiguity and paradox, one might anticipate: students find this kind of uncertainty much more difficult to accept and to cope with. They tend to want to know what is 'right': not for them the beauty of debate, the tolerance of ambiguity, the pleasures of the text that requires yet more resolution. They want prescription. They want to know which way to go on; they want to know not only the one best way but also the most foolproof recipe. To be told that there is no one 'best way', when what you wanted was an answer, is not immediately helpful even while it may be illuminating.

One response to the intellectual 'crisis' of management that has accompanied the declining intellectual currency of past prescriptive practice has been the emergence of management knowledge founded on radical relativism. Few recipe books systematically exploit different recipes for the same dish as their method. Usually the approach is one dish, one recipe. However, since Burrell and Morgan (1979) relativistic recipes have been on the menu. Morgan's (1986) subsequent *Images of Organizations* presented a smorgasbord, drawn from the culture metaphor, the machine metaphor and so on. It was left to more recent writers such as Bolman and Deal (1991), with their work on *Reframing Organizations*, to produce (or reduce) the complexity of the smorgasbord to a narrower range of choices. Today, management students can use Bolman and Deal's work to learn that there are four recipes, drawn, respectively, from culture, from politics, from human relations and from structure, and that one does not have to use just one of them. In fact, students are encouraged to switch frames, in the radical twist that they prescribe. Using each of the perspectives systematically to address the same issue, the same organization, can illuminate different facets that any one perspective would not reveal.

Palmer and Dunford cast a sceptical and empirical eye over this approach and in the course of doing so provide some basic market research on consumer preferences. This chapter reviews the theoretical ambiguities in Bolman and Deal's arguments as currently popular exponents of this relativism. Is it the generic advantage of multi-frame thinking, rather than particular frames, that is of value? It is not clear whether the concept is simply a new way of operationalizing contingency theory or whether the use of multiple frames of reference is a totally new approach. There may be many intervening variables that affect the type of action taken by managers using a multiple-frame approach. Practitioners seem happy with reframing as a tool: not for them the certainty of one best way, methodologically. Despite whatever reservations conventional organization theorists might express about 'relativism' and 'relativity', about the multiple possibilities that non-closure on singular interpretations offers, practitioners seem to find it quite comfortable because it not only illuminates practical aspects of their reality but also shows them other facets and interpretations of that reality which are useful for them. Reframing is discussed by Palmer and Dunford in terms of broader debates about the production of knowledge. There does not appear to be an empirical basis for a direct relationship between the use of varied perspectives and the ability to take more effective decisions. This raises some central questions about what contemporary management knowledge is for.

In the past, when management theory taught that there was one best way to manage, the principal risk that a scrupulous management academic might identify was that less sceptical students might become zealots. True believers, those who countenance no alternative, may be appropriate managers of doctrine, whether political or religious, but doctrine is not likely to be much use in steering complex organizations in uncertain times. This truism, at base, was one compelling reason for the popularity of contingency theory, which suggests that all organizations have a limited number of contingent factors to deal with, and that it is how they deal with them that structures these organizations. Amongst these contingencies are: the environment, as more or less turbulent; the size of the organization, as comprising more or fewer employees; the technology of the organization, as more or less routine or search-oriented in its functioning; and the culture of the host country in which the organization is located. Implicitly, the argument goes, successful managers have to identify correctly the contingencies that they are dealing with; having done that they can adopt the organization design that best fits these contingencies, according to contingency theory research (see Donaldson 1985; 1995).

Contingency theory is not the same thing as popular management theory. Nor is it the stuff of popular consultancy, which is more focused on topical solutions to recurrent management problems. The lack of popular use of contingency theory places it in a somewhat awkward position. To the extent that it does not inform the recipes that managers use in doing management, it cannot be said to be effective in practice. At best, its claims to be effective in theory have to be premised on a structualist logic: that despite whatever it is that people say that they think they are doing when reporting on management methods, causal relations between underlying contingent factors will hold. The logic of contingency theory is pure structuralism: what is beneath the surface is not available on the surface and may not even be known by those who constitute the appearance of the surface. In other words, practising managers may have many accounts of what they do, but they do not understand how what they do produces the relationships. It is not the managers' task to understand what underlies what they do. Only someone trained to decode the structural logic that is buried beneath the surface has the ability to do that. Of course, the account given of the organization, if it is to have some self-evident validity, should be translatable into the terms that managers use. The paradoxical result is a management science that is unavailable for managers to use and understand in their everyday practice as managers, by academic definition.

These academic pursuits rarely trouble practising managers. They are more likely to be concerned with the rapid turnover of popular theories as constituting their own problem of relativism, rushing to keep up with one-minute management, with quality circles, with re-engineering, with whatever. Whereas the attitude of the zealot may be the appropriate elective affinity to relate to a belief in one best way, that of the sceptic seems to be the best fit for the bewilderingly rapid turnover in theory that the managers of the last decade, in particular, have had to contend with. Ramsay, using a critical perspective, charts a course for scepticism through management theory in its fascination with phenomena such as quality circles, just-in-time and total quality management. Irrespective of what the prevailing contingencies may be, this rapid succession has seen knowledge change dramatically in the last decade.

A sceptical attitude may be called for. Certainly, this is the conclusion that Ramsay arrives at after his survey of some of the fads and fashions of management over the last sixty years. One sure-fire recipe emerges. All recipes lose popularity, and even more quickly today than in the past. For the practising manager, Ramsay suggests, the appropriate response may well be scepticism. Settle down, dig in and wait until the enthusiasm has passed. Don't get identified too closely with a particular solution: soon it will be *passé*.[7] Harness scepticism to the valuation of innovation, rather than being a fashion victim.

If it is characterized by fashion and fad, what then is the purpose of management knowledge? Scarbrough and Burrell, in their contribution titled 'The Axeman Cometh: the Changing Roles and Knowledges of Middle Managers', suggest that historically it served to further the occupational interests of managers as disparate and initially low-status employees. Management has been remarkably successful in the rise in its prestige since its inception. Warnings that it might not last have not been unknown: Colin Fletcher (1973) foresaw 'the end of management' while other writers have worried about management deskilling (Teulings 1986). Today, in ways that were not foreseeable then, management really is in crisis as 'hollowing out', 'lean production' and 'mezzanine management' all seem to herald an end to management as we once knew it. The future of management knowledge seems uncertain but it is unlikely that it will be a seamless evolution from the projects that have carried it thus far.

Management as an occupation has been the result of a remarkably successful professional project from its humble beginnings in animal husbandry to its present exalted role as the engine of economic progress. Yet, management is in crisis. Heroic managers are giving way to more ambiguous prototypes as management ranks increasingly polarize around different representational technologies, strategies of organizational restructuring and career patterns. As the world of organizations changes, becoming flatter, leaner, more virtual and less real, more technologically interconnected and networked, more premised on alliances than hierarchies, management must change also. The future of management practice may well challenge elements at the core of earlier management knowledge.

What will the management of the future look like? It is rare that management educators have an opportunity to recommend global reform of the curriculum of management education. Clegg and colleagues, as researchers for an Australian Government study into 'Leadership and Management Skills in Australia's Embryonic Industries', recently had such an opportunity, as did Clarke, through his involvement in an Inquiry into 'Tomorrow's Company' conducted for the British Royal Society of Arts.

Economic rationalism pervades most management thought in its professional project. Forms of management knowledge, like knowledge in general, should be thought of not as free-floating and disinterested truth, but as socially situated, constructed and changed. The practical relevance of this is explored in an assessment of the need for new management knowledge for the twenty-first century. At the core of the new management knowledge is a shift from a curriculum that is centred on 'competitive' models to one that is centred on 'cooperative' models. In the external environments of organizations, particularly small and medium enterprises, this entails analysis of networks, clusters and chains as major forms of firm behaviour. For all organizations, a 'feminization' of management as a form of knowledge is under way. Within the corporate sphere it points to the emergency of new norms of 'corporate governance' as the dominant knowledge code of organizations. This concluding chapter points to a transformation in the conditions governing what management knowledge is for.

Both reports were sceptical about the role of much current management knowledge. Through their recommendations and analysis, the nature of management for the future begins to emerge from the shadows of yesterday's detritus littering today's management education field. Cooperation not competition; feminization rather than machoization of management; internationalization as the recognition of cultural differences rather than their obliteration through models developed in a small number of North American universities: this is the future for management as these authors see it. It is on this note that we conclude the volume, presenting what we take to be possible management recipes for the future.

Of course, as this introduction makes clear, it would be naive in the extreme to see these recommendations as somehow immune to or outside of power – or even as a better type of power. They are a preference, a political preference, but one that, inescapably, is predicated on a recipe for power. The point is, we think, that for the foreseeable future the recipes that are proposed here are more likely to be successful, tomorrow's *nouvelle cuisine*, as it were, than some of the stodge offered up in the past. Of course, some palates are untrainable; some prefer the artlessness of stodge to the artistry of *nouvelle cuisine*. Ultimately, political preference, like taste, is a matter of past drill, of dedication to certain verities, of familiarity with what one finds comforting. Yet, at the end of the day, we believe, in management as in food, that better recipes are those that are less arteriosclerotic for the body, be it the body corporate or corporeal. New training produces new appetites.

Notes

Cynthia Hardy and Sue Jones made invaluable and detailed editorial comment on earlier drafts of this introduction.

1 Bentham's infamous Panopticon was one early architectural device for rendering these relations of proximity and surveillance manageable even where conditions of mastery of shared knowledge might be lacking (see Foucault 1977). The Panopticon consisted of a watchtower at the centre of a series of physically insulated and well-illuminated stalls that radiated from the watchtower like the spokes of a wheel. The watchtower had narrow observational slits, similar to those that archers used in medieval castles. The observer inside the watchtower could see everyone outside it, within the stalls, but they could not see the observer. The physical arrangements rendered the supervisor invisible. Consequently, supervision was less a matter of the observer watching and more a matter of the observed being aware that they might be under observation at any moment. As an architectural device

the Panopticon not only made supervision more literal: also it rendered it less necessary. The fact of potentially being seen, whatever one was doing, and of not knowing if one was being seen, was sufficient to instil supervision into the psyche of the persons under surveillance. Their behaviour would be modified by knowledge of their vulnerability to detection if they sought to 'cheat' in any way, because, at any moment, unbeknown to them, they might be under supervision. In this way the freedom of action that they might enjoy hypothetically, to 'go slow', to steal materials, to short-cut on the work, or to 'lark about', was limited. We might say that they had become subjects of bounded rationality. Of course, the Panopticon was costly, physically inflexible, and not widely successful in industry, although Robert Owen used it in his 'model industrial community' of New Lanark. Elsewhere, it found widespread application in penal and asylum design and application.

2 Where a tendency exists to act in untrustworthy ways, especially where there are small numbers of actors involved and either a high degree of unsubstitutability of one actor for another, or opportunities for collusion between them, organizations, rather than markets, handle transactions, according to Williamson (1975). Markets arrange matters of taste matter of factly through the transactions that ensue. If the buyer likes the goods on offer and can agree a price that buyer and seller accept, then the transaction stands as the consummation of the idiosyncratic taste of the buyer and the foresight of the seller in meeting it. Williamson's limits circumscribe this special meeting of minds. Outside these, discretionary behaviour is far more channelled, far less spontaneous or idiosyncratic. Managerial discretion rarely exercises itself on wholly idiosyncratic grounds: it has a modality of variation within bounds defined by various stakeholders as tolerable. Certain recipes for action are appreciated by certain stakeholders; certain other recipes, that might inflame some appetites, offend some tastes, or threaten the order of things achieved, are not. In Williamson's parlance, management is what makes hierarchies function where markets cannot.

3 His point of derparture for observation of bureaucracy was not private sector manage- ment but public sector bureaucracy. The major German political event of the nineteenth century, its unification from a confused and divided array of petty principalities under the rational disciplines of the Prussian state and military, showed the power of good management. In this case, the exemplar of good management was where the rationality of all the constituent members of the key organizations of the state and military were bounded in their rationality by rules, organized in Weber's famous fifteen precepts of bureaucracy (see Clegg 1990). Given the evident success of bureaucracy in the nation-building task, and the supremacy of military models in the nineteenth century, it was no surprise to Weber to find the serried ranks and rules of the bureaucracy mimicked in private sector organizations, such as the great industrial organizations that had sprung up in Germany and the United States, as well as elsewhere, by the turn of the century. The early spread of the bureaucratic form was a case of mimetic institutional isomorphism for Weber (Weber 1978; DiMaggio and Powell 1983; Clegg 1990).

4 Knowledge is not only a prerogative of management, as comparative perspectives on industrial relations and human resource management make evident. Unions, for example, in some national frameworks of management, such as the UK or Australia, gained knowledge- able resources to exert managerial power – for example, collective bargaining developed from stalemate compromises between rival power holders. As neither side could eliminate the other, the compromise was that unions become incorporated into the management of economic aspects of the employment relationship. The employment relationship, itself, was increasingly bureaucratized, in part as a result of the efforts of unions and the state to force implementation, throughout the organizations they represented, of what they saw as 'best practice'. Top management, to some extent, regained control by sharing it: the order that was established was to a limited degree a shared order, and the sanctions that maintained that order were divided between at least three power blocks – employers, unions and the state. The management of that order was not maintained by 'management' alone, because they did not have the power to establish the total managerial prerogative that some might have wanted. Thus, people lower in the managerial status hierarchy do manage to mobilize

resources in certain contexts and for certain issues – when they can mobilize sufficient power by collective or political action. But, as the example of unions suggests, there is no fixity to the reproduction of these relationships in past forms, as can be seen by the precipitous decline of union power, measured in terms of density of membership, and thus employment coverage, in most of the advanced societies since the 1960s. The conditions of management power, even in a classical zero-sum sense, have specific institutional conditions of existence. The extremely diverse, variable nature of national frameworks of bargaining demonstrate this point clearly (see the diverse institutional analyses collected in Moore and Devereaux-Jennings 1995 for examples).

5 In fact, cookery books and 'how-to' manuals are the genres that share the best-selling lists with books on topics like 'excellence' and 'one-minute management'. Recipes can be complex, allusive and poetical, like the classic *French Provincial Cooking* of Elizabeth David (1960). By contrast, they may be manuals of foolproof empiricism, such as those books authored by Delia Smith (1989). Much as management texts might vary.

6 Historically, following Scarbrough and Burrell's reminder of the association of 'management' with stewardship of horses, it was not always so. Chefs, for instance, were once much more prestigious in their occupation. Closer to the lord's or monarch's body in courtly society, the chef required more trust than the stablehand of the master's horses.

7 And, if the contingency theorists are right, it is less the impact of popularly espoused theories and more the subterranean implications of contingencies that are important. Perversely, contingency theory refuses to take seriously the theories that management uses. The perversity seems mutual.

References

Barnard, C. (1948) *The Functions of the Executive*. Cambridge, MA: Harvard University Press.

Bolman, L.G. and Deal, T.E.R. (1991) *Reframing Organizations: Artistry, Choice and Leadership*. San Francisco: Jossey-Bass.

Burrell, G. and Morgan, G. (1979) *Sociological Paradigms and Organizations Analysis*. London: Heinemann.

Clegg, S.R. (1990) *Modern Organizations: Organization Studies in the Postmodern World*. London: Sage.

Clegg, S.R. and Dunkerley, D. (1980) *Organization, Class and Control*. London: Routledge and Kegan Paul.

Clegg, S.R., Dunphy, D. and Redding, S.G. (eds) (1986) *The Enterprise and Management in East Asia*. Hong Kong: Centre of Asian Studies, University of Hong Kong.

Clegg, S.R. and Redding, G.S., with Cartner, M. (1990) *Capitalism in Contrasting Cultures*. Berlin: de Gruyter. Newbury Park, CA: Sage.

Cohen, M.D., March, J.G. and Olsen, P. (1972) 'A Garbage Can Model of Organizational Choice', *Administrative Science Quarterly*, 17.

David, E. (1960) *French Provincial Cooking*. London: Michael Joseph.

DiMaggio, P. and Powell, W. (1983) 'The Iron Cage Revisited: Institutional Isomorphism and Collective Rationality in Organizational Fields', *American Sociological Review*, 48(2): 147–60.

Donaldson, L. (1985) *In Defence of Organization Theory: a Response to the Critics*. Cambridge: Cambridge University Press.

Donaldson, L. (1995) *American Anti-Management Theory*. Cambridge: Cambridge University Press.

Dunphy, D. (1986) 'An Historical Review of the Literature on the Japanese Enterprise and its Management', in S.R. Clegg, D. Dunphy and S.G. Redding (eds), *The Enterprise and Management in East Asia*. Hong Kong: Centre of Asian Studies, University of Hong Kong. pp. 343–68.

Fayol, H. (1949) *General and Industrial Management*. London: Pitman.

Ferree, N.Y. and Martin, P.Y. (1995) *Feminist Organizations: Harvest of the New Women's Movement*. Philadelphia: Temple.

Fletcher, C. (1973) 'The End of Management', in J. Child (ed.), *Man and Organization*. London: Allen and Unwin.

Follett, M.P. (1941) *Dynamic Administration*. London: Pitman.

Foucault, M. (1977) *Discipline and Punish*. Harmondsworth: Penguin.

Lawler, J.L. and Atimiyanandana, V. (1995) 'Human Resource Management in Thailand', in L.F. Moore and P. Devereaux-Jennings (eds), *Human Resources Management on the Pacific Rim: Institutions, Practices, and Attitudes*. Berlin: de Gruyter. pp. 295–318.

Mayo, E. (1947) *The Social Problems of an Industrial Civilization*. London: Routledge and Kegan Paul.

Moore, L.F. and Devereaux-Jennings, P. (eds) (1995) *Human Resources Management on the Pacific Rim: Institutions, Practices, and Attitudes*. Berlin: de Gruyter.

Morgan, G. (1986) *Images of Organizations*. London: Sage.

Peters, T.J. and Waterman, R.H. (1982) *In Search of Excellence: Lessons from America's Best-Run Companies*. New York: Harper and Row.

Pugh, D. and Hickson, D.J. (1989) *Writers on Organizations* (4th edn). Harmondsworth: Penguin.

Schutz, A. (1962) *Collected Papers. Vol. I: The Problem of Social Reality*. The Hague: Martinus Nijhoff.

Schutz, A. (1964) *Collected Papers. Vol. II: Studies in Social Theory*. The Hague: Martinus Nijhoff.

Schutz, A. (1966) *Collected Papers. Vol. III: Studies in Phenomenological Philosophy*. The Hague: Martinus Nijhoff.

Schutz, A. (1967) *The Phenomenology of the Social World*. Northwestern University Press.

Simon, H. (1957) *Administrative Behaviour*. New York: Macmillan.

Smith, D. (1989) *Delia Smith's Complete Illustrated Cookery Course*. BBC Books.

Taylor, F.W. (1947) *Principles of Scientific Management*. New York: Harper.

Teulings, A.W.M. (1986) 'Managerial Labour Processes in Organized Capitalism: the Power of Corporate Management and the Powerlessness of the Manager', in D. Knights and H. Willmott (eds), *Managing the Labour Process*. London: Gower.

Townley, B. (1995) *Reframing Human Resources Management: Power, Ethics and the Subject at Work*. London: Sage.

Weber, M. (1978) *Economy and Society*. Berkeley: University of California Press.

Whitley, R. (1992) *Business Systems in East Asia*. London: Sage.

Williamson, O.E. (1975) *Markets and Hierarchies*. New York: Free Press.

PART ONE

PRODUCING MANAGERS

1

Making Up Managers: Enterprise and the Ethos of Bureaucracy

Paul du Gay

This chapter aims to open up discussion about the contemporary conduct of management. It represents an initial attempt to think through certain issues surrounding the 'making up' of the manager as an active agent in his or her own government.

However, rather than focusing upon the various technologies through which the dreams and schemes of contemporary managerial discourse are operationalized, I attempt to approach the subject through a more general analysis of the relationship between bureaucratic and entrepreneurial norms of organizational and managerial conduct. In particular, I attempt to explore some of the politico-ethical effects of the shift towards market-based forms of organizational governance upon the conduct of public sector management.

Making Up Managers

Despite the growing popularity of 'post-structuralist ideas' within British business schools, 'making up managers' still strikes students of organization and management as a rather strange phrase. So what might it mean? Well, on the one hand, making something up suggests the construction of a fiction. But in what sense can the 'manager' be represented as a fictional character? On the other hand, the idea of being 'made up' suggests a material-cultural process of formation or transformation ('fashioning') whereby the adoption of certain habits and dispositions allows an individual to become – and to become recognized as – a particular sort of person.

What both versions of making up share is a concern with invention. They serve as a corrective to the tendency to regard a given activity or characteristic as in some sense 'natural'. It is perfectly possible and legitimate to conceive of the 'manager' as a fiction, for example, because that category of person has not always existed. As Pollard (1965) amongst many others has indicated, the 'manager' only came into being at a certain historical juncture. Similarly, it is important to note that the dispositions, actions and attributes that constitute 'management' have no natural form and for this reason must be approached as a series of historically specific assemblages. To be 'made up' – in the second sense of the term – as a manager is therefore to acquire that particular assemblage of attributes and dispositions which defines the activity of management at any given period.

The term 'making up' serves to highlight the way in which conceptions of person and conceptions of activities are inextricably linked. As Rorty has argued, 'social and political conceptions of persons – conceptions of their powers, rights and limits, the criteria for their individuation and continued identity – derive from conceptions of primary, privileged activities, the activities that are thought to express human excellences and tasks. Attributes believed to be required for performing such primary tasks are designated as the essential identificatory properties of persons' (1988: 25). In other words, particular categories of person and the criteria of their identity are defined by reference to a range of activities that are regarded as 'centrally and normatively important to a culture, a historical period or an investigative context' (1988: 6).

Viewed in this way, it becomes apparent that what it means to be a manager varies historically in relation to changing conceptions of the activity of management and the associated techniques and practices that bestow upon these a material reality.

Reimagining the Manager: Managerial Discourse and the Constitution of Certain Sorts of Persons

Throughout the twentieth century the 'character' of the manager has been a regular source of public concern, debate and calls for action. Indeed, the government of economic life across the present century has entailed a range of attempts to shape and regulate the conduct of management. From 'scientific management', through 'human relations', up to and including contemporary programmes of organizational reform such as total quality management (TQM), the activities of individuals as 'managers' have become an object of knowledge and the target of expertise, and a complex series of links have been established through which the economic priorities of politicians and business people have been articulated in terms of the required personal characteristics of managers (Miller and Rose 1990; du Gay 1991).

Over the last ten to fifteen years, the character of the manager has once again become a major focus of concern. A number of reports produced during this period (discussed in Handy 1987) stressed that British companies were in danger of losing out to foreign competitors in many markets because their 'stock' of managers were not adequately trained and developed in the appropriate skills and techniques necessary to meet the challenges posed by a rapidly changing organizational landscape. In order to guarantee its position and to ensure future economic growth and success it was deemed crucial that 'Britain do more to develop her managers and do it more systematically' (1987: 15).

The importance vested in the character of the manager in general – and in the development of certain capacities and predispositions by practising managers in particular – by such diverse groupings as the NEDC, the Manpower Services Commission and the Confederation of British Industry was also reflected in the dominant discourses of organizational restructuring that emerged during this period. The discourses of human resource management, total quality management and excellence, to name but some of the most well known, all placed considerable emphasis upon the development of more 'organic', 'flexible' organizational forms and relationships which would overcome the perceived stasis, rigidity and inefficiency of bureaucratic structures, techniques and mechanisms. In particular, they indicated that such organizational change could not simply be structural but must be normative or 'cultural'. In contrast to the norms and techniques of conduct characterizing bureaucratic enterprise, both public and private – strict adherence to procedure, acceptance of hierarchical sub- and superordination, abnegation of personal moral enthusiasms and so forth – the new discourses of work reform stressed the importance of individuals acquiring more 'proactive' and 'entrepreneurial' predispositions and capacities (Peters and Waterman 1982; Peters 1987; 1992; Kanter 1990).

Within these discourses it was individual managers who were primarily charged with ensuring that these novel work-based subjects emerged. Managers were represented as having a pivotal role in securing organizational change through fostering certain market-oriented 'virtues' firstly within themselves and then among their subordinates. Thus, in opposition to the 'personally detached and strictly objective expert' characteristic of bureaucratic management, the 'excellent' manager was represented as a 'charismatic' facilitator, encouraging others to take responsibility for themselves and fostering an 'enterprising' sense of identification, commitment and involvement between employees and the organization for which they work.

Contemporary Managerial Discourse and the Critique of Bureaucratic Culture

The case against bureaucracy and for the sorts of 'organic', 'flexible' organizational forms and practices envisioned in contemporary managerial discourse begins with changes in what is termed 'the external environment'. The conditions of possibility of this 'discursive formation' rest upon a number of developments gathered together under the heading of 'globalization'. While different authors highlight differing combinations of phenomena – the dislocatory effects consequent upon the increasing deployment of 'new information technologies', those associated with the competitive pressures resulting from global systems of trade, finance and production, and so on – they all agree that the intensification of patterns of global interconnectedness has serious repercussions for the conduct of organizational life, in both the private and the public sectors. If 'globalization' constitutes the key 'predicament' for the proponents of contemporary managerial discourse then 'bureaucracy' is positioned as the crucial 'impediment' to the successful management of its effects. Globalization, it is argued, creates an environment characterized by massive uncertainty. In such an environment only those organizations that can rapidly change their conduct and learn to become ever more enterprising will survive. Because 'bureaucracy' constitutes a 'mechanistic' system of organization best suited to conditions of relative stability and predictability, it becomes the first casualty of such an uncertain environment.

> In this environment, bureaucratic institutions – public and private – increasingly fail us. Today's environment demands institutions that are extremely flexible and adaptable. It demands institutions that deliver high-quality goods and services, squeezing ever more bang out of every buck. It demands institutions that are responsive to their customers, offering choices of non-standardized services; that lead by persuasion and incentives rather than commands; that give their employees a sense of meaning and control, even ownership. It demands institutions that empower citizens rather than simply serving them. (Osborne and Gaebler 1992: 15)

In other words, the dislocatory effects generated by the intensification of patterns of global interconnectedness require constant 'creativity' and the continuous construction of collective operational spaces that rest less and less upon mechanistic objective forms and their related practices – 'bureaucracy' – and increasingly upon the development of more entrepreneurial organizational forms and modes of conduct. 'Enterprise' occupies an absolutely crucial position in this new managerial discourse. It provides a critique of 'bureaucratic culture' and offers itself as a solution to the problems posed by 'globalization' through delineating the essential principles of a new 'art' of governing organizational and individual conduct. As Gordon (1991: 43) has suggested, 'enterprise' refers to the subtle imbrication of 'economic rationality' and 'behaviourism' to produce a novel method of programming the totality of governmental action. No longer simply implying the creation of an independent business venture, the term now refers to the progressive enlargement of the territory of the 'economic' by a series of redefinitions of its object.

So what are the 'essential principles' of 'enterprise' and in what ways do these redefine the conduct of organizational life? Quite obviously one crucial feature of 'enterprise' as a principle of government is the paradigmatic status it accords to 'the commercial enterprise' as the preferred model for any form of institutional organization and provision of goods and services (Keat 1990: 3). However, of equal importance is the way in which the term refers to the 'kind of action' or project that displays 'enterprising qualities or characteristics on the part of those concerned', whether they be individuals or collectivities. Here, 'enterprise' refers to a plethora of characteristics such as initiative, self-reliance, risk-taking and the ability to accept responsibility for oneself and one's actions.

As Gordon (1991: 48) has suggested, in this latter manifestation 'enterprise' as a principle of government is intimately bound up with 'ethics'. By 'ethics' Gordon is referring to the means by which individuals come to understand and act upon themselves in relation to the true and the false, the permitted and the forbidden, the desirable and the undesirable. Thus, 'enterprise' as an 'art of governing' promotes a conception of the individual person as an 'entrepreneur of the self' (Gordon 1987: 300).

This idea of an individual human life as an 'enterprise of the self' suggests that there is a sense in which no matter what hand circumstance may have dealt a person, he or she remains always continuously engaged (even if technically 'unemployed') in that one enterprise, and that it is 'part of the continuous business of living to make adequate provision for the preservation, reproduction and reconstruction of one's own human capital' (Gordon 1991: 44). As Rose (1990) has suggested, an 'enterprising self' is a calculating self, a self that calculates about itself and works upon itself in order to better itself.

Governing organizational life in an 'enterprising' manner therefore involves the reconstruction of a wide range of institutions and activities along the lines of the commercial firm, with attention focused, in particular, on its orientation towards the 'sovereign consumer'. In other words, the free-market system with its emphasis upon consumer sovereignty provides the model through which all forms of organizational relation should be structured. At the same time, however, guaranteeing that optimum benefits accrue from the restructuring of organizations according to the dictats of free-market rationality necessitates the production of certain forms of conduct by all members of an organization. Restructuring organizational life in this sense involves 'making up' new ways for people to be; it refers to the importance of individuals acquiring and exhibiting particular 'enterprising' capacities and dispositions.

Refracted through the gaze of 'enterprise', bureaucratic culture appears inimical to the development of these virtues and hence to the production of enterprising persons. The bureaucratic commitment to the norms of impersonality, adherence to procedure, hierarchical sub- and superordination and so forth are seen as antithetical to the cultivation of those entrepreneurial skills and sensibilities which alone can guarantee a 'manageable' and hence sustainable future.

While 'enterprise' constitutes all forms of bureaucratic conduct as subjects of conscientious objection, it is the perceived failure of bureaucracy in opening up people's personal involvement and ideals which comes in for the most severe criticism (Peters and Waterman 1982: 29–86; Kanter 1990: 351–65). Because bureaucratic norms are assumed to be founded upon an unhappy separation of reason and emotion, the public and the private, and since this state of affairs is deemed to be inimical to individual self-realization, personal responsibility and other enterprising virtues, bureaucracy is represented as fundamentally unethical. In other words, for advocates of 'enterprise', bureaucracy is represented as a flawed means for the realization of moral personality.[1]

The Ethos of Enterprise and the Critique of Bureaucratic Personality

According to its critics, the flawed moral character of bureaucracy is directly related to its atomistic effects. For proponents of 'enterprise' the identity of bureaucracy is founded upon a traumatic and ultimately disastrous 'split' or separation. They suggest that the establishment of bureaucratic organization is always likely to involve significant human, and hence financial, cost because the privilege it accords to 'instrumental rationality' involves the simultaneous repression and marginalization of its Other – the personal, the sexual, the emotional and so forth. Thus, bureaucracy is based upon a series of 'foundational' exclusions whose 'absent presence' erupts onto the organizational surface in the form of cumulatively disabling 'dysfuntions'. To back up this claim advocates of 'enterprise' continually point to, amongst other things, a perceived lack of commitment, motivation and identification amongst the bureaucratic workforce which they attribute directly to 'rationalist' systems 'that seem calculated to tear down their worker's self-image' (Peters and Waterman 1982: 57).

In this reading, inefficiency, waste and inertia are directly related to the fact that bureaucratic organization does not function as an instrument of self-realization for its members. Instead, its very 'essence' is based upon a separation of 'work and life', 'reason and emotion', 'pleasure and duty' which is disastrous for the productive health of the nation, the corporation and the moral and emotional character of the individual human subject.

In contrast to the constitutive splits deemed to characterize bureaucracy, the 'entrepreneurial' corporation is represented as all of a piece. It constitutes, in Charles Sabel's (1990) words, a 'Möbius strip' organization whose inside and outside imperceptibly blur. In such an organization, work and leisure, reason and emotion, pleasure and duty are once more conjoined and thus the human subject is again a plenitude, restored to full moral health. But how exactly does this feat of reintegration come about?

Once again, the story begins with the market. As a variety of social spheres have become increasingly 'market dependent' their differing modes of operation and calculation have been subsumed under the overriding logic of one form of rationality: the 'economic' (Bauman 1987). The 'levelling function' that this process performs ensures that formerly diverse institutions, practices, goods and so forth become subject to judgement and calculation almost exclusively in terms of market-based criteria; in other words, this process of de-differentiation or implosion involves the increasing dominance of what Lyotard (1984) terms 'the performativity principle'. However, it would be misguided to view this development as simply the latest and purest manifestation of the irresistible rise of 'economic rationality'. Rather, the subtle imbrication of economy and culture leaves neither untouched. 'Market dependency' and 'the performativity principle' may well involve the colonization of the cultural by the economic but the resultant economic formation is itself distinctly 'aesthetic'. In other words, even as 'market dependency' effaces 'culture' as an autonomous sphere of existence it simultaneously positions artifice at the very heart of reality.

This blurring of boundaries has significant repercussions for individual human conduct. For if the process of differentiation inaugurated distinct spheres of existence to which specific ethical protocols applied then the process of de-differentiation implies that one overarching ethos is now constitutive of all human activity. Thus, 'market dependency' implies the reconfiguration of human conduct around one universally appropriate benchmark or principle and that principle is 'enterprise'.

As I indicated earlier, 'enterprise' allows an alignment to take place between what traditionally have been recognized as separate realms of human endeavour by representing an individual human life as an 'enterprise of the self'. Because a human being is considered to be continuously and exclusively engaged in a project to shape his or her life as an autonomous individual driven by motives of self-fulfilment, life for that person is represented as a single, essentially undifferentiated arena for the pursuit of that endeavour.

In this vision there are no longer distinct spheres each with its own particular ethos but rather a single continuum within an overarching rationale: enterprise. Enterprise brooks no opposition between the dispositions and capacities required of 'workers' and those required by 'consumers', for example. Being a good, virtuous worker or consumer means being an entrepreneur of oneself because 'enterprise' offers the means of obtaining self-realization and self-perfection. Thus, the character of the entrepreneur is no longer represented as one among many ethical personalities but assumes an ontological priority.

Unsurprisingly, the character of the entrepreneur is firmly established at the heart of contemporary programmes of organizational reform. Breathing strange new life into the old artistic ideal of the 'organic' – of 'the unified moral personality' and 'life as a work of art' (hence the comments made earlier about 'enterprise' positioning 'artifice' at the centre of reality) – characterizes work not as a painful obligation imposed upon individuals, nor as an activity only undertaken by people for instrumental purposes, but as a vital means to self-fulfilment and self-realization. As Kanter (1990: 281) comments, life in the entrepreneurial corporation has 'a romantic quality'.

By reimagining work as simply part of that continuum along which 'we' all seek to realize ourselves as particular sorts of person – autonomous, self-regulating, self-fulfilling individual actors – 'enterprise' seeks to 're-enchant' organized work by restoring to it that which 'bureaucracy' is held to have crassly repressed: emotion, personal responsibility, the possibility of pleasure etc.

> In the traditional bureaucratic corporation, roles were so circumscribed that most relationships tended to be rather formal and impersonal. Narrowly defined jobs constricted by rules and procedures also tended to stifle initiative and creativity, and the atmosphere was emotionally repressive. the post-entrepreneurial corporation ('because it takes entrepreneurship a stage further'), in contrast, with its stress on teamwork and cooperation, with its ecouragement of imagination and commitment to the process of building the new, brings people closer together, making the personal dimension of relationships more important. (Kanter 1990: 280)

Contemporary organizational success is therefore premised upon an engagement by the organization of the 'self-fulfilling impulses' of all of its members, no matter what their 'formal' role. This is to be achieved by allocating particular 'enterprising' dispositions and capacities to employees through the medium of a variety of mutually enhancing technologies and practices. The latter include such devices as techniques for reducing dependency by reorganizing management structures ('delayering'); for cutting across and transcending traditional organizational boundaries (the creation of 'special project teams'); for encouraging internal competitiveness (through 'small group working'); and for eliciting individual responsibility and self-management through the peer review and appraisal schemes. In this way, 'enterprise' plays the role of relay between objectives that are economically desirable and those that are personally seductive, 'teaching the arts of self-realization that will enhance employees as individuals as well as workers' (Rose 1989: 16).

This 'autonomization' and 'responsibilization' of the self, the instilling of a reflexive self-monitoring which will afford self-knowledge and therefore self-control, makes paid work (no matter how 'objectively' alienated, deskilled, or degraded it may appear to social scientists) an essential element in the path to self-fulfilment and provides the *a priori* that links work and non-work, reason and emotion, the public and the private, together. As I indicated above, the 'employee', just as much as the 'sovereign consumer', is represented as an individual in search of meaning and fulfilment, looking to 'add value' in every aspect of existence. For the organic, aesthetic 'entrepreneur' the relations between work life and non-work life and identity – between what is properly inside and what is properly outside the orbit of the organization – are progressively blurred.

Although both managers and workers are represented as equally amenable to 'entrepreneurial' reconstitution, the former are held to have a particularly important role in ensuring organizational change through fostering 'enterprise' amongst the latter. In opposition to the personally detached bureaucratic manager, 'entrepreneurial' management is represented as calculatingly 'charismatic' in essence. Managers are charged with 'leading' their subordinates to the promised land of 'self-realization' by encouraging them to make a project of themselves, to work on their relations with employment and on all other areas of their lives in order to develop a style of life and relationship to self that will maximize the worth of their existence to themselves. In other words, managers are charged with reconstructing the conduct and self-image of employees: with encouraging them to acquire capacities and dispositions that will enable them to become 'enterprising' persons. The current interest in identifying and allocating key 'personal' management competencies and in developing 'competence architectures' within organizations is seen as fundamental to this process (Boyatzis 1982).

To sum up: according to advocates of 'enterprise', the efficient and effective governance of organizational life – whether 'private' or 'public' it matters not – is premised upon an engagement by the organization of the 'self-fulfilling' impulses of all its members. Seen from the perspective of 'enterprise', 'bureaucratic' forms of organizational governance are inefficient and ineffective because they fail to open up and incite people's personal involvement and ideals. These 'personalist' failings are traced back to a tragic separation of reason and emotion, pleasure and duty, public and private, which 'bureacracy' both engenders and perpetuates.

Bureaucracy, Enterprise and the Liberal Art of Separation

While proponents of 'enterprise' (Kanter et al. 1992: 146; Osborne and Gaebler 1992: 12–16) are not averse to admitting that bureaucratic norms and techniques have proved appropriate under certain circumstances, they clearly believe that such circumstances are no longer to be found, nor are they likely to recur in the foreseeable future. The implication is that for organizations to survive and flourish in the dislocated environments of the present require the cultivation of an appropriate entrepreneurial competence and style through which at one and the same time organizations conduct their business and persons conduct themselves within those organizations.

As I indicated above, because the discourse of enterprise presupposes that no organizational context is immune from the effects of globalization, it therefore assumes that ostensibly different organizations – schools, charities, banks, government departments and so on – will have to adopt similar norms and techniques of conduct, for without so doing they will lack the capacity to pursue their preferred projects (Peters 1987; 1992). The urgency with which such claims are deployed gives the impression that 'there is no alternative'. As Kanter, for example, forcefully declares, organizations 'must either move away from bureaucratic guarantees to post-entrepreneurial flexibility or they stagnate thereby canceling by default any commitments they have made' (1990: 356).

However, instead of simply accepting the case that this entrepreneurial confusion of realms represents a uniformly positive as well as inherently necessary development, it may be worth attempting to evaluate some of the consequences involved in such a manoeuvre. The process of evaluation would need to be conducted on a case by case basis. A blanket assessment would merely reproduce the kinds of 'forced' options' that I have just criticized advocates of 'enterprise' for deploying.

We may, for example, wish to enquire into the political and ethical consequences of reimagining public sector bureaucrats as entrepreneurs – paying particular attention to whether such a move is sufficiently pluralist (presupposing as it does a single ethical hierarchy with the entrepreneur at its apex). In order to conduct such an enquiry it would be necessary to specify what the bureaucratic ethos consists of, to indicate what sort of conceptions and practices of personhood the bureau gives rise to and to delineate the relationship between these and the 'liberal art of separation' (Walzer 1984). It is to this task that I now turn.

Office as a Vocation: Delineating the Bureaucratic Ethos

The idea that public sector bureaucracies need reforming has achieved a somewhat axiomatic status. To what extent and in which directions remain a matter of some debate. In recent years, however, one particular approach has become pre-eminent and it is this approach which underpins many of the public sector reforms currently taking place across the advanced economies.

This new *modus operandi* is termed 'entrepreneurial governance'. According to two of its main proponents, Osborne and Gaebler, the latter consists of ten 'essential principles' which link together to form a functioning network:

> Entrepreneurial governments promote competition between service providers. They empower citizens by pushing control out of the bureaucracy, into the community. They measure the performance of their agencies, focusing not on inputs but on outcomes. They are driven by their goals – their missions – not by their rules and regulations. They redefine their clients as customers and offer them choices – between schools, between training programmes, between housing options. They prevent problems before they emerge, rather than simply offering services afterward. They put their energies into earning money, not simply spending it. They decentralize authority, embracing participatory management. They prefer market mechanisms to bureaucratic mechanisms. And they focus not simply on providing public services but on catalysing all sectors – public, private and voluntary – into action to solve their community's problems. (1992: 19–20)

The identity of entrepreneurial governance is constituted in relation to that which it is not – namely, the public service bureaucracy. The latter is represented as the enemy of 'good governance' for the reasons outlined earlier: for example, bureaucracy is represented as inefficient and ineffective because it fails to open up and incite people's personal involvement and ideals.

However, it is possible to suggest that this representation of bureaucracy as colossal immodesty does not in fact tell us very much about the technical, ethical or social organization of the bureau. Instead its main role appears to be to frame the difference between the vocational ethics of the bureaucrat and those of the entrepreneur from the perspective of entre-preneurial principles. In other words, rather than describing the ethos of office the entrepreneurial critique seeks to assess bureaucracy in terms of its failure to realize objectives which enterprise alone has set for it.

However, in his classic account of bureaucracy Weber (1968) refuses to treat the impersonal, expert, procedural and hierarchical character of bureaucratic reason and action as a symptom of moral deficiency. Instead he makes it clear that the bureau consists in a particular ethos or what he terms *Lebensführung* – not only an ensemble of purposes and ideals within a given code of conduct but also ways and means of conducting oneself within a given 'life order'. In other words, the bureau must be assessed in its own right as a particular moral institution and the ethical attributes of the bureaucrat must be viewed as the contingent and often fragile achievements of that socially organized sphere of moral existence.

According to Weber, the bureau comprises the social and 'spiritual' conditions of a distinctive and independent organization of the person. Among the most important of these conditions are, first, that access to office is dependent upon lengthy training in a technical expertise, usually certified by public examination; and second, that the office itself consti-tutes a 'vocation', a focus of ethical commitment and duty, autonomous of and superior to the bureaucrats extra-official ties to class, kin, or con-science. In Weber's discussion of bureaucracy these conditions delineate the bureau as a particular department of life, and they provide the bureaucrat with a distinctive ethical bearing and mode of conduct.

The ethical attributes of the good bureaucrat – strict adherence to procedure, acceptance of sub- and superordination, commitment to the purposes of the office and so forth – do not therefore represent an incompetent subtraction from a 'complete' entrepreneurial conception of personhood. Rather, they should be viewed as a positive moral achieve-ment in their own right. They represent the product of particular ethical techniques and practices through which individuals develop the disposition and ability to conduct themselves according to the ethos of bureaucratic office (Hunter 1991; Minson 1993).

Instead of lending support to the entrepreneurial stereotype of bureau-cracy as inimical to self-realization, Weber points to the historical specifi-city of the 'rational' character of bureaucracy. Rather than representing the denial of personal involvement in, or the possibility of deriving personal pleasure from, the conduct of office, Weber's (1968: 359) stress on the 'impersonal', 'functional' and 'objective' nature of bureaucratic norms and techniques refers simply to the setting aside of pre-bureaucratic forms of patronage. What is to be excluded as 'irrational' by this form of conduct is not personal feelings *per se* but a series of 'private' group prerogatives and interests which 'governed as they were by a completely different ethos, it was at other times deemed quite legitimate and "reasonable" to pursue' (Minson 1991: 15). Thus the normative scope of bureaucratic rationality is quite particular. As Weber remarks, decisive is that this freely creative administration would not constitute a realm of free arbitrary action and discretion, of personally motivated favour and valuation as we find among the pre-bureaucratic forms. (1968: 973)

Weber proceeds to indicate that bureaucratic rationality does not operate to exclude all sentiment from organizational existence. Such a characterization – levelled, as I indicated earlier, by the advocates of enterprise amongst many others – completely misses the point that bureaucratic culture engenders no antipathy towards emotional or personal relations within the domain of the office as long as these do not open the possibility of corruption through, for example, the improper use of patronage, indulging in competence or the betrayal of confidentiality. As Minson argues, 'the supposition of an essential antipathy between bureaucracy and informal relations such as friendship hinges on a romantic identification of such relations with freedom from normative compulsion, spontaneous attraction, intimacy, and free choice' (1993: 135). When Weber describes bureaucratic conduct as precluding 'personally motivated' actions, it is therefore important not to follow the advocates of enterprise and extend his intended reference from the exercise of personal patronage to the universal exclusion of the personal and/or 'private' realms.

In a similar move, Weber also indicates that far from being morally and emotionally vacuous, 'formally rational' modes of conduct do have an ethical basis. As Charles Larmore (1987: xiii–xiv) has argued, Weber's concept of 'formal rationality' has been consistently misappropriated and made to serve a function he never intended it so to do. It differs from its twin concept of 'substantive rationality' not by being narrowly 'instrumental' and dependent upon arbitrarily given ends, as the advocates of enterprise suggest, but rather by taking account of the heterogeneity of morality. In other words, while the ethos associated with formal rationality is certainly premised upon the cultivation of indifference to certain moral ends, that very indifference is predicated upon an awareness of the irreducible plurality of and frequent incommensurability between passionately held moral ends and thus of the possible moral costs of pursuing any one of them. Viewed within this frame, formal rationality is associated not with the development of an amoral and colossally immodest instrumentalism but rather with the cultivation of a liberal pluralist 'ethics of responsibility' which does take account of the consequences of attempting to realize essentially contestable values that frequently come into conflict with other values.

In this sense, the bureau represents an important ethical and political resource in liberal democratic regimes because it serves to divorce the administration of public life from private moral absolutisms. It has become, as Larmore indicates, 'a condition of freedom' because it permits 'a significant and liberating separation of the public and the private' (1987: 41–2). Without the emergence of the ethical sphere of the bureau and the persona of the bureaucrat, the construction of a buffer between civic virtues and personal principles would never have become possible.

Instead of heralding the disintegration and fragmentation of a previously integrated political-moral personhood, the emergence of distinct public and private modes of personal comportment that bureaucracy helps to effect represents a contingent but hard-won political and ethical achievement.

'Businessing' Bureaucracy: Enterprise and Public Service

The ethos of office, with its chief point of honour, the capacity to set aside one's private political, moral, regional and other commitments, should not therefore be regarded as obsolete. The question then remains as to what effect a shift to entrepreneurial forms of governance is likely to have upon this ethos.

As I have indicated, the very identity of the entrepreneurial project is constituted in opposition to bureaucratic culture. Advocates of enterprise tend to represent 'bureaucracy' in language which leaves little room for any positive evaluation. Peters (1987: 459), for example, informs his readers that he regularly incites the managers who attend his seminars 'to develop a public and passionate hatred of bureaucracy'. Such rhetoric is unlikely to leave its audience concerned to understand, let alone maintain or enhance, the bureaucratic ethos.

However, it is only possible to begin to answer the question posed above by indicating the ways in which the norms and techniques of entrepreneurial governance outlined earlier might pose a threat to the bureaucratic 'art of separation'.

According to Amélie Rorty (1988: 7) the 'art of separation' is most often challenged when the concerns of one particular context or 'life order' are imposed on other different departments of life. It is possible to suggest that the discourse of enterprise is involved in just such an attempted imposition or 'takeover bid' by seeking to render a variety of discrete ethical domains amenable to one particular style of government.

As Burchell, for example, has indicated, the defining characteristic of entrepreneurial government is the 'generalization of the "enterprise form" to all forms of conduct – to the conduct of organizations seen as being non-economic, to the conduct of government, and to the conduct of individuals themselves' (1993: 275). Through a variety of mutually enhancing techniques and practices this form of government 'encourages the governed to adopt a certain entrepreneurial form of practical relationship to themselves as a condition of their effectiveness and of the effectiveness of this form of government'. In other words, this form of government 'makes up' the governed as entrepreneurs of themselves, as enterprising sorts of persons. Or, to put it in Tom Peters's words, entrepreneurial organizational governance 'businesses' people: 'emerging organizational forms will permit – and the market will demand – that each employee be turned into a businessperson' (1992: 235).

In this way, a certain conception of the person as an entrepreneur, which derives from and properly belongs to a particular sphere of existence (the life order of the marketplace), is imposed upon other departments of life (each of which has given rise to its own conceptions and practices of personhood). In so doing distinct spheres of existence become confused and the liberties, equalities and freedoms predicated upon 'separation' are put into question.

As Weber, for example, argued, the ethoses governing the conduct of the 'bureaucrat', the 'entrepreneur' and the 'politician' are not identical. In addressing the different kinds of responsibility that these 'persons' have for their actions, Weber insists upon the irreducibility of different spheres of ethical life and on the consequent necessity of applying different ethical protocols to them.

> An official who receives a directive he considers wrong can and is supposed to object to it. If his superior insists on its execution, it is his duty and even his honour to carry it out as if it corresponded to his innermost conviction and to demonstrate in this fashion that his sense of duty stands above his personal preference. This is the ethos of office. A political leader acting in this way would deserve contempt. He will often be compelled to make compromises, that means, to sacrifice the less to the more important. 'To be above parties' – in truth, to remain outside the struggle for power – is the official's role, while this struggle for personal power, and the resulting political responsibility, is the lifeblood of the *politician* as well as the *entrepreneur*. (1968: 1404, emphasis added)

By demanding – in the name of the 'market', the 'customer' or whatever – that the ethical conduct of the public administrator be judged according to the ethos of the entrepreneur, the discourse of enterprise in fact requires public sector bureaucrats to assume the role of business persons. As Larmore (1987: 99), for example, argues, such 'confusion of realms' can have disastrous consequences. In seeking to instil a strong sense of personal 'ownership' for particular policies amongst public administrators, for example, proponents of 'enterprise' (Osborne and Gaebler 1992) seem to have completely lost sight of the bureau's crucial civic and ethical role in separating public administration from personal moral enthusiasms.[2]

Such 'forgetfulness' is inscribed within all too many of the public sector reforms currently taking place across liberal democratic societies. In Britain, for example, the introduction of 'entrepreneurial' norms and techniques into the civil service as a result of the Next Steps initiative seems destined to undermine the bureaucratic ethos. Top civil servants, it would appear, are increasingly being encouraged to adopt a 'can do' style of conduct characterized by 'decisiveness and an ability to get things done, rather than the more traditional approach which lays greater emphasis on analysis of options and recommendations for action based upon that analysis' (RIPA 1987). The obvious danger here is that public servants are now required to develop 'personal' enthusiasms for particular policies and projects and as a consequence the bureaucratic (liberal pluralist) 'ethos of responsibility' is being abandoned. As Chapman has argued with regard to these reforms, 'the emphasis on enterprise, initiative, and a more business-like style of managment seems oddly at variance with the expectations of officials working in a bureaucracy' (1991b: 3).[3]

The central mechanism of Next Steps – the replacement of a 'unified' civil service by a host of 'autonomous' agencies – is explicitly represented as a means of enterprising up the public sector. The 'new' agencies, it is argued, are structured to enable civil servants to 'obtain a sense of ownership and personal identification with the product' (Goldsworthy 1991: 6). In other words, rather than seeking to moderate the perfectly understandable enthusiasms of public officials for particular projects and policies the agency system seems designed to incite them.

> Staff, we are told, now often think of themselves as belonging to a particular department or agency, not to a wider civil service. They work in units that, far from displaying a team spirit with a common ethos, compete with each other. Efforts are now made to stimulate feelings of enterprise and initiative in them and there can be no doubt that these have resulted in a fundamental change from an ethos which contributed to the identity of the civil service. (Chapman 1991b: 3)

The advocates of these reforms seem unable to imagine that business management and public administration are not identical in every respect. While there is a sense in which the state and the business concern are both rational 'enterprises' deliberately and explicitly directed towards advancing goals and objectives in an efficient and effective manner, public administration differs from business management primarily because of the constraints imposed by the political environment within which the management processes are conducted. Simply representing public bureaucracy in economic terms as an inefficient form of organization fails to take account of the crucial ethical and political role of the bureau in liberal democratic societies. If bureaucracy is to be reduced or abandoned and an entrepreneurial style of management adopted then it must be recognized that while 'economic efficiency' might be improved in the short term, the longer term costs associated with this apparent 'improvement' may well include procedural neutrality, impartiality, complex equality, pluralism, and other crucial 'qualitative' features of liberal democratic government. As Chapman argues:

> When attention is focused on public sector management as distinct from management in other contexts, a distinctively bureaucratic type of organization, with accountability both hierarchically and to elected representatives, may mean that far from being inefficient it is in fact the most suitable type of organization. Consequently, regarding bureaucracy as an inefficient type of organization may reflect a superficial understanding of bureaucracy and, perhaps, a blinkered appreciation of public sector management. Bureaucracy may be more expensive than other types of organization, but that is not surprising when democracy is not necessarily the cheapest form of government. (1991a: 17)

We are in no danger of forgetting the disasters and dangers to which bureaucracies are prone if we remind ourselves every now and again of the threats – including those posed by an unbridled entrepreneurialism – against which they offer protection.

Concluding Remarks

There may well be a compelling case for making certain bureaucracies more responsive to the publics they serve. It is also possible that particular 'entrepreneurial' approaches to such a project are not without merit: certain services currently supplied by state bureaucracies might be better run by civic organizations, enhancing rather than endangering the liberal democratic art of separation. However, these decisions should be made on a case by case basis. Admitting the sagacity of such a move in one case does not mean that all services can or should be removed from public bureaucracies and handed over to civic organizations. To harbour the desire that they should is to lose sight of the bureau's crucial political and ethical role in separating public administration from moral absolutism. In other words, while reforms of this institution – such as reductions in its size and cost – may be welcomed, they should not be carried through to the point at which they are liable to undermine the bureau's political and ethical role as outlined above.

Similarly, arguing that there are distinct limits to the efficacy of deploying entrepreneurial norms and techniques within the public sector does not amount to saying that such forms of governance are uniformly bad. It simply means that such norms and techniques and the conceptions of personhood they give rise to should not be unilaterally imposed upon other spheres of existence.

Notes

Different versions of this chapter have appeared as 'Making Up Managers: Bureaucracy, Enterprise and the Liberal Art of Separation', *British Journal of Sociology* 1994, and 'Colossal Immodesties and Hopeful Monsters: Pluralism and Organizational Conduct', *Organization* 1994. I would like to thank Stuart Hall, Ian Hunter and members of the History of the Present network in London for their comments on an earlier draft of this chapter. The concerns of the chapter develop from the work on 'making up managers' that I am currently conducting with Graeme Salaman. The financial support of the ESRC (grant no. R000234869) is gratefully acknowledged.

1 It is at this juncture that the 'entrepreneurial' critique of bureaucratic culture becomes almost indistinguishable from that deployed by communitarian critics of managerialism (MacIntyre 1981; Anthony 1986) and some feminist critics of 'bureaucratic rationality' (Ferguson 1984; Pringle 1989).

2 As Ian Hunter has suggested, it is all too easy to forget, as proponents of political romanticism are apt to do, that the capacity of the bureau to divorce politics from absolute principles is a historically contingent and fragile achievement that those of us who live in pacified societies should not take for granted.

3 There are a number of famous examples of the disasters that can befall when public officials act in a manner befitting the conduct of an entrepreneur or a politician. With regard to British public administration see, for example, Chapman's (1988: 302–3) discussion of the Crichel Down case.

References

Anthony, P. (1986) *The Foundations of Management*. London: Tavistock.

Bauman, Z. (1987) *Legislators and Interpreters*. Cambridge: Polity Press.

Boyatzis, R. (1982) *The Competent Manager: A Model of Effective Performance*. London: Wiley.

Burchell, G. (1993) 'Liberal Government and Techniques of the Self', *Economy and Society*, 22 (3): 266–82.

Chapman, R.A. (1988) *Ethics in the British Civil Service*. London: Routledge.

Chapman, R.A. (1991a) 'Concepts and Issues in Public Sector Reform: the Experience of the United Kingdom in the 1980s', *Public Policy and Administration*, 6(2): 1–19.

Chapman, R.A. (1991b) 'The End of the Civil Service?', *Teaching Public Administration*, 12(2): 1–5.

Du Gay, P. (1991) 'Enterprise Culture and the Ideology of Excellence' *New Formations*, 13.

Ferguson, K. (1984) *The Feminist Case against Bureaucracy*. London: Sage.

Goldsworthy, D. (1991) *Setting Up Next Steps: a Short Account of the Origins, Launch and Implementation of the Next Steps Project in the British Civil Service*. London: HMSO.

Gordon, C. (1987) 'The Soul of the Citizen: Max Weber and Michel Foucault on Rationality and Government', in S. Whimster and S. Lask (eds), *Max Weber: Rationality and Modernity*. London: Allen and Unwin.

Gordon, C. (1991) 'Governmental Rationality: an Introduction', in G. Burchell, C. Gordon and P. Miller (eds), *The Foucault Effect*. Brighton: Harvester Wheatsheaf.

Handy, C. (1987) *The Making of Managers*. London: MSC.

Hunter, I. (1991) 'Personality as a Vocation: the Political Rationality of the Humanities', *Economy and Society*, 19(4): 391–430.

Kanter, R. (1990) *When Giants Learn to Dance*. London: Unwin Hyman.

Kanter, R., Stein, B. and Jick, T. (eds) (1992) *The Challenge of Organizational Change*. Reading, MA: Addison-Wesley.

Keat, R. (1990) 'Introduction', in R. Keat and N. Abercrombie (eds), *Enterprise Culture*. London: Routledge.

Larmore, C. (1987) *Patterns of Moral Complexity*. Cambridge: Cambridge University Press.

Lyotard, J.F. (1984) *The Postmodern Condition* (trans. G. Bennington and G. Massumi). Minneapolis: University of Minnesota Press.

MacIntyre, A. (1981) *After Virtue*. London: Duckworth.

Miller, P. and Rose, N. (1990) 'Covering economic life', *Economy and Society*, 19: 1–31.

Minson, J. (1991) 'Bureaucratic Culture and the Management of Sexual Harassment'. Institute for Cultural Policy Studies Occasional Paper no.12, Griffith University.

Minson, J. (1993) *Questions of Conduct*. Basingstoke: Macmillan.

Osborne, D. and Gaebler, T. (1992) *Re-Inventing Government*. Reading, MA: Addison-Wesley.

Peters, T. (1987) *Thriving on Chaos*. Basingstoke: Macmillan.

Peters, T. (1992) *Liberation Management*. Basingstoke: Macmillan.

Peters, T. and Waterman, R. (1982) *In Search of Excellence*. New York: Harper and Row.

Pollard, S. (1965) *The Genesis of Modern Management*. Harmondsworth: Penguin.

Pringle, R. (1989) *Secretaries Talk*. London: Verso.

RIPA (1987) *Top Jobs in Whitehall: Appointments and Promotions in the Senior Civil Service*. Royal Institute of Public Administration Working Group Report.

Rorty, A. (1988) *Mind in Action*. Boston: Beacon Press.

Rose, N. (1989) 'Governing the Enterprising Self'. Paper presented to a Conference on the Values of the Enterprise Culture, Lancaster University.

Rose, N. (1990) *Governing the Soul*. London: Routledge.

Sabel, C. (1990) 'Skills without a Place: the Reorganization of the Corporation and the Experience of Work'. Paper presented to the BSA Conference, University of Surrey, Guildford.

Walzer, M. (1984) 'Liberalism and the Art of Separation', *Political Theory*, 12(3): 315–30.

Weber, M. (1968) *Economy and Society* (3 vols). New York: Bedminster.

2

The Mentality of Management: Self-Images of American Top Executives

Klaus P. Hansen

Each age reveres its own type of hero. The Renaissance revered disco-
verers; the eighteenth century kings, poets and philosophers; and the
nineteenth century statesmen and generals. We, however, the last generation of the twentieth century, get enthusiastic about top athletes, rock
musicians, film stars and all the other darlings of the media. Every epoch
admires what it deserves.

Recently, though, we've added a new idol and one whose previous
reputation had been rather low or at any rate ambivalent. I refer to
business managers, entrepreneurs, the 'captains of industry' who control
large parts of the American economy. They've almost become cult figures
and seem to awaken in us the same kind of fascination the older generation
in Great Britain used to feel for royalty. They are surrounded by an aura of
high achievement, leadership positions, power, huge bank accounts,
stretch limousines and luxury.

This dramatic move up the ladder of public esteem only became possible
because business people acquired a new *image*. We can see signs of this
almost everywhere: just think of the television series 'Dallas' for instance
or (something new in journalism) glossy, mass-circulation magazines
devoted to business. Over the course of time business people have
naturally had any number of different images but they usually weren't very
flattering. The Renaissance saw them on a scale between royal merchant
and *nouveau riche* moneybag, and in the period of industrialization their
image vacillated between technical pioneer and inhuman exploiter.

That this ambivalence has given way to admiration can also be seen in
another phenomenon: business people are now considered worthy of
autobiography. In the nineteenth century sitting down in old age to record
the wisdom of a lifetime was a privilege reserved for theologians,
statesmen, philosophers and poets. For centuries such a thing would have
been unthinkable for a merchant or any other kind of business person.
After all, it was well known that it would be easier for a camel to go
through the eye of a needle than for a rich man to enter the Kingdom of
Heaven, and this biblical condemnation of merchants and money changers
had a lasting effect.

Meanwhile, however, the eye of the needle has become an arch of triumph. In the United States, where traditional ways of thinking are more readily abandoned than in Europe, even the heroes of the industrial revolution began writing autobiographies: Andrew Carnegie for example or Henry Ford, the man who supposedly invented the assembly line. These books naturally did not go unnoticed by their contemporaries but they were not enough to establish entrepreneurial autobiography as a literary genre. It is only in our own day that they've found successors.

In 1984 the autobiography of Lee Iacocca appeared, the man who had been at the top first of Ford and then of Chrysler; in 1988 Donald Trump followed with *The Art of the Deal*; and in 1990 Thomas J. Watson Jr published the story of his and his father's life *Father, Son and Co.*, which is also a history of IBM. The broad cultural acceptance of these autobiographies can be seen in the fact that they soon made their way to the top of the best-seller lists.

Heroes create curiosity. This accounts for the huge editions of Watson, Trump and Iacocca. People buy these books because they want to find out what makes these big-time operators different from themselves; what it is that makes their achievements so unusual. In his best year, before the fortunes of Chrysler Corporation began declining again, Lee Iacocca pulled down $20 million, and Donald Trump was at one time worth $2 billion – unimaginable sums for the average person on the street.

But how do these people who actually ought to know see the secrets of their own success? What does it take to become the head of an enormous corporation and make a success of it? I'd like to pursue this question using the three autobiographies I've mentioned. Just to round off the picture I'll take brief glances at the memoirs of Carnegie and Ford. I won't try the reader's patience, however, with too many individual details and intend to concentrate on the essential core which my authors have in common.

Apart from hard work, which is a truism, my authorities on business success, Iacocca, Watson and Trump, all emphasize three abilities as absolute prerequisites: leadership; decisiveness; and an intuitive feeling for the market. In other words: these three character traits are a must for any business person who wants to succeed. They will be familiar to us since they are also expected by any company hiring an executive. Let's go through these three qualities one by one, by asking ourselves the question: are these qualities really essential for success in business?

All three autobiographers insist that someone at the top must have strong leadership qualities. Donald Trump for example is proud of his aggressiveness, his toughness and his strong will. He tells us that he had these qualities already as a child and that when a teacher slapped him he slapped the teacher right back. In some sections of the book he poses as a sort of Nietzschean 'superman' who fearlessly mows down every form of opposition without regard for the consequences. Watson Jr has similar things to tell us. He admires the unrelenting mercilessness of his father and sums up the insights of both father and son as follows: 'a business is a dictatorship, more efficient than a government with checks and balances'.

As we can see from this quotation, business leaders seem to admire dictatorships. Henry Ford was no exception to this and ruled his corporation with an iron hand. He was unrelenting in his conviction that his famous Model T was the great invention of the century and even when sales began to go down he refused to consider any new design conceptions. Once when Henry Ford was absent from the firm for a considerable period his son Edsel took advantage of the situation and began experimenting with a six-cylinder motor. When his father finally returned, the son proudly wanted to present the results of these experiments. He was delighted when his father suggested assembling the whole firm for this occasion. But dictator Henry Ford used the audience for dramatically destroying the prototype, thus giving a warning to anybody who might think of not following his orders.

The son Edsel Ford died of a stomach ulcer at the age of fifty; and in the meantime, although the company was in the red, Henry Ford still refused to give up his Model T. He even hired a prize-fighter to intimidate the board of directors. Finally, his wife and the widow of his son got together and threatened to sell their shares. This would have meant that the corporation would no longer be in the control of the Ford family and Henry was forced to relent. And so two cunning women outwitted the tyrant.

Biographers usually talk about senility in such cases but actually they're missing the point. Senility only becomes dangerous when the person afflicted by it has absolute power which makes it difficult to remove him when he is no longer competent. Shortly before Watson Senior's death at the age of eighty his doctor confided the following diagnosis to his son: 'Your father's stomach looks like the battlefield of the Marne.' But the battles which produced this scarred stomach tissue weren't only about business. They also took place at home and had consequences for others as well. The younger son (who wrote his autobiography) suffered from depression and had to give up his career at fifty because of heart trouble; his brother suffered from severe asthma attacks; and his daughter was still unmarried at thirty because her father had driven away any potential suitors.

A tyrant at home, Watson Sr behaved towards his employees like the petty dictator of a banana republic. His picture was on the wall of every office; each morning every employee had to sing the IBM hymn, and on their lunch hours they were strongly encouraged to read his editorials in the company newspaper. Using such methods he was naturally able to whip up a sort of 'corporate identity' but his style of leadership can't have been highly motivating for everyone. As a matter of fact it very nearly resulted in IBM missing out on electronic data processing altogether. Watson Sr still believed in his punch cards and the Hollerith machines that IBM had begun with. His son, however, saw the potential for electronic data and a terrible struggle for power ensued, the outcome of which was determined not by arguments but by a war of nerves which the son luckily won.

Our autobiographers praise strong leadership but at the same time and without realizing it they also show us the other side of the coin. They don't seem able to see how easily autocratic rule can turn into obstinate high-handedness. While almost every other sector of society has abandoned the idea of autocracy, the business world has stuck to it tenaciously. People in politics know that a dictatorship is simply impractical because it leaves too much scope for arbitrary despotism. And what applies to an enterprise such as the state also applies to commercial enterprises: they too have to be ruled by structures rather than individuals. An enterprise can only function efficiently if it is ruled by a system, by a structure which is almost independent of individuals and their idiosyncrasies – something the Japanese figured out long ago. In Europe and the United States, however, people still believe in Schumpeter's notion that the kind of drama produced by the personal element is somehow productive.

But there is another factor as well: teamwork has become increasingly important in the solution of complex problems. We can see this in the sciences but also in any research and development department where engineers, scientists and marketing specialists all work together. The logic behind this is simple and obviously just good common sense: two heads are better than one. In a world which becomes more complex from day to day, a wide variety of technical knowledge and professional experience is vastly more efficient than the lonely decisions of an all-powerful leader.

But let us now turn to the second of the supposedly indispensable prerequisites for a successful business person. Watson Junior's former boss Charlie Kirk introduced him to decision-making. 'I learned how to make decisions for Kirk was excellent at making them fast and making most of them right.' For a simple minded lay economist like myself this seems a little odd. After all, isn't the whole point of decision-making to find the *right* decision? But here the *speed* with which a decision was made matters more than whether it was right or wrong. And this isn't just some peculiarity of Watson's. Decisiveness is expected of any top executive and it means rather the capacity for speedy and enthusiastic decision-making than the ability to make the right decisions.

When Watson was first confronted with anti-trust proceedings and had to deal with highly complex legal questions his first reaction was to 'fight like hell'. He immediately hired the 'toughest' lawyer he could find but then didn't quite know what to do with the rest of all his 'fighting spirit'. The slow pace of legal proceedings frustrated him because it thwarted his main character trait: 'All my life my answer to complicated circumstances has been to make a dramatic and decisive move, but this time there were no such moves to make.' The logic behind this is that the more complicated a Gordian knot is, the quicker and fiercer it has to be slashed. Watson relies less on informed competence and rational analysis than on action for its own sake which he describes using military imagery.

But when we take a closer look at the concrete examples these men use to document their passion for quick and dramatic decision-making, another picture begins to emerge. In his Chapter 6 Iacocca describes one of the most important decisions in the history of the Ford Corporation, the decision in favour of one of their most successful models, the Ford Mustang. The chapter begins with an attempt to evoke the spirit of the age: old-fashioned, grandfatherly Dwight Eisenhower was replaced in the White House by a man who fascinated America's young people; all America was caught up in a move toward 'new frontiers' and encouraged by an economic boom. Ford's emphasis on models with a low purchasing price and low operating costs therefore seemed outmoded. Iacocca put together a team of experts which soon came to the conclusion that the market could do with a model that was more like a sports car. Then, in order to test this theory, an extensive programme of market research was initiated. Soon, a number of basic trends became clear: the relative size of the generations had changed in favour of young people; a higher percentage had a college degree; people starting their careers were earning more money; and so on. These perceptions then formed the basis for an idea. They would design a medium-sized car, but one which *looked* like a sports car. As soon as there were reliable data, a prototype was made and the whole question was discussed throughout the firm.

Finally, after many meetings of numerous different committees and commissions, the project was approved. And where was Iacocca's love of quick decision-making in all this process? Nowhere, of course. In this procedure, which is typical for large corporations, Iacocca's role was not that of a fearless leader making lonely judgements in splendid isolation from the rest of the firm. Instead, he was a coordinator who gave impetus to a developmental process which was based on teamwork and reached its conclusions almost automatically.

Just as with their decisiveness, the third quality these men praise, namely intuition, is no less problematic. Watson Jr tells us for example that his father had 'run the company out of his vest pocket' (which is another way of saying 'intuition') and that he wanted to replace this with 'professional management'. And Carnegie emphasized that when a company reached a certain size it needed organization and structure rather than 'rule of thumb' management. But in another section of his book Watson Jr seems to be pleading for the exact opposite. Unlike Charlie Kirk whose approach he described as 'analytical', he personally claimed to prefer a style which was more 'intuitive'. Here, the reader is confronted with the paradox that the young boss whose goal was to professionalize IBM's management prefers instinctive to rational approaches. One might resolve the conflict this way: the lower and medium levels of the firms are the realms of systematic and rational decision-making, while at the top, where really important decisions are made, intuition is required. Iacocca always surrounded himself with analytic minds and experts but the rational proposals they worked out were then evaluated not according to rational standards but by the 'gut feeling' of the top management. Both Iacocca and Watson use professional analysts but at the same time they feel superior to them. Iacocca had a special dislike for graduates of the Harvard Business School and used to call them 'bean counters'. He based this judgement on his conviction that real life could not be accounted for by the theories of system-makers, and Watson agrees with him in this: 'Management is no science; it is much too human to qualify.'

The dubious, even dangerous quality of such instinctive decision-making can be seen in the way one of the twentieth century's most far-reaching management decisions was made. Let's take a look at how Watson Jr describes the way IBM decided to get into the computer business. Of his father's position he says: 'Having built his career on punch cards, Dad distrusted magnetic tape instinctively.' And a paragraph later he describes his own views: 'I knew in my gut we had to get into computers.' Here we have a confrontation between instinct and intestines – one that's not likely to be solved rationally. If we don't just dismiss these statements as business jargon and take what Watson Jr says seriously, then that means that the future of IBM was dependent on an irrational struggle between two different instincts.

Donald Trump is the most radical proponent of intuition. 'Too much structure' (which for him means any hint of organization) is something he rejects utterly because it supposedly inhibits spontaneous decisions. Assertively, though a bit ungrammatically, he propounds: 'One is to listen to your gut, no matter how good something sounds on paper.' Structure and paperwork, planning, systematization and organization, are all things which Trump feels are unworthy of a business leader and hold him back. But if one takes a closer look at Trump's successes, this soon seems very doubtful indeed. He planned, financed and constructed huge projects such as hotels and casinos so perfectly that he usually stayed 'in time and on budget'. This shows that he was a brilliant planner, organizer and construction manager. But these are qualities that he never mentions in his self-portrait where he much prefers to see himself as spontaneous and irrationally intuitive.

Well, what have I done so far? I examined the assertion – a very common one – that the aforementioned three qualities are a prerequisite for success in business or for running a corporation. I found out that the assertion is not true. It's a cliché, it's a stereotype to say that leadership, decisiveness and intuition are the most important capabilities of a business tycoon. And clichés are seldom in keeping with reality. But I want more than just to add another cliché to the long list of those already detected. I want to draw the reader's attention to the fact that outstandingly successful business leaders like Iacocca and Watson do not understand the nature of their own successes. They have false ideas about why they are successful. In other words there is a discrepancy between their practical actions and their theoretical interpretation of these. In the field of their highest expertise they misunderstand themselves. And this is a thought-provoking insight.

First, however, we have to answer another question. Since the three abilities are not the real foundation of success, why and how did they come into being? The answer is that each was an offspring of a certain epoch of our economic history.

If one compares the autobiographies from the 1980s with those of the beginning of the century, one thing is immediately noticeable. Whereas Ford and Carnegie both stress strong leadership, neither of them speaks of intuition or enthusiastic decision-making. And if one goes back even further to the eighteenth century one can no longer even find the idea of strong leadership. You don't find it in Benjamin Franklin's autobiography although he was a successful businessman, too. What seemed then most important was respectability. From this we can conclude that the individual abilities which go to make up the cliché developed during different periods of economic history and came into being as a result of specific circumstances of the times.

Carnegie and Ford were not only among the first great industrialists, they were also the first such authors to be in favour of strong leadership. The reason is simple. One result of the process of industrialization was that the corporations and plants grew bigger and bigger. This impressed their contemporaries so much that they used military metaphors to describe the mass of employees and labourers. They spoke of divisions or of a whole army. And an army, of course, needs a general or a commander with unlimited powers to control it. In using the military vocabulary one ignored, however, that an army is a well-structured unit which is supervised by a large bureaucracy. Only because of this is the general able to lead it. He would not be able to do it through his strong hand alone. Seen in this light, from the very beginning the idea of strong leadership has been a half-truth or a myth.

Decisiveness and intuition can also be traced back to historical economic conditions. Watson Jr can help us date the moments of their respective appearances. He mentions both traits only when talking about himself, never about his father. For the generation which was active between the wars they don't seem to apply; they only become important for those who took over control after the Second World War. The economic history after the war was dominated by two factors. On the one hand there was an increase in technological complexity, while at the same time the market was gradually becoming saturated.

Henry Ford still constructed his engines himself, and he was able to fully understand the technology of the cars leaving his factories. Watson Sr also knew just exactly how a punch card machine worked. His son, however, understood nothing of the electronics he was selling and had no real notion of how or why his computers functioned so well or so badly. The degree of technological complexity had increased to such an extent that it was no longer possible to be both a technician and a merchant at the same time. For executives this meant that they had to make decisions on matters which were actually outside their competence. When for example Watson Jr had to choose between magnetic tape and disks he had no clear technical knowledge of the nature of his options. He listened to his engineers argue with each other but had no possibility of exercising independent, rational control. The more complex a product is, the more entrepreneurial decisions have to be made on the basis of second-hand information that business people themselves are unable to check. This kind of calamity led to the propagation of non-rational qualities. It gave birth to the idea of decisiveness. To make a decision about something you don't really understand requires courage and a conscious effort. The glory which business people attribute to decisiveness makes a virtue of necessity by pretending to love something they actually fear.

A second condition of modern economies is that the market is essentially saturated. Most consumers already have everything they really need and even more than that. Quite rightly Henry Ford assumed that the function of the economy was to satisfy basic human needs such as transportation, and therefore he saw the market as predictable. But as soon as everybody already had a car, times grew more difficult. As soon as the basic needs have been satisfied, business has to create new, artificial needs. In this situation marketing skills begin to be dominant.

But this situation makes entirely new demands on business people. They are expected to develop new products which are supposed to sell well even though no one really needs them. Creating new needs, however, is largely a matter of aesthetics. Once real needs have been satisfied and products perfected to the point that significant improvements are no longer possible, competition takes place on the level of images and symbols. A product's design and the aesthetic symbols which constitute its image can, however, only be successful if they are accepted by the majority of the proposed target group. The crucial problem for business people and one which determines the fate of their companies is that they have to predict the trend, and that means to predict the cultural acceptance of new products. Since, unlike nature, culture is not subject to strict laws, making such predictions seems extraordinarily difficult. A decision made in this kind of diffuse atmosphere is considered non-rational and because of this gets relegated to the realm of instinct or intuition. Here, too, one makes a virtue of necessity: nebulous problems are transferred to equally nebulous abilities.

As I have already indicated, the three qualities which are supposed to solve the problems of management simply don't work. Strong leadership alone isn't capable of dealing with the enormous quantitative problems of a modern economy: there has to be an organization, a structure and, yes, even though economists do not like the word, a bureaucracy. Even the most dynamic decision-maker is no substitute for rational analysis and paying the kind of critical attention to experts which is possible even without specialized technical knowledge. Predictions about cultural acceptance cannot and will not simply dispense with rationality. Carried through with the proper methodology, results can be produced which are as reliable as those in the humanities or social sciences. Iacocca showed us how it was done. When the Mustang was developed he didn't just look at factors like personal income, he also paid attention to the cultural indicators of his time (Kennedy's election, the new youth culture, etc.). And he interpreted them correctly (new political beginnings, a move away from the post-war mentality). He based the whole conception of the new model not on some wild, intuitive insight but on a rational and systematic analysis of cultural factors.

These three characteristics we've been looking at are a reaction to economic conditions, but from the beginning they were a false reaction. When the business tycoons of today repeat them they are still false. But why do they repeat them? That men like Trump and Iacocca, despite all their practical experience, despite their success, still seem to delude themselves requires another explanation. We don't have to look far to find it. Executives, after all, also have to market themselves. This function is splendidly fulfilled by our three characteristics. They create a mythic aura. The cliché creates an image of strong-willed people at the top, making decisions in a way that only they could. Just like a great statesman or general, the top executive has intuitive insights and their quick decisions have no need of time-consuming analysis because they spring from the depths of their genius.

But why do people such as these who are held up as models for our very complex civilization still have the need for this kind of atavistic swaggering and irrationality? The three characteristics have one thing in common: they can't be learned. Strong leadership isn't on the curriculum of any school and you can't major in decisiveness or intuition. That's why Iacocca, Watson and Trump all advise against attending a university. In other words, the abilities you need to be a truly great businessleader are ones you either have or you don't. And the few chosen ones, the select, have had them from birth. These monarchs of the managerial level adorn themselves with unlearnable abilities, reserved for a small number of extraordinary individuals. But why this need to make themselves seem so special? Here one begins to get suspicious. Particularly in the United States, the heads of large corporations have managed to transcend the usual income level. Even compared to the top ranks of income, to physicians, lawyers and high government officials, all of whom are very well paid, the business executives are far ahead. In this income level, which begins at a million dollars a year, we find only media stars, pop musicians, some top sports people and a few top executives – chief among them our three autobiographers. But since income is supposed to be dependent on what one actually accomplishes, it can only be justified if the work these people are doing is also something vastly beyond everyone else. And here we have the reason not only for their supposed uniqueness but also for the ways they've exploited the cult of the genius and the cult of the leader.

References

Carnegie, A. (1920) *The Autobiography of Andrew Carnegie*. Boston and New York.

Ford, H. and Crowther, S. (1922) *My Life and Work*. London.

Iacocca, L. and Novak, W. (1984) *An Autobiography*. New York.

Trump, D. and Schwartz, T. (1988) *The Art of the Deal*. London.

Watson, T.J. Jr and Petre, P. (1990) *Father, Son and Co.: My Life at IBM and Beyond*. New York.

3

The Role of Social Identity in the International Transfer of Knowledge through Joint Ventures

John Child and Suzana Rodrigues

The world-wide growth of foreign direct investment (FDI) has far exceeded that of domestic investment and gross domestic products in the years since 1958. FDI is not merely a means of physical capital formation and employment generation; it also transfers at least some of the knowledge, practices and cultures of the investing companies. FDI is therefore an extremely important potential vehicle for the international transfer of managerial and organizational knowledge, especially to developing economies and/or those transforming into market systems.

By far the most important agents for this investment are transnational corporations which by 1994 totalled about 40,000 with some 250,000 foreign affiliates. Their investment is often introduced into an organization in which there is a mixture of foreign and host-country management. This may be an existing firm which is wholly or partly acquired or it may take the form of a new joint venture based on shared equity, or a contractual agreement or franchising. These international business ventures face a double learning challenge: that of ensuring an effective transfer of knowledge to the host unit and that of appropriate adaptation by the international partner to local conditions including the complementary strengths of the local organization.[1] The difficulties experienced by many international business ventures, and comments made by their managers, suggest that the achievement of this learning is problematic (Bleeke and Ernst 1993).

One of the reasons for the problematic nature of knowledge transfer (learning) in international business ventures lies in the phenomenon of social identity. This derives from people's awareness that they belong to one group (the 'in-group') to the exclusion of other groups ('out-groups'). Social identity becomes an important concern whenever people and differing backgrounds have to interact. International ventures bring people and different nations and organizational cultures together in the management of business activities. The phenomenon of social identity assumes particular complexity in the case of joint ventures between a local and a foreign firm in which they together create and share responsibility for a new firm, which is 'legally distinctive' from the parents (Geringer and Hebert 1989). There are at least three collective entities involved in a joint venture, each potentially being a reference for the members' social identity.

The intention of this chapter is to advance the thesis that the process of international knowledge transfer is bound up with the social identity of the participants in that process. It argues that social identities are consequential for the quality of learning that takes place and hence for realizing the full potential value of the knowledge being transferred. In turn, the knowledge being transferred and the way this is done can impact upon participants' social identities, particularly those of the recipients. These issues are explored with particular reference to *joint ventures* between foreign transnational corporations and local domestic companies. For the sake of simplicity we assume that there are only two such partners to the venture. Although there is reference to some examples drawn from investigations conducted by the authors and colleagues,[2] the intention is not to report findings but rather to encourage discussion of a neglected aspect of international knowledge transfer. The chapter begins by addressing the concept of social identity, and then proceeds to its manifestation in international joint ventures. Following that, the relevance of social identity for knowledge transfer is considered with reference, first, to the types of knowledge being transferred and, second, to the transfer process itself.

Social Identity

Research on social identity is as yet a relatively unexplored area in organizational theory (Borys and Jemison 1989) and, in general, there has been insufficient theoretical development of the subject (Weigert et al. 1986). Social psychologists view social identity as a subjective but social phenomenon whereby the individual definition of the self is based (at least in part) on how a person defines the fellows in his or her own group and others in equivalent groups (Tajfel 1982). This means that identity makes sense in so far as comparison between groups is possible. Within this approach, collective identity is a metaphor which captures, simultaneously and in a condensed form, group uniformity and distinction. Accordingly, identity is like a mirror with two faces: one face reflects what a particular group has in common – values, beliefs, ideologies, experiences, practices – whereas the other face reflects how this same group is distinguished from other groups in these same respects. It involves a sense of belonging to particular groups as opposed to others. Social identity theory views personal identity as inseparable from collective identities. It draws attention to interaction among groups which are culturally and/or ethnically distinct and also to the question of individual identification and commitment to a particular group, but in the context of the relative attractiveness of other reference groups.

Additionally, social identity theory does not treat personal identification as an episodic and disconnected phenomenon. Rather, this is seen to arise from the meanings that individuals attribute to their interaction with socially diverse groups during their lifetimes; for example, through familistic or particularistic relations (Parsons and Shils 1951). In other words, identification can derive from a person's family group, work group or other social groups (Berger and Luckmann 1964). The substantive meaning of individuals' identification can therefore be understood in the context of the family, work or community relations they have had within their biography and/or career (Giddens 1991).

Within this perspective, a manager's identification constitutes a set of meanings arising from his/her interaction with different reference groups during his/her life and career. The significance of each particular reference group will vary in accordance with the meanings of each experience for the construction or reinforcement of the manager's perceived self (Tajfel 1982). Thus, managers may simultaneously feel attracted towards and/or repelled by particular groups.

The managerial role, especially at the senior level where it integrates diverse functions, means that incumbents must be flexible and adapt their approach as they move between individuals and institutions both within the workplace and in other social contexts (e.g. with suppliers, customers or occupational groups). The existence of different role identities (Burke and Tully 1977; McCall and Simmons 1978) means that it is possible for the individual to identify with different and sometimes contradictory social groups. Consequently, social identity cannot be considered as a unitary phenomenon. Rather, it can be desegregated into several types and degrees of individual and collective embracement and distancing. For example, a manager may embrace the values of his/her national or age group, yet at the same time identify with colleagues in the same functional area.

By embracement we refer to commitment to, and involvement with, a particular institution, group or activity (Snow and Anderson 1987). Social identity, however, does not always manifest itself through the embracement of particular values and practices. It can also take the form of individual and group distancing. When people enact roles, associate or have to interact and negotiate with groups or institutions which are inconsistent with their self-concepts, they may reject, resist or cognitively distance themselves from those roles and institutions. In fact, group identity and embracement can manifest itself through distancing from other groups and people. Distancing itself can be the glue which sustains the sense of group cohesion and belonging. Collectively, feelings of embracement and distancing stem from how groups define and compare themselves in terms of various dimensions including skills, values, behaviour and performance.

Understanding social identity is not simply a matter of discovering its essence but one of discerning the social practices which create and sustain it. As collective modes of action and practice, national, organizational and occupational cultures are also important sources of meaning for identity. Symbols of identity like cars, dress, political and professional attachments are defined by social, bureaucratic and legal conventions. In other words, modes of behaviour are inscribed through interactions of the individual with and within institutions. Cultures are internalized ways of thinking and behaving. We can only make sense of a nation, a bank, a school, or a computer manufacturer in terms of a framework of shared meanings. A national identity, for example, consists of the attributes which are collectively conceived to be specific to a particular nation (Poole 1992: 16). Similarly, an organizational identity is a metaphor used to describe and simplify 'distinctive and enduring organizational characteristics' (Albert and Whetten 1985: 280). National, organizational and occupational identities comprise the total feelings held by members, respectively of, the nation, the organization or the occupation about those values, symbols and shared histories that identify them as a distinct group. Nevertheless, these identities may express themselves as quite different social outcomes.

Thus a strong national identity among managers may express itself in the form of a determination to offer employment to fellow nationals rather than to foreigners, a reluctance to socialize with foreign personnel, an insistence on communicating only in the national language, and an adherence to customary national modes of behaviour. A strong organizational identity might express itself in the form of close adherence to corporate policies and norms, and an assumption that career advancement will be within that company. A strong occupational identity may express itself in the form of adherence to a specialist functional perspective, hostility to the members of other specialist areas, and an assumption that career advancement will be within the occupation rather than through staying with the one company.

Social Identity in International Joint Ventures

International joint ventures (IJVs) contain a number of social reference groups for identity. There are at least three collective organizational entities involved in an IJV, namely the parents and the venture itself; each is a potential focus for the social identity of the personnel concerned. There are at least two national reference groups, and this applies to other forms of international business collaboration as well. In the case of joint ventures there could be more, as when companies from several nationalities decide to establish a collaborative venture or when the partners decide to bring in a management team from a third country (as in the case of some international joint venture hotels). There will also normally be a range of occupational groups within an IJV whose identities may extend across national and organizational boundaries, but differ significantly among themselves.

The venture itself may be a self-directed and autonomous organization, with its inherent properties distinguishing it from 'significant others', its parents and similar organizations (Foote 1951). This will depend on the outcome of the play of interests between the parent companies and on their expectations as to the joint venture's future. Studies in this area suggest, however, that such a high degree of joint venture distinctiveness is not often found. In the first place, loyalty is problematic (Gregersen and Black 1992). Role theory indicates that individuals in organizations experience multiple attachments to multiple constituencies (Gouldner 1958; Aldrich and Hecker 1977; Reichers 1985). In order to maintain IJV managers' loyalties to their company of origin, parent companies design specific strategies. For example, they guarantee the salary level of their managers and prepare them for repatriation; this lends a feeling of impermanence to their jobs as IJV managers. Secondly, there is the question of how far one of the parents seeks to impose its own culture and practices on the joint venture company, and the level to which this will be accepted by the other company/companies involved in the IJV.

It is widely recognized that the success of international joint ventures is limited by the difficulties that managers and staff coming from different parent organizational cultures have in understanding and accepting other collective modes of organizing and managing. These difficulties are likely to be compounded when the social differentiation between the groups is national as well as organizational. Peterson and Shimada (1978), for example, attribute the instability of American and Japanese alliances to the contrasting perspectives held by their two groups of managers. The difficulties of doing business with the Japanese and with the Chinese (Child et al. 1994) have been attributed to the Japanese reluctance to acknowledge organizational cultures different from their own (Sethi 1975) and to the general suspicion of foreigners embedded in Chinese culture (Campbell and Yee 1991).

Social identity theory thus appears to be highly relevant for an understanding of international organizations since it takes personal identity and consequent action to be inseparable from collective identities. It draws attention to interaction among groups which are ethnically, corporately or occupationally distinct, with particular reference to the question of how individuals commit to a particular group in the context of the relative attractiveness of other potential reference groups. The creation of a joint venture brings new potential reference groups into being, such as the venture itself and the other parent company/companies involved.

Our preliminary investigations of IJVs have so far focused on the national cultural sources of social identity though, as has been noted, these are not the only social bases for the phenomenon and there is always the danger of slipping into, and reproducing, cultural stereotypes. These studies nevertheless indicate that feelings of embracement and distancing are expressed in how the members of their constituent groups define and compare themselves in contrast to others. For example, the Brazilian manager of a Brazilian-Japanese joint venture defined his Japanese counterparts as 'a detailed and particular people who lose too much time in checking information, take too long to make decisions, have a rigid hierarchy and make an unnecessary fuss to their parent company about problems in the joint venture'. In the same IJV, Brazilians were seen by the Japanese as people who 'do not know how to systematically organize and who work for themselves rather than for the company' (Drummond 1992). The two faces of the mirror are quite clear when these statements are compared. Such statements, expressing a sense of distance between managers identifying with different social groups within IJVs, also begin to indicate how the emotional significance of such distancing can create problems for the smooth transfer of knowledge.

To take another example, the senior Chinese manager of a Sino-American joint venture said that work relationships between American and Chinese personnel had been tense because, when endeavouring to introduce new methods, the 'foreigners shouted at the (Chinese) staff and did not understand that in China the workers are the masters of the house.' A particular conception of status and self-respect among the Chinese had clashed with foreign patterns of behaviour leading to a reinforcement of separate social identity through distancing and consequently to problems in knowledge transfer.

In the same IJV, a foreign manager criticized the Chinese approach to marketing: 'They do not believe in distribution. Our partner believes they make the products and it is enough to put them on the floor so that people will come and buy them. We do not see it in this way because if we want a long term business we have got to do things properly.' Again, the social distancing of one collaborating national group from the other accompanied a perceived difference in behaviour.

An identity conflict frequently fosters social categorizations and stereotyping. In the process of social categorization, individuals make negative and positive evaluations of themselves, the group they belong to, and other groups in a way that makes sense to them (Tajfel 1982). Goffman's (1959) concept of the 'performed self' suggests that individuals use their engagement in social interaction in order to improve their self-concept. People's evaluation of others tends to be favourable to their own self-image and self-concept. Thus, while relationships with others inform self-definition, self-definition in turn guides and sets the parameters for ideas regarding others. By a similar social process, groups conceive themselves as being superior or inferior to other reference groups. The relative superiority of 'the dominant group' stems from forcing upon 'the inferior group' a negative image, as the former is in a position to lay down rules and impose a definition of the situation which is favourable to their skills, resources, and competencies.

By joining managers of different national and organizational identities into the common task of running a business, IJVs provide the ground for contested or conflicting identities.[3] Managers of different parent companies bring to the IJV different maps of meanings which are not only in their minds but explicitly defined through organizational practices. These maps of meanings, 'maps of belief structures' (Markóczy 1992: 16), reflect not only internalized managerial practices but managers' national culture and other biographical characteristics such as age, education and experience. Child and Markóczy (1993) argue that managers also develop attitudes consistent with the institutional context. Managers who worked in planned economies are likely to have different ideas about managing a business to those of their Western counterparts. For example, Hungarian managers in IJVs complained that 'foreigners do not really understand the Hungarian market, the regulatory conditions and the other rules of the game, and therefore push for actions and make business decisions which are inappropriate under Hungarian conditions' (Markóczy 1992: 11). Although maps of meanings are not equivalent to identities themselves, they embody collective beliefs about dimensions of social life, including conceptions on how an organization should be managed.[4]

In management the way of doing things has a symbolic relevance in creating proximity and distancing between groups. In other words, the sense of 'us' and 'them' is defined primarily by the way of doing things and accepted modes of self-expression. The corporate cultures of joint venture partners may contrast significantly in these respects, particularly when the match is between a transnational and a local domestic company. Transnational corporations usually bring to foreign countries standard practices which have proved to be successful elsewhere. However, what the foreign partner sees as 'rational and objective practice' may be considered by the domestic partner as inappropriate or even illegitimate in the local social and political environment (Markóczy and Child 1995). The lack of understanding of each partner's logic of action can easily change a disagreement over an issue into a struggle over spheres of legitimate authority. Once the issue becomes one of 'territory', the factor of social identity will be brought into play (Royce 1982). In other words, a conflict over what is seen as 'the rational' way of doing things as opposed to 'the traditional' way may lead to a division within joint venture management whereby managers have a heightened sense of the distinctiveness of each parent company. The social identity of the management groups and conflict between them become mutually reinforcing. In this kind of situation, managers will tend to identify with their parent companies and they may find it difficult to create and propagate aims and practices suited to the joint venture itself.

National cultural differences in the partners' orientations constitute a further sensitive area in the management of an IJV and may foster feelings of distancing and conflict between them. Take, for example, the dimension of collectivism–individualism identified by Hofstede (1991). Brazilian managers distance themselves from foreign counterparts not only in their location along the dimension but also in the forms of collectivism they espouse. In the first place, they frequently complain about the difficulty of conforming to the formal system of communications required by most foreign business partners. This appears to reflect a Brazilian preference for individual idiosyncratic behaviour within organized contexts. However, it also appears that Brazilian and Japanese managers value different aspects of collectively oriented behaviour. The Japanese reject the Brazilian managerial practice of employing friends and relatives in the organization. At the same time, the Japanese adherence to consensual decision-making is seen by the Brazilians as a waste of time in a highly unstable economic environment.

Some societal cultures tend to be more ethnocentric than others and do not value any culture different from their own. As collective modes of action and practice, some cultures can only patronize or underestimate the alternatives they encounter (Dumont 1986). Thus, although 'developed' and 'developing' countries are familiar expressions, the idea of development is far from being unequivocally unidirectional. In IJVs, the partner companies from both developed and developing countries are likely to expect respect for their social identities and to believe that the other partner has something to learn from them.

In the international business context, ideas of national superiority may manifest themselves not only through categorizing partner attitudes and culture as negative, but also through professional attitudes whereby learning is conceived as a one-way process, especially by transnational partners. For example, the foreign managers we interviewed in Brazilian IJVs always saw Brazilian informality in communications as negative and as preventing the development of formal reports and communication. In reality, personal communications can speed matters up as well as effectively elicit personal commitments to action, and they may not necessarily be in competition with formal methods of communication. The interviews with the foreign managers of Sino-American joint ventures suggest that their attitudes towards Chinese managers tend to be patronizing as well: 'they don't understand the market'; 'their way of thinking is not right, they should change it'; 'they should learn from us'; these and similar views were frequently expressed.

In joint ventures, the definition of one partner as superior can serve the political purpose of maintaining that partner's hegemony or as a justification for the division of power and distribution of resources. Further, the perception of a hierarchy among the partners may lead to a rather fragmented business policy and disconnected actions, especially when there is low trust between them. Social categorization involves a cognitive and emotional segmentation, an interpretation of the social world in such a way that it psychologically unifies and identifies people from one side and separates and isolates people from the other. At best, it may lead to an acquisition of technical knowledge accompanied by resistance to the partner's managerial practices and thinking which could inhibit the effective utilization of the technical knowledge. At worst, it may lead to a situation in which exchanges are unbalanced, information is concealed and people are excluded from opportunities to learn.

Types of Internationally Transferred Knowledge

Transnational corporations see themselves in relation to developing or transforming economies as purveyors of business and managerial expertise. Local managements also rationalize their linkages with foreign firms as a means of acquiring not only technology but new managerial thinking and practices as well. The foreign parent is therefore likely to identify itself as the active partner in knowledge transfer and to legitimate this through an identity with its tried and proven track record in other parts of the world. Those transnational corporations providing goods or services which are international brands, such as the cola companies and hotel chains, are especially concerned to transfer knowledge and practice which support their product or corporate brands. In these cases, knowledge and practice are likely to be highly standardized, and supported by a strong organizational culture. Villinger comments that a Western branded consumer goods company 'through brands . . . establishes a strong cultural image which is generally not a flexible image for the host country. These firms, particularly those from the United States, are inflexible with respect to image, brand and corporate identity' (1993: 2). She notes further that 'corporate identity is a critical feature of the BCG [branded consumer goods] company' (1993: 3). In the case of American BCG companies which are foreign joint venture partners, a corporate belief in the necessity of applying international standards to protect the brand and image may join with a national belief in the need to introduce good (American) management practices such as human resource management, giving rise to an aggressive and inflexible approach to knowledge transfer which is supported by strong organizational and national identities.

This probably represents the more extreme case of an attempt to transfer knowledge in a predetermined standardized form without any substantial adaptation to the local context. This approach is most likely to arise in sectors where the foreign parent is providing goods or services the very standardization of which is seen to be a guarantee of brand integrity, and where the national business identity of that foreign parent is reinforced by a belief in its corporate management approach which has developed through a long history of international activity. It stems from the claim to international identity and credibility on the part of the foreign partner. It contrasts, and is likely to conflict strongly, with considerations of adaptation to the local environment which is part and parcel of the identity of host-country managers. Adaptation to local environments is the focus of cultural ecology, which has generated the concept of an 'ecological niche', referring to the fit of a group into its specific environment in such a way that it is able to exploit it successfully (Steward 1955).

Organizations adapt to their ecological niches when they make choices which are consistent with their local environment. Ecological adaptation on the part of IJVs concerns those behaviours which are peculiar to doing business in a particular region. It may imply rational behaviour but not always. It does not necessarily lead to efficiency gains, but it is linked to survival in the local environment. The use of professionals to disentangle documents or to secure authorizations from the Brazilian bureaucracies is an example of ecological adaptation to the inefficiencies of Brazilian public administration. The exercise of the 'Brazilian little way' (Da Matta 1981) is also manifest in many transactions, even though it may not be rational. Thus an identity card is usually required in Brazilian commercial transactions as if it provided a payment warranty. This widespread practice is not necessarily efficient since it is not legitimized by financial institutions and cannot guarantee payment.

The kind of adaptation to local conditions which develops among partners in international organizations depends on the inherent nature of those conditions. An instance might be how far trust or opportunism defines the features of economic transactions in the host country. In high-inflation economies like Brazil, many practices are created to ensure trust and to avoid opportunism. In China, many practices have been created to ensure employees' loyalty to the party. One way to capture ecological adaptation in international organizations is to compare what is standardized locally with what reflects an international practice. Forms of adaptation to the ecological niche may become clear if one is able to compare areas where standardization is local to the sector with what is common to international practice. In some situations, the 'self-presentation' of joint ventures is more Brazilian or Chinese than reflective of international practice.

Cultural anthropology suggests that the deep need to preserve their social identity drives different groups to find ways of maintaining their distinctive cultural boundaries, even when at the same time they have to learn a *modus vivendi* by incorporating features of the other group or by creating new practices which incorporate features of both cultures. The viability of each group in an international business collaboration therefore requires some preservation of the manifestations of its distinct social identity. Consequently, even the most standardized organizational practices imported from abroad will always incorporate some local practices and attitudes. Thus, despite the effort made by McDonald's to train local managers and staff in its standard practices, the style of dealing with customers remains Brazilian, Chinese, Hungarian or Russian. For example, all of the McDonald's outlets in Brazil have modern tills, but many for some time maintained the practice of writing manual receipts for customers, in this way following the practice of Brazilian retail outlets.

The knowledge that is available for international transfer in an IJV involving a foreign and a local partner therefore has two main sources which are also points of reference for identity: international and local. The former is adapted to international business practice, more precisely that of the transnational corporation, whereas the latter is adapted to the ecological niche. In the long run an IJV is unlikely to be successful unless its management can absorb, reconcile and apply both types of knowledge. One would expect this constructive reconciliation to be achieved when the managers coming from different partner groups can overcome the distancing inherent in their social identities and develop sufficient mutual trust to lay the foundation for shared understanding associated with an element of shared identity with the joint venture.

In addition to the distinction between the international and the local origin of knowledge transferred through IJVs, there is the further consideration that such knowledge is not intrinsically all of a kind. It is possible to distinguish three categories of such knowledge, each of which is likely to be perceived differently by the parties concerned in terms of their social identities. The three categories are, respectively, technical knowledge, knowledge about the design of systems and procedures, and strategic understanding.

Technical knowledge involves the acquisition and implementation of new techniques such as statistical quality control and market forecasting. Learning at this level may be confined to individuals or small specialist groups. It could amount merely to the acquisition of personal skills and does not necessarily have any wider behavioural or relational consequences. It is therefore not anticipated that the transfer of purely technical knowledge will normally raise significant questions of social identity or be seen as a threat to it. Indeed, the improvement of personal competencies may be perceived as enhancing professional occupational identity as well as the capacities of the receiving IJV partner. Much technical knowledge will be transferred between groups of people who share a similar occupational identity and who may therefore actually serve as a bridge for this transfer between the IJV partners. It is probably for these reasons that the international transfer of technical knowledge in IJVs has not, in our experience, normally generated much conflict or resistance – indeed, usually the contrary.

The international transfer of *systemic knowledge* refers to the introduction and operation of new systems and procedures. Examples are production control and budgeting systems, as well as those defining responsibilities and reporting relationships. These normally impact on relationships and coordinated behaviour within an organization, involving large groups if not the whole organization. For example, a new information system can require that people in an organization communicate with each other more directly than before and without the facility of ignoring messages from other departments. New remuneration systems may well establish different criteria for reward than were previously applied and these may well be experienced as exerting strong pressures to modify behaviour. Since new systems and procedures do normally require a change in workplace behaviour and relationships, they are liable to generate considerable sensitivities for social identity. If the systemic knowledge is being transferred from abroad, it is likely to be seen as threatening locally based norms of conduct.

Strategic understanding concerns the mindsets of senior managers, especially their criteria of business success and their mental map of factors which are significant for achieving that success. Many of the public articulations of business people and politicians in developing and transforming countries stress the benefit of acquiring new strategic understanding as a fundamental requirement for learning how to operate under competitive conditions, both in the international market and in developing domestic markets. Whereas, for instance, the critical environment for enterprises under an economic system reliant on state paternalism was one of public institutions and their normative expectations, that for enterprises in a market system is the strategic environment in which new managerial competencies are required to evaluate the enterprise's positioning in its sector (strengths, weaknesses) and the competitive threats and opportunities open to it (Child 1993).

The transfer of new strategic understanding presents a significant challenge to the self-perceived competencies of senior managers. These competencies were in many countries acquired in the course of leading the enterprise within a different set of institutional rules and often through managing a different set of key external relationships. The challenge to them is therefore likely to be interpreted as a threat to the very basis of their social identity as senior managers, since it was nurtured by a special set of competencies and relationships which identified them as a social group of standing and (often) privilege. This means that something more fundamental and personally challenging than a substantial rethinking of conceptual principles is required, though this itself is not easy to achieve for people who have taken these principles for granted through an often lengthy career. It is not surprising therefore to find many foreign managers reporting that the greatest problems of knowledge transfer have occurred in the area of strategic understanding (Child et al. 1994). Moreover, strategic decisions are of consequence for the organization as a whole. If the partnership with a foreign corporation substantially changes the priorities which lie behind such decisions, such as a greater emphasis on the pursuit of core business objectives at the expense of providing social welfare functions, then this may provoke widespread opposition because it threatens both material interests and values widely held within the local community. These changes will almost certainly be interpreted as threats to host-country identity.

This threefold categorization has emerged from preliminary field studies of IJV development. It contrasts with the distinction, advanced by Fiol and Lyles (1985) from their review of the literature, between 'lower-level' and 'higher-level' organizational learning. Fiol and Lyles identify lower-level learning as being primarily behavioural and at the level of organizational routines, while by contrast higher-level learning is primarily cognitive and at the level of understanding patterns of causation which affect the whole organization. The correspondence between the two schemes is not particularly close. The acquisition of technical knowledge involves cognitive learning, albeit within a restricted field and with the proviso that a mere imitation of technical practices could amount to little more than behavioural learning. The transfer of systemic knowledge could impinge on those affected primarily in the behavioural sense of learning new routines to follow; to this extent it corresponds with Fiol and Lyles's lower-level learning. However, the transfer of knowledge on systems design is primarily cognitive. The transfer of strategic understanding falls more clearly into the higher-level learning category.

The threefold categorization appears in the light of early investigations to distinguish more adequately between the forms of knowledge transfer within IJVs than does the Fiol and Lyles scheme. It draws attention both to the intrinsic difficulties of knowledge transfer, where an increase in the cognitive element may be assumed to present an additional learning challenge, and to the social difficulties of knowledge transfer, where social identity plays a role.

Our analysis suggests that both the source and the type of knowledge being transferred internationally in IJVs are relevant to the question of whether issues of social identity are likely to become involved in the transfer process. Looking at the matter from the perspective of the effectiveness of knowledge transfer, technical knowledge is least likely to be perceived as threatening local social identities. This is because (1) technical knowledge often adds to existing practices rather than replacing them, (2) it may have very few ramifications for the social life of the organization, (3) it is usually transferred between specialist groups sharing a similar occupational identity, and (4) it may not be perceived as conveying strong national or corporate values. Both IJV partners normally agree that the process of technical knowledge transfer is beneficial.[5]

Systemic knowledge is more closely tied to social identity because procedures and systems impinge upon culturally based norms of conduct. The more that systems introduced from abroad are concerned with ways of organizing and managing people, the stronger the implications for social identity are likely to be. In these areas, systems and procedures imported from abroad bid to usurp already existing practices, in contrast to those related to new and specialized issues such as procedures for conducting market research. Systems dealing with organizational and human resource matters impinge on issues that are already deeply embedded in people's consciousness of the appropriate social order: issues such as authority, power distance, relationships, personal dignity and social equity. Moreover, it is by no means always obvious that the foreign systems dealing with these matters are superior in terms of what is claimed for them by way of efficiency and financial criteria. It is difficult to establish proof of superiority for imported systems dealing with organizational and human resource issues. So it is in this sphere of international knowledge transfer that social identity is likely to be offended and negative reactions generated. In so far as there is a strong chance of resistance from the domestic side and the superiority of the foreign approach is not demonstrable, wisdom points to the sharing of knowledge and experience between the partners in order to achieve a mutual approach to the formulation of IJV systems.

The case of strategic understanding is different again. For here, both partners may agree that an input of foreign strategic knowledge is necessary to match the changing conditions of doing business in the host country and/or the aspirations of the host company to export into the international market. The underlying problem lies in the fact that the domestic partner is obliged to adopt a learning role, which implies an inferior right to strategic control over the joint venture and so threatens the basis of the host management's social identity and status. This may help to explain the fact, noted in some Sino-foreign IJVs, that senior local managers, on the one hand, accept the need to acquire new strategic understanding yet, on the other hand, criticize their foreign partners for failing themselves to understand the peculiar strategic requirements of doing business within the Chinese system. While this view may be accounted for rationally by reference to the differences between the overseas and domestic business contexts of Sino-foreign IJVs (albeit that the latter is fast changing), it also appears to express a perceived dilemma on the part of Chinese managers who are not sure how to cope with the threat posed to their social identity by the transfer of a new strategic understanding. Mutuality and compromise are not obvious solutions to this problem in the short term, if a substantial increment of strategic knowledge on the part of local managers is necessary for the success of the venture.[6]

The likelihood that the international transfer of different categories of knowledge is accomplished with varying degrees of difficulty because of its impact on social identities, and that there may be contrasting ways of accommodating to this problem, raises two further issues which are considered in the next and closing section. These are, first, the relationship between the social identity of the participants in knowledge transfer and the mode of transfer that is followed, and, second, the possibility that the process of knowledge transfer passes through different stages as the IJV matures.

Identity and the Process of International Knowledge Transfer

Our recent research suggests that the transfer and implementation of knowledge within IJVs can occur through different processes, or 'modes'. Four such modes have so far been identified and these are set out in Table 3.1. Distinctions are made between them according to whether changes in behaviour and cognition take place. The table is therefore a typology of ways whereby practical knowledge is transferred and adopted rather than of learning *per se*. It includes categories where only behaviour changes without a significant change in understanding.[7] The typology can in principle be applied separately to each of the three categories of knowledge which were identified earlier. Table 3.1 also postulates connections between the mode of knowledge transfer and the predominant social

Table 3.1   *Modes of knowledge transfer in international joint ventures*

Mode of transfer	Change in: Behaviour	Cognition	Predominant identity of IJV managers
1 Forced	Yes	No	With parent companies
2 Dependent:			
imitation	Yes	No	Foreign group: with parent company
			Domestic group: weakly with IJV
internalized	Yes	Yes	Foreign group: with parent company or IJV
			Domestic group: with IJV
3 Segmented	Part	Part	With parent companies
4 Mutual	Yes	Yes	With IJV

This representation assumes that the international transfer of knowledge is from foreign to domestic management groups.

identity of IJV personnel, and these are discussed as we now review each of the four modes.

There were indications from our studies that the likelihood of one mode of knowledge transfer prevailing rather than others could be influenced by two factors. The first is the *relative power in the venture of the foreign and domestic partner*, a feature much emphasized in the literature since Killing (1983) claimed that dominance by one partner facilitated the joint venture management process and was conducive to success. Dominance may be founded upon a formal basis, through majority ownership and control of board and senior managerial positions; it may also be achieved through control over scarce resources, market access, and knowledge. The second factor is *partner compatibility*. This is the product of several features including the compatibility of the partners' objectives, the complementarity of the resources they each bring to the joint venture and the compatibility of their organizational practices and cultures. One can appreciate how the cultural component of each partner group's identity, and the extent to which the groups distance themselves from each other in defining those identities, are among the elements of compatibility.

The first mode of knowledge transfer is 'forced' in the sense that the staff of a dominant partner insist that those of the other partner accept their techniques, systems or strategic priorities. When this dominant approach is not attractive to the other partner's personnel, because of incompatibilities in national or organizational culture which are not offset by other perceived benefits from the partnership, the recipients of the new knowledge are likely to experience resentment. Resistance to the new knowledge is more likely if the receiving group has a strong sense of its own identity which leads it to distance itself from foreign personnel. In turn, the resort to an aggressive mode of introducing new thinking and practices is likely to increase such distancing, so that the negative process becomes self-reinforcing. The probable consequence is that while the recipients of the new knowledge may modify their behaviour, they resist internalizing the rationale behind the changes they are obliged to accept. This mode of transfer will not therefore provide a sound basis for the longer term development of an IJV. If the dominant partner in such cases is the foreign investor, then it cannot rely on host-country personnel to take over the eventual running of the organization along lines it believes to be necessary to ensure sound performance. If the dominant partner is that of the host country, then forcing its approach on foreign personnel may destroy its chances of importing knowledge from abroad.

A situation where the process of international knowledge transfer is forced is likely to convince each group that it is right and the other is wrong. Their social identities will be further distanced with each group clinging strongly to its respective parent company as an identity referent.

A second situation is where there is an asymmetrical balance of power between the partners, but at the same time there is compatibility between them. For instance, the non-dominant partner believes the managerial approach introduced by the other to be beneficial. This partner seeks to acquire new techniques from the other or accepts that it can benefit from new systems and/or strategic acumen. In these respects, the dependent, knowledge receiving group is prepared to embrace the other group rather than distance itself from it. In such circumstances, a 'dependent' mode of knowledge transfer is likely to arise, which in turn can take two forms. If the receiving group accepts the new knowledge as superior without fully understanding the rationale behind it, then 'imitation' takes place and the effect is likely to be just a change of behaviour. If, on the other hand, it does comprehend the rationale behind the new approach, then the transfer becomes 'internalized' and learning is also achieved.

In this situation, the social identity of foreign personnel is likely to remain strong and oriented towards the parent corporation. The identity of the host group with its parent company will probably weaken over time in favour of a stronger identity with the joint venture itself. This emerging identity in turn provides a receptive ground for the transfer of further knowledge from abroad so long as it is seen to be beneficial to the joint venture.

A third mode of knowledge transfer within IJVs may be termed 'segmented'. This is more likely to arise in circumstances where the partners' power is relatively balanced, but their compatibility in terms of objectives and/or approach to management is low. This low compatibility is likely to be accompanied by a moderately high sense of separate identity. The segmented solution, observed quite frequently in joint ventures based in Russia (Hertzfeld 1991; Cattaneo 1992), is usually manifested by the partners taking responsibility for the organization and conduct of different areas of IJV activity. There is an obvious danger of suboptimization, if not disintegration, under this arrangement, and the transfer of knowledge and competencies between the partners is limited. The absence of an integrated upward communication of information under a segmented regime is also likely to jeopardize the quality of strategic decision-making in the IJVs concerned. Segmentation does not therefore offer a viable basis for the long term development of IJVs, or for them to be effective agents for knowledge transfer. It is likely to continue to sustain a sense of separate identity among the two partner groups.

A fourth mode of knowledge transfer within IJVs is 'mutual' in the sense that staff appointed to the IJV by both parent companies endeavour to address each other's experience and knowledge in a receptive and sensitive manner, in all probability learning from each other in the attainment of a new approach that is both mutually acceptable and suited to the IJV's specific situation. The preconditions favourable to mutuality are a relatively balanced distribution of power between the partners and a high level of compatibility between them. These factors are likely to minimize any sense of distancing between them. This mode of knowledge transfer is integrative in the sense noted by Mary Parker Follett in that it enables differences between the parties to be accommodated through a process of mutual problem solving which usually gives rise to an innovative solution (Metcalf and Urwick 1941). It is the transfer mode most likely to offer a basis for the long term development of an IJV as an organization with its own identity.

Our analysis suggests that social identity within IJVs is related to both knowledge transfer mode and its preconditions. In other words, the factors encouraging a particular transfer mode also have some direct impact upon social identity. Parent power will, *inter alia*, be manifest in control over appointments and reward criteria, and hence over the possibility of offering attractive future career opportunities to IJV managers and staff. It seems reasonable to assume that the availability of attractive rewards and career opportunities will, *ceteris paribus*, tend to strengthen their identity with whichever organization is offering these – parent company or joint venturer.

Partner compatibility is also likely to impact directly on identity. In IJVs where compatibility is low, managers and other personnel may well retain a strong identity with their separate parent companies. When compatibility is high, there is more chance that they will develop an identity with the joint venture itself, especially when the process of knowledge transfer is a mutual one and is producing solutions that are specific to the IJV rather than being derived from one or more of the parent companies. However, there is one category of IJV personnel who may identify with the joint venture even when partner compatibility is low. These are people appointed to work specifically for the joint venture and who do not, therefore, perceive the availability of a career path within one of the parent companies.

The considerations which we have raised draw attention to a fundamental paradox within IJVs, the resolution of which constitutes one of the greatest challenges facing their management. On the one hand, IJVs present special risks because they are collaborations between partners having a separate identity in which the control available to any one partner is limited. This creates a keen awareness of issues of control and power among their managers, which has been reflected in the literature (e.g. Killing 1983; Schaan 1988; Geringer and Hebert 1989). On the other hand, for IJVs to perform successfully, both as recipients in their own right of relevant new knowledge and as the means for knowledge transfer from one parent company to another, the parents have to learn how to cooperate and the members of the IJV have to achieve a degree of shared identity. In both respects, a learning process has to be accomplished. What the foregoing discussion has revealed is how difficult it may be to reconcile this need for learning with the social dynamics inherent in IJVs. Investigation of the adaptation modes in IJVs as they develop over time promises to reveal new insights into how this dilemma can be handled.

International joint ventures contain a problematic set of dynamics inherent in the relationship between their parents. The power balance and compatibility in their relationship can modify over time, in line with changes in the parents' commitment to the IJV, the venture's own success and other circumstances. The extent to which the IJV continues to be a recipient of international knowledge transfer rather than developing its own know-how and managerial approach is also likely to vary between cases, as the example cited in note 6 suggests. These sources of differential IJV development over time also give rise to an expectation that the issue of social identity between their constituent groups will be resolved in contrasting ways.

There is a need to investigate how these dynamics of international business collaboration work out over time and the paths of development to which they give rise. The following hypothetical examples of such paths are derived from the analysis presented earlier and they are certainly not exhaustive of every possibility. The purpose of presenting them is as a means of drawing the strands of our argument together and also of indicating what the authors believe is a challenging way forward for research.

Path A   The IJV begins with a dominant foreign partner and there is conflict or antipathy between personnel appointed by the partners owing to low compatibility. The social identities of the two groups are highly distanced. Over time the conflict reduces and trust grows. The foreign partner eventually lowers its (direct) dominance by granting more autonomy to the IJV, probably relying on host-country personnel whom it has trained. The result is a management shared between foreign and domestic partners. The likely path of development will be $1 \rightarrow 2 \rightarrow 4$ in Table 3.1, with the dominant mode of knowledge transfer changing from forced to dependent to mutual. As the IJV develops in this way, so its members will increasingly identify with it rather than with the parent companies.

Path B   The IJV begins with a balance of power between the partners but low mutual attractiveness. The social identities of the two groups are highly distanced. Areas of control are divided between the partners and the use of knowledge is therefore segmented with a foreign approach prevailing in some areas (e.g. finance and marketing) and a domestic management approach prevailing in others (e.g. production and human resource management). The resulting lack of management integration jeopardizes the IJV's performance. In order to prevent the IJV from fragmenting and disintegrating, the foreign partner comes to insist on greater control and imposes its approach to developing the IJV through a forced transfer of knowledge and practice. The result is an IJV dominated by the foreign partner which has in effect become a subsidiary of that partner. Eventually conflict reduces and some trust grows as the performance of the IJV improves and this may lead to a situation of dependent knowledge transfer. The path of development postulated here is $3 \rightarrow 1 \rightarrow 2$, with the transfer mode changing from segmented to forced to dependent. In this process, the partners' sense of separate identity is likely to rise at first and then subside.

Path C   The IJV begins with a balance of power between the partners and high mutual attractiveness. The social identities of the two groups are not highly distanced and each is willing to accept new knowledge from the other. The domestic management acquires new techniques from its foreign partner, which, however, takes the view that it also has to learn how to adapt to the domestic ecological niche. As the knowledge transfer matures, the foreign partner may withdraw from an active participation in IJV management since it is satisfied with the IJV's performance and also believes that its domestic partner's managers can cope adequately on their own. The path of development postulated here remains in category 4, with the IJV becoming a collaboration under domestic management control. This is likely to mean that the IJV is managed relatively autonomously under host-country management, with the IJV rather than the domestic parent company providing the main source of identity for that management.

Path D   The IJV begins with an imbalance of power and a low mutual attractiveness. The social identities of the two groups are highly distanced. The dominant partner attempts to force its approach on the other but the result is to generate resistance to change which leads the dominant partner to cut its losses and reduce its commitment to the IJV. The imbalance of power consequently reduces but mutual antipathy remains high, leading eventually to the collapse of the IJV either through the withdrawal of one partner, or through a decision by both partners to close it down, or because of a performance failure by the IJV. The path of development postulated here is $1 \rightarrow 3$ and then failure. In this example, the problem of incompatible social identities is never resolved.

Conclusion

The transfer of managerial and organizational knowledge is not a socially neutral process. Such knowledge is applied to practice and therefore impinges on organizational members' mental constructs and norms of conduct. Their social identity derives from a sense both of sharing such ways of thinking and behaving, and of how these contrast with those of other groups. The process of transferring practical knowledge between different managerial groups will be interdependent with the degree of social distance that is perceived between the parties involved. Thus, if initially this distance is high, the transfer is likely to be impeded. If the transfer is conducted in a hostile manner or in threatening circumstances, then the receiving group is likely to distance itself from those initiating the transfer. There is a clear possibility of virtuous and vicious circles emerging in this interaction.

While IJVs and other types of international business linkage are extremely important means for the international transfer of managerial and organizational knowledge, they introduce special sensitivities into the process. IJVs are the products of inter-company alliances that are often uneasy with respect to accommodating the interests of their constituent groups and managing the cultural contrasts between them. These differences contribute to a sense of separate social identity between staff who are attached or beholden to the respective partners.

Some types of internationally transferred knowledge impinge on group social identity more than others. This is particularly true of knowledge relating to new systems and strategic understanding. Resistance to the transfer of such knowledge is likely to heighten the separate identities of the partner groups, including those doing the knowledge transfer for whom persuading their recalcitrant colleagues may take on the nature of a crusade. The relation between social identity and international knowledge transfer is a dynamic one, in which contextual factors such as the performance of the joint venture also play a part through inducing changes in factors which condition the process, such as partner dominance and compatibility.

We have attempted to outline a way of thinking about these phenomena, in the hope that this might clear the ground for their eventual empirical investigation. Such investigation still faces a number of problems, one of them being the operationalization of social identity which remains a nebulous concept. Moreover, much closer work needs to be undertaken on the forms of knowledge being transferred, particularly if our argument is correct that the distinction between them is consequential for social identity and the role it plays. Last, but not least, we have argued that international knowledge transfer should be regarded as a process through time, the conditions of which may well change as the IJV develops along one of a number of possible paths.

Notes

An earlier version of this chapter was presented at the 11th EGOS Colloquium in Paris, July 1993. The authors wish to thank the members of Group 4 in the Colloquium for their constructive comments on the chapter which have assisted its further development.

1 It is assumed that foreign-investing companies will normally seek to transfer knowledge to their international business ventures and to harness the strengths of their host-country partners in developing those ventures. Nevertheless, the extent to which they wish to do this remains an open question. Many companies investing internationally restrict their transfer of technology, and/or local access to it, for fear that full and open transfer might be used later to their competitive disadvantage. Some investing companies may want their overseas joint ventures to function as branch operations rather than as full-blown businesses in their own right. The stance adopted by companies on these issues is likely to affect their preferences for the different modes of knowledge transfer discussed in the chapter, including that of non-transfer. This possibility is not addressed specifically in this chapter, but deserves attention in future research.

2 For reports on these investigations, see Child et al. (1990; 1994), Child and Markóczy (1993), Drummond (1992), Markóczy and Child (1995), Markóczy (1995).

3 We argue that members of an IJV are likely to retain their own social identities in contrast to those of other groups, such as foreign staff, even though they were attracted to membership of the organization by favourable employment conditions and opportunities. In transforming and developing countries with relatively low levels of personal income, many people may welcome employment in higher-paying foreign-funded companies but neverthe-less retain their own social identities.

4 It is interesting to note in this regard that Markóczy's findings in American-Hungarian joint ventures suggest that occupation may be a stronger predictor of managerial mental maps than nationality or corporate attachment (Markóczy 1995).

5 This does not mean that local managers will not question the suitability of the techniques being transferred from a foreign partner on grounds such as the inadequacy of local competences to utilize them or the unreceptivity of the local environment to them. There was an instance of the latter in an American-Hungarian joint venture where local management complained that the American technique of relying on big advertising campaigns rather than on personal contact with customers was not appropriate to the local market.

6 Despite what is said here, the transfer of strategic knowledge can soon become a two-way process in some circumstances. In the case of a Sino-British IJV, knowledge transfer of all kinds was initially from the British to the Chinese partner. Once this had been achieved, British managerial and technical personnel were withdrawn. The joint venture was expected to develop export markets in East Asia which had not hitherto been significantly penetrated by the British partner. The venture's Chinese management learned how to do this, with an Oriental emphasis on nurturing close personal relationships with customers allied to a Western emphasis on product superiority. Its success in countries such as South Korea far exceeded the expectations of its British partner, which then found itself in a learning role so far as East Asian strategy implementation was concerned.

7 The case of non-transfer of knowledge, where there is neither behavioural nor cognitive change, is not included. However, as discussed in note 1, it is possible that IJV partners may not wish to have certain knowledge transferred to their partners through the medium of the joint venture.

References

Albert, S. and Whetten, D.A. (1985) 'Organizational Identity', *Research in Organizational Behavior*, 7: 263–95.

Aldrich, H.E. and Hecker, D. (1977) 'Boundary Spanning Roles and Organization Structure', *Academy of Management Review*, 2: 217–30.

Berger, P.L. and Luckmann, T. (1964) *The Social Construction of Reality: a Treatise in the Sociology of Knowledge*. London: Allen Lane, Penguin Press.

Bleeke, J. and Ernst, D. (1993) *Collaborating to Compete: Using Strategic Alliances and Acquisitions in the Global Marketplace*. New York: Wiley.

Borys, B. and Jemison, D.B. (1989) 'Hybrid Arrangements as Strategic Alliances: Theoretical Issues in Organizational Combinations', *Academy of Management Review*, 14: 234–49.

Burke, P.J. and Tully, J. (1977) 'The Measurement of Role Identity', *Social Forces*, 55: 881–97.

Campbell, N. and Yee Cheng (1991) 'Relationship Management in Equity Joint Ventures in China: a Preliminary Exploration', *Advances in Chinese Industrial Studies*, 2: 217–27.

Cattaneo, E. (1992) 'Managing Joint Ventures in Russia: Can the Problems be Solved?', *Long Range Planning*, 25: 68–72.

Child, J. (1993) 'Society and Enterprise between Hierarchy and Marketing', in J. Child, M. Crozier, R. Mayntz et al., *Societal Change between Market and Organization*. Aldershot: Avebury.

Child, J., Boisot, M., Li, Z., Ireland, J. and Watts, J. (1990) *The Management of Equity Joint Ventures in China*. Beijing: China–European Community Management Institute.

Child, J. and Markóczy, L. (1993) 'Host-Country Managerial Behaviour and Learning in Chinese and Hungarian Joint Ventures', *Journal of Management Studies*, 30: 611–31.

Child, J., Markóczy, L. and Cheung, T. (1994) 'Managerial Adaptation in Chinese and Hungarian Strategic Alliances with Culturally Distinct Foreign Partners', in Sally Stewart (ed.), *Joint Ventures in the People's Republic of China*. Advances in Chinese Industrial Studies, vol. 4. Greenwich, CT: JAI Press.

Da Matta, R. (1981) *Carnavais, malandro e heróis: para uma sociologia do dilema brasileiro*. Rio de Janeiro: Zahar.

Drummond, A. Jr (1992) 'Joint ventures internacionais do Brasil'. Tese de Mestrado, Universidade Federal de Minas Gerais.

Dumont, L. (1986) 'Collective Identities and Universalist Ideology: the Actual Interplay', *Theory, Culture & Society*, 3: 25–33.

Fiol, C.M. and Lyles, M.A. (1985) 'Organizational Learning', *Academy of Management Review*, 10: 803–13.

Foote, N.N. (1951) 'Identification as a Basis for a Theory of Motivation', *American Sociological Review*, 16: 14–21.

Geringer, J.M. and Hebert, L. (1989) 'Control and Performance of International Joint Ventures', *Journal of International Business Studies*, 20: 235–54.

Giddens, A. (1991) *Modernity and Self-Identity: Self and Society in the Later Modern Age*. Oxford: Polity Press.

Goffman, E. (1959) *The Presentation of Self in Everyday Life*. London: Allen Lane.

Gouldner, A.W. (1958) 'Cosmopolitans and Locals: toward an Analysis of Latent Social Roles', *Administrative Science Quarterly*, 15: 176–89.

Gregersen, H.B. and Black, J.S. (1992) 'Antecedents to Commitment to a Parent Company and a Foreign Operation', *Academy of Management Journal*, 35: 65–90.

Hertzfeld, J.M. (1991) 'Joint Ventures: Saving the Soviets from *perestroika*', *Harvard Business Review*, January–February: 80–91.

Hofstede, G. (1991) *Cultures and Organizations*. London: McGraw-Hill.

Killing, J.P. (1983) *Strategies for Joint Venture Success*. London: Croom Helm.

McCall, G.J. and Simmons, J.L. (1978) *Identities and Interactions* (2nd edn). New York: Free Press.

Markóczy, L. (1992) 'Measuring Managerial Beliefs about Business in International Mixed Management Organizations (IMMOs) located in Hungary'. Unpublished paper, Judge Institute of Management Studies, University of Cambridge.

Markóczy, L. (1995) 'Barriers to Shared Belief: The Role of Strategic Interest, Managerial Characteristics and Organisational Factors'. Unpublished PhD Thesis, University of Cambridge.

Markóczy, L. and Child, J. (1995) 'International Mixed Management Organizations and Economic Liberalization in Hungary: from State Bureaucracy to New Paternalism', in T. Howard, D. O'Neal and J. Kelly (eds), *Strategic Renaissance and Business Transformation*. Chichester: Wiley.

Metcalf, H.C. and Urwick, L. (eds) (1941) *Dynamic Administration: the Collected Papers of Mary Parker Follett*. London: Pitman.

Parsons, T. and Shils, E. (1951) 'Values and Social Systems', in Jeffrey C. Alexander and Stevin Seidman (eds), *Culture and Society: Contemporary Debates*. New York: Cambridge University Press.

Peterson, R.B. and Shimada, J.Y. (1978) 'Sources of Management Problems in Japanese-American Joint Ventures', *Academy of Management Review*, 3: 796–804.

Poole, R. (1992) 'A Response to Jonathan Rée', *Radical Philosophy*, 62: 14–19.

Reichers, A.E. (1985) 'A Review and Reconceptualization of Organizational Commitment', *Academy of Management Review*, 10: 465–76.

Royce, A.P. (1982) *Ethnic Identity: Strategies of Diversity*. Bloomington, IN: Indiana University Press.

Schaan, J.-L. (1988) 'How to Control a Joint Venture Even as a Minority Partner', *Journal of General Management*, 14: 4–16.

Sethi, S.P. (1975) *Japanese Business and Social Conflict*. Cambridge, MA: Ballinger.

Snow, D.A. and Anderson, L. (1987) 'Identity Work among the Homeless: the Verbal Construction and Avowal of Personal Identities', *American Journal of Sociology*, 92: 1336–71.

Steward, J. (1955) *Theory of Culture Change*. Urbana, IL: University of Illinois Press.

Tajfel, H. (1982) 'Instrumentality, Identity and Social Comparisons', in H. Tajfel (ed.), *Social Identity and Intergroup Relations*. Cambridge: Cambridge University Press.

Villinger, N.D. (1993) 'Between Dependence and Independence in the Branded Consumer Goods Industry: a Study of the Management of International Corporate Alliances in East Central Europe', Unpublished paper, Judge Institute of Management Studies, University of Cambridge.

Weigert, A.J., Teitge, J.S. and Teitge, D.W. (1986) *Society and Identity: toward a Sociological Psychology*. New York: Cambridge University Press.

PART TWO

COMPARATIVE CULTURAL RECIPES FOR MANAGEMENT

4

Lean Production: the Myth which Changes the World?

Bengt Sandkull

Many critics of contemporary industry characteristic of North America and West Europe claim that the well-known and well-established adversarial corporate model is no longer adequate in the global competitive race (Mathews 1989; Piore and Sabel 1984). Japanese industrialists have understood the benefit of having a compliant workforce. They have been able to combine a Fordist-inspired production model with a human-oriented management model that far exceeds that of their competitors. They also early understood the importance of throughput in mass manufacturing (Johnson and Kaplan 1986).

The rationalization of industry and the growth of the modern corporation as described by Alfred Chandler (1962; 1977) improved greatly the operative efficiency of the production system but was accompanied by increasing administrative inertia. The solution to that problem which Alfred Sloan envisaged and implemented was the transition from a functional unitary organizational form to a multidivisional corporate structure (but not fully independent business divisions as in Williamson 1975). This simplified management at the top but it could not prevent for long the growth of expensive and sluggish administration in the automotive industry (see Keller 1989; De Lorean 1979). However, the ongoing pursuit of rationalization at the operating level was able to protect the managerial structure until quite recently.

The organizational form of Toyota inspired the team of the MIT research project known as the International Motor Vehicle Program (Womack et al. 1990), who labelled their interpretation of this phenomenon *lean production*. When the success of the Toyota model had been proved, it was emulated by other Japanese auto manufacturers and in several transplants in North America and Europe. After the severe crisis in 1982 even Ford restructured its operations along the same principles very successfully (Womack et al. 1990).

The concepts of mass production established by Henry Ford around World War I and modified by Sloan did not become the norm for organizing manufacturing until the decades after World War II. Will the concept of lean production spread rapidly and become the new dominating standard for the industry, or is it possible to find alternatives that may allow a reversal of the division of labour and provide a more human work setting?

The Decay of the Fordist Model

It was already clear to many observers by the 1970s that the Fordist model of manufacturing had reached its saturation point. Reports appeared on the problems of quality and workers' dissatisfaction in terms of absentee-ism, turnover and low productivity in many factories in North America and Europe. Car buyers showed their preferences and the sales of Japanese cars soared in the US and later also in those European markets not practising trade restrictions (for details and comparisons of productivity see Womack et al. 1990).

Attempts to break out of this dead-end were primarily through two different routes. The automation track was followed by General Motors and Fiat (Bonazzi 1992; Berggren 1992). Both experienced spectacular failure and could not handle varying demands for a range of models at reasonable cost. After some time both companies abandoned these attempts to eliminate their dependency on skilled workers. The other track was trying to learn from Toyota, which Ford did in the 1980s and GM has attempted to do in the 1990s.

The characteristics of the two large American car manufacturers include not only the design of the production system, but also the relations with suppliers and customers and the managerial structure. The production system reflects the following Tayloristic principles:

- dedicated technology
- horizontal division of labour with strict specialization
- vertical division of labour
- hierarchy of control
- planned production against stock.

In the original Fordist model the problem of compliance (how to get the workers to work harder) is solved by the standardization of the production system in which the workers are expected to follow narrowly defined standard operating procedures. The employees' relation to the company is characterized by the principle of the cash nexus, i.e. the workers sell their labour for a reasonable payment (Baldamus 1961). A great number of job classifications is used to specify the work. In order to defend the income of the workers the unions are bound to become guardians of that classification.

Originally the two large car makers established integrated systems for the supply of parts and components. In the 1950s Ford began another approach and asked independent firms to bid against detailed specifications for components previously supplied from within. The best bidder usually won a one-year contract.

In the 1980s GM followed a similar track in order to reduce the costs of parts and components. In this way the supply of parts and components is transferred from internal distribution to a market exchange relation with outside firms. No consideration is given to trust or long term development. When demand slumps the contracts with suppliers are reduced.

The car manufacturers make sales predictions and expect the car dealers to do their best to fulfil these targets. The dealers usually do not provide any particular service for customers and do not attempt to establish any long term relations with buyers. The market exchange principle also governs relations with customers.

The whole system of manufacturing and selling cars is characterized by the market principle and does not promote trust and long term development.

The Lean Production Myth

Lean production is lean because it uses less of everything compared with mass production American style. Despite the fact that there is a greater variety of product, results are achieved at lower costs and with fewer defects. However, lean production is not equivalent to Japanese manufacturing methods.

After a visit to Ford's Rouge plant in Detroit in 1950, Eiji Toyota returned with some ideas on how to improve the system of mass production and adapt it to conditions in Japan (Cusumano 1985). Thanks to the new techniques of die changing discovered by Taiichi Ohno, Toyota could now introduce modern manufacturing methods for small batches. The domestic market in Japan demanded many different types of cars in numbers far below the Detroit standard of one million cars for economic production.

It took many years to fully implement the Toyota production system, the cornerstones of which became just-in-time and small batches based on order. To implement this system a skilled and a highly motivated workforce was required.

Relations between management and workers were very strained just after the war. After a period of conflict and negotiations the former president had to step down before a settlement was reached which included two important concessions to the employees: lifetime employment, and pay based on seniority and tied to company profitability. As later became known, Toyota was reluctant to grant this condition to all the workers (Kamata 1973).

It is not sufficient to understand the Toyota production system only as lean production, because it was firmly embedded in a particular societal setting as a consequence of the special situation after World War II. The extreme post-war conditions in Japan were met by Toyota and other industries by providing housing, welfare and medical care to their workers. These arrangements of social responsibility ('company town') are known from early industrialization in Europe and the US. They have similarities with solutions established in China and the former socialist countries in East and Central Europe, which also tie welfare to employment.

> By focusing on the nature of skill, we can easily explain many features of Japanese industrial relations. The most famous are undoubtedly seniority wages and permanent employment. Seniority wages simply reflect the nature of the skill; skill is developed in a career over a long period within a firm, and accordingly the age–wage profile is positively sloped . . . the skills of Japanese blue collar workers in large firms are partly of an intellectual character – determining the causes of problems and adjusting to minor changes on the shopfloor – and this intellectual character of skill is shared with white-collar workers in general. Therefore, seniority wages are not a uniquely Japanese feature; the Japanese feature, if any, is the extension of white-collar wages to a section of blue-collar workers. (Koike 1987)

The Toyota production system kept the basic Tayloristic principles: horizontal division of labour, vertical division of labour and hierarchy of control. These basic features of the Fordist model were combined with a general technology and a system for planning production based on order. Specialization was however less strict than in the American firms and foremen were replaced by working team leaders. The teams became responsible for the quality of their work.

Relations with suppliers were established on the principle of mutual benefit and long term development. The first-tier suppliers took part in the process of designing new parts. In terms of manufacturing each firm received assistance from Toyota to implement the ideas of the Toyota model.

The dealer groups affiliated with the car maker tried in their turn to establish long term relations with buyers. These efforts were manifested by dealers offering to take care of the compulsory and strict government safety inspection required three years after purchase. In contrast to the American way, the Toyota model was based on trust and mutual benefit all the way from the suppliers to the customers. The decision-making process in Toyota and other Japanese firms is also based on collaboration, not bureaucracy.

In terms of costs both mass production and lean production benefit very much from smooth manufacturing. Although Japan has had steady economic growth, the demand for cars has fluctuated somewhat. Toyota has met these fluctuations by lowering prices and increasing sales efforts.

One of the main principles of the Toyota model is always to stick to the work pace. When new methods which increase efficiency are introduced in the factory, unneeded workers are moved to other jobs. To maintain the challenge of continual improvement it is regarded as necessary to keep the same intensity of work. This is also one of the weaknesses of the model, because when the workers get older they have difficulties in meeting the established work pace. Young people are no longer so eager to join Toyota.

Toyota has so far apparently been successful in establishing its production regime both in Japan and overseas. It has proved possible to transfer the manufacturing philosophies and practices to the USA and UK, but not the political and social support which the wider social context of Japan provides. The success of the almost slack-free production system is dependent on total management control of labour. In Japan this is achieved through combining a tight social system and a particular factory regime that puts claims not only on everybody's physical capabilities but also on their mental ones. Outside Japan, similar compliance has been achieved through a very selective recruitment process.

In North America and the UK the labour market has created favourable conditions for a Toyota-type production system. Toyota has transplanted its personnel practices selectively to create sufficient protection against disturbance. Compared with traditional Fordist management practices, the workers have, at least initially, regarded the Japanese regimes as much more enlightened. All are not happy, though: 'They promised us a rose garden. They gave us a desert' (Phil Keeling of the UAW at Mazda, Flat Rock, in Berggren et al. 1991).

The Toyota regime may be regarded as superior to the old Fordist system in many respects. The workers are more skilled and they work in teams. The system does allow the workers to solve projects at the point of production, but only within narrowly defined limits. The concept of lean production stresses the efficiency of the production system but it does not take into consideration the wear on the workers and the damage it causes them. The lean production system is not lean to the individuals, and they have to bear the costs inflicted on themselves. Their ability to influence events is restricted to the point of production (the quality circles).

Alternatives

The Swedish manufacturers Volvo and Saab began their operations in a small market and, like Toyota, had to cope with scales of production far below the Detroit standard. They too introduced the basic Tayloristic principles: horizontal division of labour, vertical division of labour and hierarchy of control. In contrast to Toyota they specialized on a few models and could therefore use dedicated technology. The production planning system which originally built on manufacturing for stock was gradually adapted to allow for custom orders. The specialization of the workers was, however, less strict than in the American firms and only a few job classifications were used.

The Swedish firms had to rely on outside suppliers to a greater extent than the American firms, and therefore relations were very much based on trust and long term commitment. From the start they embarked on a system embracing all their major suppliers which offset their competitors' supposed economies of scale. Despite its small size, Volvo at least was competitive compared with much larger European and American car makers.

Spurred by the shortage of labour willing to work on a traditional production line and beset by problems of quality, the Swedish manufacturers had already introduced a number of workplace reforms by the 1970s. The importance of the workers' consent to the production process was recognized.

These reforms at Kalmar and Trollhättan aimed at improving motivation in the workplace. They took a psychological (i.e. socio-technical) approach and shied away from the broader socio-political aspects of participation and control concerning the factory regime and the manufacture of consent (Burawoy 1979; 1985).

In retrospect we can see that the Kalmar plant and the other new plants in the Volvo group represented a great achievement in production technology and initially much improved working conditions. The Kalmar factory was the world's first assembly plant without mechanically driven assembly lines. By introducing space for inspection and adjustments in the team area, quality was made a top priority. However the MTM methods still prevailed, and opportunities for good work (despite the longer cycle times, about 25 minutes) and worker participation remained meagre (for a full account of all these attempts see Berggren 1992). The original innovative assembly docks which allowed for buffers were later removed (the last in 1984). Standard line pacing returned and control became centralized. Assembly time per car was about 25 per cent lower than in the main plant in Gothenburg, and time for adjustments almost 50 per cent lower.

Saab in Trollhättan used a less technical approach to introduce teamwork and foster responsibility in combination with authority at the point of production. Responsibility for quality was, however, unfortunately not included. Productivity improved but was later offset by increasing quality problems. The corporate management of the Saab group was not in favour of the new ideas of work design. As a consequence the new organization fell into disrepute after some years and became an issue of controversy in the company. As in Volvo from the 1970s onwards, management in Saab became more and more elaborate and bureaucratic; it was also very conflictual because there was no clear leadership from the corporate summit.

During a period of booming sales (owing to a favourable dollar exchange rate) the Saab management decided to build a new factory which would incorporate increased worker responsibility. The company attempted a higher degree of mechanization on the line, but met great problems. The design process of the new factory was beset with conflict, but there resulted a solution based on team work with quality responsibility on parallel lines.

The cycle time was extended to about 20 minutes (compare with Kalmar). This plant started operation in 1989 when demand had already fallen, and closed after two years.

In continuing to refine its labour process, Volvo management has favoured the increased mechanization of production in combination with schemes for inculcating greater loyalty and more responsibility into the workforce. The strategy for transforming assembly work into skilled work seemed to belong to the realm of rhetoric until the establishment of the new Uddevalla plant (closed in April 1993). The changes in the Volvo Components Corporation were extremely ambitious but so far they have failed to break away from the old tradition of submission, or even to recognize it.

An intrinsic dilemma of the Fordist corporate organization in its modern form is the question of the legitimacy of hierarchy. The formal control necessary to uphold hierarchy is practically impossible without normative rules accepted by the employees. This was discovered early by Simon: 'unless a subordinate is himself able to supply most of the premises of a decision, and to synthesize them adequately, the task of supervision becomes hopelessly burdensome' (1952: 193).

For some years it seems that industry, in response to increased competition, has tried to apply strategies which have the potential to mobilize a larger set of human resources. However, such a strategy presupposes the creation of a different form of legitimacy than that under a Fordist factory regime.

Managers attempting to introduce post-Fordist flat organization find themselves in a dilemma because they need to replace the previous order of enforcement and remuneration with a new combination of rewards and norms that can maintain the continuity of the basic dominance. The principles of total quality control, for example, presuppose that those working at the point of production are also allowed to and are capable of solving the problems appearing in daily work. This clearly goes against the norms of the functional organization.

It seems that few managers have that understanding which would allow them to handle properly the issues of legitimacy inherent in a different corporate order. Thus many grope in the dark for 'corporate culture' or something else perceived as a quick-fix remedy, or they stick stubbornly to the old practices (Howard 1985).

A production system embodies the production process which is simultaneously a process of manufacturing (a concrete transformation), a process of creating a surplus (value added through the labour process), and a social process (reproduction of labour) (Sandkull 1984; see also Litteler 1982). The design of a production system has its origin in the product and is based on an analysis of which operational steps are necessary to complete the transformation from input to a finished product. The sequence of the operational steps specifies the machine work and as a consequence the flow of additional materials and the need for direct labour. The physical flow in

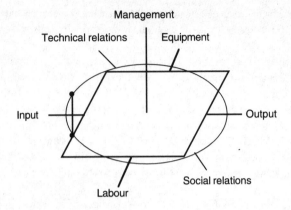

Figure 4.1   *The production system model*

the production follows from the layout of machinery and other equipment in the plant.

The production system comprises an additional number of operations which are usually not incorporated into the physical flow, such as maintenance and repairs of tools and machinery, quality control and adjustments, cleaning, and keeping of records. Very often activities like maintenance are carried out in separate workshops; these workshops can be regarded as production systems in their own right, although dependent on the main system. The outcome of all these decisions is called the technical relations of production (Burawoy 1979).

In a plant where the principles of mass production reign, the division of labour is strict and any one worker has only a very limited range of tasks. To him this limitation excludes responsibility for the product or the equipment. Instead that responsibility has been allocated to special workers in departments of quality control and maintenance. The core of the conditions and rules that regulate the work of the employees is the horizontal and vertical divisions of labour (the social relations of production: Burawoy 1979).

Any modern production system reflects two different forms of logic. One, techno-economic logic, dominates the other, human logic, which is based on the actions and communication between human beings (Habermas 1971; Israel 1979). The actual situation in a particular plant is modified by the attitudes and actions of the production management and the factory regime, and the ways the workers cope with it. The dialectic is expressed by the relations between the technical and the social relations of production in the model in Figure 4.1. This model enables us to distinguish between different forms of production systems and to clarify the idea of 'post-Fordism' which has been discussed for some time (see, for example, Kern and Schumann 1984; Mathews 1989).

Taylor's basic contribution to the theory of production system design was to separate work from the worker. In this way, not only the components of a good became standardized but also the work operations necessary to manufacture it. When new methods of production were introduced which employed standardized methods and produced standardized outcome, managers and engineers could develop the technical relations without paying much regard to the social relations. The mass production system of Ford thus became the blueprint for organizing most industrial activities.

Even in modern industrial production all work cannot be standardized, for example tool making, machine repair and product design. The irregular nature of these tasks has, however, not prevented production engineers from trying to bring them under their control. Nevertheless, workers retain a degree of discretion in their work because their knowledge is not easily standardized.

The different thinking in the design of the Toyota production system is to regard the whole chain from the suppliers to the customers as a machine which can cope with the external world by increasing sales efforts and lowering prices. To maintain it as a machine despite its human components, these had to be integrated in a different way than in the Fordist solution. The integration is achieved by the design of a socially tightly knit system, exposing people continuously to the requirements of the customers.

The concept of commodification (Esping-Andersen 1990) is useful in comparing the different societal conditions. In the USA as well in Japan most workers' benefits are tied to employment. The general benefits from society are at a minimum. Hence the degree of commodification is high. The seniority pay system and the restricted mobility in the labour market give an extra sharpness to labour's subordination in Japan. In contrast the degree of commodification in Sweden is low because the common welfare benefits (health care, unemployment pay, retraining facilities and so on) are quite generous and are independent of any one employer.

Another aspect related to the above is the workers' access to 'voice' in dealings with employers. A strong labour movement which has had political control for a long period, and a strong labour union movement (almost 90 per cent coverage), provide a socio-political climate in Sweden that has been able to establish a dialogue between different interests. The situation is very different in the USA where no labour movement exists and the labour unions are entrenched in a defensive position (both Ford and Sloan were strong opponents of labour unions). Japan has a labour movement but it has not been able to loosen the political stronghold of the ruling Liberal Party. The labour unions have been confined to company level and forced to play a minor role.

Conclusions

Lazonick (1990) argues that 'in the face of Japanese challenge, the 1980s saw a search for new structures of labor–management cooperation and new models of workplace relations that stressed commitment rather than control.' On the other hand he contends that 'a century of managerial obsession with taking skills, and initiative, off the shop floor is not easily overcome.'

My reading of the Japanization process is that the control motive is seldom far away. Despite the claims of the MIT group, lean production is not a single unambiguous concept, but encompasses a diverse number of imputed elements, all not necessarily mutually compatible. In a Tayloristic strong tradition, lean production is likely to retain much of the control perspective; whereas in a Swedish participative tradition, lean production tends to resemble 'semi-autonomous' groups, even if that has now become a despised expression. The conflict between democratic participation in the community and subordination in the workplace was not resolved during the boom of the 1980s, which hampers the new attempts to mobilize still more of the human resources of the employees.

It seems to me that lean production builds on a fundamental contradiction when it is regarded as an integrated process involving customers, manufacturers and suppliers. The integrated lean production process is like a machine which has to run at a preset, even pace in order to work. In a world of global competition in which numerous manufacturers vie for the favours of customers, machine stability seems less than probable: rather, we would expect turbulence.

Although lean production ideas are likely to be propagated in the automotive industry, in other areas of large-scale industry they will be less prevalent. Small firms in loose coalitions have a better chance in a turbulent world. We can also note a tendency in the mature industries to move workplaces from countries with strict labour legislation and high social taxes to countries where labour can be exploited with only the minimum of restrictions.

Even if many industrial leaders pay lip-service to the claims of lean production and adopt that vocabulary, their practice will still to a large extent reflect the particulars of their own trade. Because lean production at present is in the form of an ideology, it is being introduced with little reference to the reality of particular cases. It readily becomes managerial rhetoric, a device to maintain established power structures, the inertia of which precludes learning.

References

Baldamus, W. (1961) *Efficiency and Effort*. London: Tavistock.
Berggren, C. (1992) *The Volvo Experience: Alternatives to Lean Production in the Swedish Auto Industry*. London: Macmillan.
Berggren, C., Björkman, T. and Holländer, E. (1991) 'Are They Unbeatable?'. Department of Work Science, Royal Institute of Technology, Stockholm.
Bonazzi, G. (1992) 'A Gentler Way to Total Quality? The Case of the Integrated Factory at Fiat Auto'. Paper presented to the 10th Annual International Aston/UMIST Conference on Organization and Labour Process, Birmingham.

Burawoy, Michael (1979) *Manufacturing Consent: Changes in the Labour Process under Monopoly Capitalism.* Chicago: University of Chicago Press.

Burawoy, Michael (1985) *The Politics of Production: Factory Regimes under Capitalism and Socialism.* London: Verso.

Chandler, A. (1962) *Strategy and Structure.* Cambridge, MA: MIT Press.

Chandler, A. (1977) *The Visible Hand: the Managerial Revolution in American Business.* Cambridge, MA: Harvard University Press.

Cusumano, M. (1985) *Japanese Automobile Industry: Technology and Management at Nissan and Toyota.* Cambridge, MA: Harvard University Press.

De Lorean, John Z. (1979) *On a Clear Day You Can See General Motors.* Grosse Point, MI: J. Patrick Wright.

Esping-Andersen, G. (1990) *The Three Worlds of Welfare Capitalism.* Cambridge: Polity Press.

Habermas, Jürgen (1971) *Towards a Rational Society.* Boston: Beacon Press.

Howard, Robert (1985) *Brave New Workplace.* New York: Elisabeth Siftington.

Israel, Joakim (1979) *The Language of Dialectics and the Dialectics of Language.* Copenhagen: Munksgaard. London: Harvester Press. New York: Humanities Press.

Johnson, H.T. and Kaplan, R.S. (1986) *Relevance Lost: the Rise and Fall of Management Accounting.* Boston: Harvard Business School Press.

Kamata, S. (1973) *Japan in the Passing Lane: an Insider's Account of Life in a Japanese Auto Factory.* New York: Pantheon (English translation 1982).

Keller, M. (1989) *Rude Awakening: the Rise, Fall and Struggle for Recovery at General Motors.* New York: William Morrow.

Kern, Horst and Schumann, Michael (1984) 'Work and Social Character: Old and New Contours', *Economic and Industrial Democracy*, 5: 1–70.

Koike, K. (1987) 'Human Resource Development and Labour Management Relations', in *The Political Economy of Japan.* Stanford University Press.

Lazonick, W. (1990) *Competitive Advantage on the Shop Floor.* Cambridge, MA: Harvard University Press.

Litteler, Craig, R. (1982) *The Development of the Labour Process in Capitalist Societies.* London: Heinemann.

Mathews, John (1989) *The Age of Democracy: the Politics of Post-Fordism.* Melbourne: Oxford University Press.

Piore, Michael J. and Sabel, C.F. (1984) *The Second Industrial Divide.* New York: Basic Books.

Sandkull, Bengt (1984) 'Managing the Democratization Process in Work Cooperatives', *Economic and Industrial Democracy*, 4: 359–89.

Simon, Herbert A. (1952) 'Decision Making and Administrative Organization', in R.K. Merton (ed.), *Reader in Bureaucracy.* Chicago: Free Press.

Williamson, Oliver E. (1975) *Markets and Hierarchy: Analysis and Antitrust Implications.* New York: Free Press.

Womack, James P., Jones, Daniel T. and Roos, Daniel (1990) *The Machine that Changed the World.* New York: Rawson.

5

The International Popularization of Entrepreneurial Ideas

José Luis Alvarez

It hardly seems surprising that the popularization of knowledge has to do not only with its intellectual merits but also with the political, social and ideological positions and dispositions, to use Boudon's (1986) terms, of the social actors who generate, disseminate and consume that knowledge, as well as with the external events that affect them. However, regarding economic ideas in general and business knowledge in particular, works that empirically study their processes of diffusion and institutionalization have been very scarce until recently (among those that did exist before the current interest on the topic we could mention Barley et al. 1988 and Cole 1985).

This paucity of research was very surprising, given the existence of a number of reasons that should years ago have prompted the development of a sociology of business knowledge aimed at the explanation of the processes of diffusion and institutionalization of management knowledge, from academic constructs to social ideas. One such reason is the outstanding precedent set by Bendix in *Work and Authority in Industry* (1974), which views ideologies of management as a key factor not only in the intellectual mobilization required for economic development but also in the legitimation of industrial societies and organizational hierarchies. While a group of authors (Braverman, Burawoy, Edwards and others) criticized management knowledge as playing an ideological role in the maintenance of the status quo of the economic system, their critique remained mostly at the level of ideas. The concrete, institutional and social mechanisms relating business knowledge to group interests, for instance, or to political movements, were left mostly unexplored.

Another argument for the development of a sort of sociology of business knowledge lies in the sociology of organizations itself. An approach has been developed over the 1980s – the neo-institutional school – that points up the importance of the beliefs held by organizational actors and their normative ideas for explaining practices *vis-à-vis* supposedly rational and contingent answers to the demands of the environment. Hence, the importance of attending to the origin, legitimation, reception and consumption of business knowledge, ideas and ideologies.

Recent sociological works by authors like Wuthnow, Zaret, Boudon and others, using historical and institutional perspectives, have opened up the study of ideologies, that until recently, owing to a tradition of highly emotional and ideologized debates, had been a dead-end. These new developments are very important for the study of business knowledge, since the epistemological structure of the latter is, to an important degree, analogous to that of ideologies. The extreme complexity of managerial tasks – highly interdependent, contextual and systemic, relatively under-standardized, changeable and developing, combining both the mainten-ance of structures and their change, rarely generating visible and separable inputs (Whitley 1989a) – demands the use of several types of knowledge by practitioners: from technical knowledge to decision-making habits, to organizational savvy, to assumptions about the social features of human nature. These kinds of knowledge are typical components of ideologies, and as such they fit together not in ordered patterns, but rather in the way of a *bricolage* (Bourricaud 1980). Moreover, like ideologies, management know-ledge is composed of ideas aimed both at making sense of the countless data out there in the business world, and at social action upon that world.

A final factor for pursuing the opportunity of developing a sort of sociology of business knowledge arises from uncertainty about the real influence of management concepts on actual organizational practices, derived from the innumerable variables and redundancies at play in organizational action (Hackman 1985). There are no final and purely academic regulative evaluations of the usefulness of business notions. As a consequence, administrative knowledge needs to be perceived as socially legitimated by, for instance, prestigious business schools, business media, management gurus, and other mediating institutions, in order to be adopted by practitioners and to impact on practices (Cohen and March 1986). This explains the high number of faddish episodes in the populariza-tion of business ideas (Abrahamson 1991). Concepts and methods of the sociologies of art, fashion, and other fields can then represent an oppor-tunity for the advancement of our understanding of the spread of business ideas and resulting practices. In turn, the epistemological nature of business knowledge and the character of managerial practices – between science and art – make them a privileged topic of research for attempting the articulation between the two cultures, the sciences and the humanities, whose division has handicapped the sociology of culture and knowledge.

In sum, while the links between ideologies and politics on the one hand and business knowledge on the other have been posited and widely recognized, there has been a dearth of studies on this relationship either empirical or comparative. The purpose of the research summarized by this chapter is to start filling that void.

Purpose of the Study

In the 1980s entrepreneurship was a huge success in management educa-tion: a new domain of academic literature emerged, new scholar associations were launched, courses were made obligatory, chairs were endowed, research centres were created. It was also a great success as an economic and political idea, being situated within wider trends, such as the reinstatement of enterprise as the most important institution of economic life, and the diminishing economic role of the state (Bourricaud 1986); and in the social and cultural domains, entrepreneurship has obvious links with the demands for high psychological and professional rewards, the re-evaluation of personal merit and the parallel devaluation of egalitarian tendencies (Stevenson and Sahlman 1986). Moreover, entrepreneurship has become an ecumenical movement, spreading across countries – regardless of their level of development.

This chapter summarizes a study made of the causes of the populariza-tion in the 1980s of the business idea of entrepreneurship (here termed the entrepreneurship movement) in three countries: Britain, Mexico, and Spain.[1] It focuses on three processes: (1) those by which entrepreneurship has come to be a part of management education, both formal (academic) and informal (popular business publications); (2) those by which the promotion of entrepreneurship became a task undertaken by governments of all political stances; and (3) those by which the eulogy of entrepreneur-ship has become the core of pro-business ideologies in the 1980s. Special attention is paid to the reception, in these three countries, of knowledge and ideas on entrepreneurship transmitted from traditional exporters of management knowledge, especially the US.

Methods and Main Hypothesis

The research uses a comparative method for two basic reasons. First, the entrepreneurship movement took place in both developed and underdevel-oped countries. Although the three countries selected – Britain, Mexico, Spain – do not constitute a representative sample of any possible universe, preliminary data suggested that they might be illustrative enough for the purposes of this study. There is an early industrialized country, Britain, which shares a similar political and economic system with Spain, a late industrialized society, although it sharply differed with the latter in the political orientation of its government in the 1980s. Mexico, a developing country with a highly interventionist state, is quite an attractive case, because of the abrupt transition towards a market economy under the presidency of Carlos Salinas de Gortari, and again, links between Mexico and Spain and the US have provided opportunities for assessing knowledge diffusion mechanisms.

A second reason for a comparative approach is that variance among the three societies in the timing, content and impact of entrepreneurship ideas (entrepreneurship movement, EM) will depend on the economic and political contexts of each country, as well as on the respective national social actors involved in the dissemination of entrepreneurial ideas (see Figure 5.1). The three-country comparison will allow development, then,

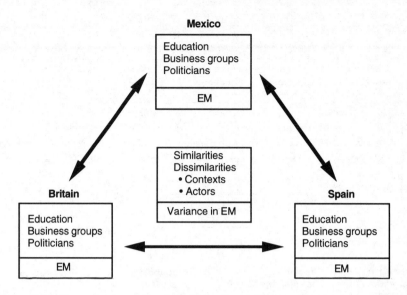

Figure 5.1 *Comparative national analysis of entrepreneurship movement*

of hypotheses on the relationship between social groups and external events, on the one hand, and the popularization of business knowledge, on the other.

An analysis of the sociological literature was made in order to account for the main agents intervening in the processes of diffusion and institutionalization of knowledge analogous to business knowledge and ideas. The literature generally coincides on the three most relevant groups for a social idea to become popularized. The first is educators. These are divided into two groups. On the one hand, there are scholars in institutions of management education. On the other, there are the agents of so-called informal education, such as groups of intellectuals, management gurus, and media that diffuse non-academic business knowledge in magazines, in publishing houses specialized in how-to books, and so on. The second group is politicians; and the third, specifically for this case, is business people. Two resources – cultural and organizational – are viewed as necessary for these groups to be able to receive, legitimate and disseminate knowledge.

Moreover, most authors have ordered the processes leading to the popularization of social ideas in similar sequences (Table 5.1). These sequences propose, first, that there should be environmental conditions in the economic, social, and political realms acting as prompting events, by de-legitimating old ideas and opening the need for new ones. Second, necessary conditions or institutional contexts are needed. Carriers or social agents – producers, transmitters, and consumers of business knowledge with their cultural and organizational resources – are affected by those

Table 5.1   *Processes leading to the diffusion of ideas*

	Mohr (1982)	Wuthnow (1989)	Berger et al. (1974)	Boudon (1986)	Weber, Mannheim
Prompting events	External directional forces	Environmental conditions	Professional groups	Situation	
Social actors			Primary carriers	Professional groups	
Organizational resources	Necessary conditions	Institutional contexts	Secondary carriers	Institutional factors	Carriers
Cultural requirements				Cultural factors	
Social action	Probabilistic processes	Action sequences			

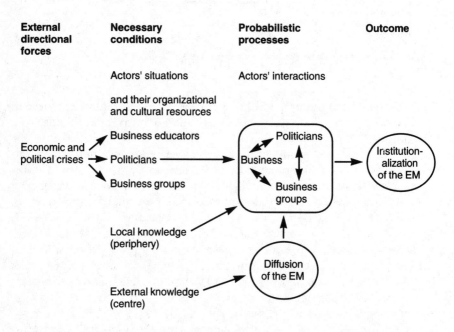

Figure 5.2   *Diffusion and institutionalization of entrepreneurship ideas*

external directional forces. The third requirement is probabilistic processes or action sequences: these social actors' actions and reactions, based on their positions and dispositions, of selection, dissemination, consumption and reproduction of ideas. The outcome of these processes is the diffusion and institutionalization of ideas. Since prompting events and social actors and their resources are mostly defined on a national basis, the popularization of ideas should present specific national intensities and contents. Figure 5.2 shows a graphic summary of this framework as applied to the process of diffusion and institutionalization of entrepreneurship ideas (entrepreneurship movement, EM).

The Data

The data gathered on the international popularization of pro-entrepreneurship ideas, following the framework of Figure 5.2, are summarized next.

Management Education

In Britain, education on entrepreneurship stands in sharp contrast to that of Mexico and Spain. It started much sooner, in the early 1970s, after the publication in 1971 of the Bolton Report, an inquiry made on behalf of the government and leading industrialists to confront the British economic decline. This report recommended the promotion of small firms as a way to revitalize the decaying industrial fabric. Among other consequences, the report prompted a wave of research of small firms and of new entrepreneurship courses, in many cases supported by public agencies, which in the long run enabled British management academia not to be dependent upon foreign sources of entrepreneurial knowledge and pedagogical materials, producing its own entrepreneurship knowledge, mostly on small firms, and also distributing it directly, through special programmes, to professionals launching new businesses and owners of small firms, and through MBA and university courses to business students. Business educators also provide mediators of business knowledge – business journalists, for instance – with a good deal of the raw materials upon which they base their articles in newspapers and in the numerous magazines and publications that appeared in the 1980s on start-ups, small business and joint ventures.

In Britain, the entrepreneurship movement presents a dominant theme. There is a coherence between a good portion of the academic teaching and research, centred on small firms, and the content of the sections on entrepreneurship in periodicals and books on the topic, also mostly devoted to small firms. Figure 5.3 summarized the main flows of agents and audiences in British entrepreneurship education (Figures 5.3 and 5.4 are based on Boudon 1986).

The most important characteristic of entrepreneurship education in Mexico, both formal and informal, is also its strong thematic cohesiveness and clear-cut content. Entrepreneurship in Mexican management schools, at both undergraduate and graduate levels, means, almost always, micro-firms and self-employment. This orientation was not the result of deliberate decisions but the consequence of the lack of research and lower curricular capabilities of Mexican business schools and universities.

In Mexico the formal education front of the entrepreneurship movement developed in two phases. In the first, the Mexican school pioneering in entrepreneurship education, the Instituto Tecnológico y de Estudios Superiores de Monterrey (ITESM), the most prestigious private university

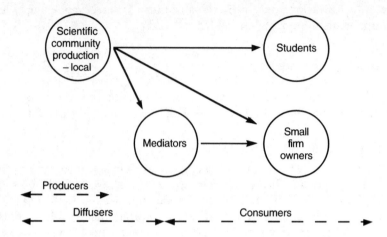

Figure 5.3   *Agents and audiences in British entrepreneurship education (based on Boudon 1986)*

in Mexico, initiated it for predominantly socio-political reasons. The business groups of Monterrey – the most powerful in the country, the most oriented to the US as political, social and economic models, and the founders and financial backers of the Institute – in order to help change the economic culture of Mexico, modified in 1983 the institutional goals of ITESM, and entrepreneurship education became obligatory in all programmes. This change was not random. In 1982 the Mexican government nationalized the banking system, and business groups, fearing for the fate of the private sector, initiated an offensive, at the level of ideas, that is, an ideological offensive, to promote the social legitimation of private enterprise in the country, and the idea of entrepreneurship became one of the most important vehicles for that legitimation.

However, the lack of autochthonous entrepreneurship knowledge and curricular development capabilities forced ITESM to import foreign pedagogical material, from course outlines to slides ready for classes. Most of these materials were imported from US Junior Achievement, an organization that through courses on how to start micro-firms promotes free enterprise in US high schools, and which had a delegation in Mexico. Instructors of Mexican Junior Achievement were recruited by ITESM where, thanks to their enormous resources, they could develop their activities to a much higher degree. The very basic level of the materials drawn from Mexican Junior Achievement, which in turn were copied, almost literally, from US Junior Achievement, made them easy to adopt by ITESM's faculty, of easy general application across all types of programmes, and of non-problematic acceptance by students.

In the second phase, most of the other Mexican universities and schools started to teach entrepreneurship courses responding to a more typical mimetic motivation, as the new-institutional school of organizational

Table 5.2   *Courses offered at Mexican management schools*

School	Knowledge origins	First entrepreneurship courses		
		College	MBA	Others
ITESM	US/Mexican Junior Achievement	1986	1989	1989
UNAM	US/Mexican Junior Achievement	1989	1989	
ITAM	US/Mexican Junior Achievement	1987	1989	
IPADE	IESE (Spain)/Harvard (US)		1976	
La Salle	US/Mexican Junior Achievement	1990		
Anahuac	Local			1986

theory would recognize: to follow the succcessful example of ITESM. From this institution they copied most of their materials, and thus the very basic and motivational entrepreneurship knowledge produced and used by US Junior Achievement has been imported, literally translated without significant adaptation, at least until the end of the 1980s, and spread throughout most Mexican educational institutions. Table 5.2 shows the dates in which courses on entrepreneurship started to be offered at the main management schools of the country. A few years after the nationalization of the banking system, and of the consequent reaction of business groups promoting their social legitimation, entrepreneurship education became a widespread phenomenon in management education in Mexico.

In regard to informal education it is worth emphasizing the importance gained in Mexico by a handful of intellectuals of entrepreneurship. Through frequent articles in the most important newspapers, and through other media like books, seminars and the like, they reach an adult audience of owners of small firms or of family businesses. The message of these entrepreneurship gurus is very motivational and ideological, articulating the occupational concerns and strains of their audiences into signs of a social identity that had never until the second half of the 1980s been fully appreciated by the Partido Revolucionario Institucional (PRI) ideology which had been dominant for decades. In Mexico, then, there is one basic message – micro-firms and self-employment – and the message is transmitted in one basic style, motivational and ideological. It is conveyed (see Figure 5.4) to two different audiences or social groups through two main channels: first, through universities to young students, and second, through popular business media to adult entrepreneurs.

Although Spain presents most of the manifestations of the popularization of entrepreneurial ideas that exist in Britain and Mexico, they lack thematic unity and intensity. For instance, while there are entrepreneurship courses in the main business schools, Spanish entrepreneurship education is not as generalized as in Mexico, or as research-oriented or institutionalized as in Britain. It was after the economic crisis that entrepreneurship became an established part of the curricula of Spanish graduate business education. Even at IESE, the most internationally recognized Spanish business school, where a pioneer course on the launching and managing of new firms started in the mid 1970s, it was only

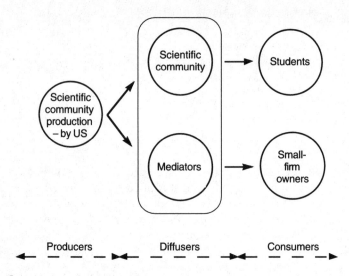

Figure 5.4   *Agents and audiences in Mexican entrepreneurship education (based on Boudon 1986)*

well into the 1980s, after the economic crisis, that research was systematically done, a faculty group interested in the field was formed, international academic links were established, and so on.

The diffusion and institutionalization of entrepreneurship education in Spanish business schools has followed an international mimetic pattern: institutions in the periphery (or, like Spain, in the semi-periphery) follow the model of US institutions in the centre, trying to legitimate themselves through their similarity with these, adopting as soon as possible their latest innovations, etc. However, an important specification has to be made regarding these isomorphic dynamics. These were not the result of organizational mimesis, the consequences of the academic pressure built into those institutions for incorporating a new academic field, of decisions taken by the boards of the Spanish business schools, or even of the pressures of business people giving donations to these schools. These courses were the product of particular initiatives of professors with academic education and contacts in the US. These professors were the carriers (sociologically and literally, of cases, teaching notes, course outlines, books, and so on) of entrepreneurship courses to Spanish business schools. That is, the mimesis was more professional and personal than strictly organizational, and the importance that entrepreneurship education has reached in Spanish business schools has depended on the political skills of the professors who, at their own risk, in a somewhat academic entrepreneurial way, pushed for an acknowledgement of the importance of the field in their own organizations.

At the same time, the role of informal entrepreneurship education in Spain is very small: there are no specific media, like magazines, or social champions for entrepreneurship. In sum, the absence of a dominant theme, such as micro-firms in Mexico and small firms in Britain, and the lack of social visibility give to Spanish entrepreneurship education a very amorphous character.

Politicians

The idea of entrepreneurship has gone well beyond academic domains, also imposing itself as positive to politicians of all ideological stands who, in the 1980s, enthusiastically jumped onto the bandwagon of entrepreneurship with an ardour that even the *Financial Times* qualified as 'banal attitudes and exaggerated claims' (quoted by Rainnie 1985). This enthusiasm of politicians and public administrators has also surprised researchers in the three countries, who have frequently stated that their own research – statistics on entrepreneurship and on its actual impact on job creation are very difficult and disputable – does not give cause for such uncritical acceptance (see for instance, for the British case, the following numerous caveats by researchers: Curran and Stanworth 1982; Hall 1986; Gallagher and Doyle 1986; Bannock and Peacock 1989; Whitley 1989b).

The timing of the entrepreneurship movement's emergence in the realm of public administration is similar to that in the educational domain. In Britain, the Bolton Report, early in the 1970s, was also the starting point of a series of legal measures aimed at the promotion of small firms. As it is well known, Mrs Thatcher's coming to power added a political discourse, situating small firms as the epitome of her enterprise culture, which in turn was the ideological centrepiece of her economic discourse, even of her whole endeavour.

In Mexico, the movement's academic and government fronts do not share a single source, like the Bolton Report in Britain, but they do have the same timing. It was between two to three years after the external debt crisis of 1982 that the goverment started to promote entrepreneurship, especially micro-firms and self-employment. As in the case of education, this reaction would not have been possible in Mexico without the reception of knowledge from other countries: foreign experiences on the promotion of new firms and micro-firms was facilitated for the Mexican Government after 1983 through the United Nations Organization for Industrial Development. The impact of this foreign influence is similar to that in business education: as the pedagogical materials imported from the US were literally reproduced in Mexican classrooms, some of the recommendations of the UN agency were also reproduced verbatim in programmes and laws on self-employment and micro-firms enacted after 1985 by the Mexican Government (no specific laws were promulgated then on small and medium firms).

In the case of Spain, the activity of the central government and local authorities started, as did most entrepreneurship education, after the economic crisis, which peaked in 1979. As in Mexico, foreign influence has been determinant: most public support to new and small companies, from

financial aid to data bases, comes from European Community programmes. However, the fact that Spain is the only European country
without laws differentiating companies by size (the only initiative to fill this
lacuna relies on French legislation) reinforces the lack of profile and
intensity of the Spanish entrepreneurship movement, already present in its
educational front.

There is a common urge behind the eagerness of governments for
celebrating and promoting entrepreneurship: the struggle against unemployment, the most recalcitrant problem for the monetarist and neo-
classical economic policies that spread after the energy crises of the 1970s.
But there has been more than a search for employment sources in the
political front of the entrepreneurship movement. The generalized political
adoption of the idea of entrepreneurship – which implies the notion that
the creation of enterprises, and consequently of employment, takes place
within the private economic domain – was also one of the main justifica-
tions for politicians of all ideologies to drop from their political discourse
the idea of government's responsibility for employment, which was a
constant in Keynesian economics and corporatist politics. Entrepreneurship has been the occasion for a retreat in the economic and employment
expectations that the public domain had set for itself after World War II.

Business Groups

The actions of business people – the social group with the highest stake in
the spread and acceptance of entrepreneurship, since this constitutes a part
of its identity and legitimacy – further reinforced some of the ideological
motives for the popularization of entrepreneurial ideas. It can be said that
business groups shared a basically similar position in the 1980s: the
exhaustion – signalled by the deep crises of the late 1970s – of the
corporatism in place since the Cárdenas presidency in Mexico, the end of
World War II in Britain, and the end of the Civil War in Spain, with which
business groups collaborated in general. But business participation in this
corporatism was not backed by a self-legitimating ideological discourse,
and business became, by default, merely justified by the general economic
crisis and a legitimation crisis (Useem 1984). Despite this common
denominator, important differences among countries and among business
people's dispositions still existed. The reactions to these dissimilar circumstances gave plurality to the diffusion of entrepreneurial ideas.

The literature (among others, Useem 1984) posits that in general there
are two main variables for explaining business groups' activism. The first is
the incentives that these groups may have for participating in political
activities – which are very relevant given traditional business reluctance to
become involved in them. The urgency of the incentives of business people
in each country varied greatly. In Britain, decreasing profits and the
increasing role of the state under Labour were the trigger for political
activism. In Mexico, the incentives were much more powerful: the very

legitimacy of private business was at stake, and consequently business groups became hyperactive in their goal of changing a political regime perceived as not fully committed to private enterprise (as the 1982 nationalization of the banking system showed). The great opportunity for a pro-business offensive was the external debt crisis of 1982, which questioned the most important basis of PRI regime legitimacy: economic development. Whereas the strongest motivations for a high-profile social offensive were present in Mexico and Britain, in Spain the possible incentives were quickly diminished both by a constitutional agreement recognizing the market economy's hegemony and by a brilliant economic recovery.

The second variable necessary to explain processes of institutionalization is the resources these groups have for social action – from self-organization, to financing, to political skill, to slogans. Only Mexican business people, because of their control over important universities, were able to launch massive campaigns of entrepreneurial education in order to increase their social legitimation. In Britain, the most liberal wing of the Conservative Party was even ahead of business people themselves in initiating an ideological offensive and in promoting the enterprise culture. However, in Spain, business people had neither the backing nor the pull of an openly pro-business party for launching anything like Mrs Thatcher's enterprise culture campaign, nor do they own prestigious educational institutions.

In sum, the generalized ideological offensive of business groups in the late 1970s and the 1980s was based upon an active self-legitimating discourse defending the autonomy and pre-eminence of the market economies and business people's irreplaceable role in them. Entrepreneurship – the fruit of civil society, independent of the state, which even helps to defeat unemployment – became for business people an ideal concept upon which to base their increased ideologization, as well as their retreat from corporatism. The position, incentives and resources of business groups in each country have made the importance and content of entrepreneurial ideas vary. Whereas in Mexico entrepreneurship as self-employment is the main self-legitimating idea for business people of all categories, and in Britain the management of small firms (more than start-ups) has been the idea representing the social virtues of the enterprise culture, in Spain entrepreneurship was not the core of a generalized, but themeless, social acceptance of capitalist values in the 1980s.

Summary of the Data

The popularization of entrepreneurial ideas presents a fundamental contrast. It has taken place quite simultaneously in Britain, Mexico, and Spain, as well as in most other countries; and, owing to the important international circulation of business knowledge, some of its manifestations are fairly isomorphic across societies. Yet the movement presents very

Comparative cultural recipes

Table 5.3   *Entrepreneurship movement profiles in three countries*

	Triggering events	Social champions	Diffusing institutions	Dominant theme	Origin of knowledge
Britain	British decline and energy crisis, 1970s	Conservative politicians	Enterprise culture and education	Small firms	Local
Mexico	External debt crisis, early 1980s	Business groups	Entrepreneur-ship education	Micro-firms	USA
Spain	Energy crisis, late 1970s	No leaders	No salient institutions	No dominant theme	USA

different profiles in the three countries where it has been studied, as Table 5.3 summarizes.

In Britain the entrepreneurship movement began to develop about a decade earlier than in Mexico and Spain as one of the first reactions to the decline of Britain as an industrial power. At the beginning of the 1970s, the Bolton Report started a tradition of research on small firms, probably the strongest in Europe. It also prompted a series of government actions for the support of small businesses, and gave the entrepreneurship movement in Britain its dominant theme: small firms.

The arrival of Margaret Thatcher to power added a high-profile ideological and political dimension to this tradition. Entrepreneurship, represented by small firms, became one of the most important ideas integrating the enterprise culture, promoted by the liberal and populist wing of the Conservative Party, pulling after it the most active groups of business people. This enterprise culture was to be one of the key elements for the expected economic revitalization of Britain and for the end of the Keynesian consensus in place since the end of World War II. During the years of Conservative Government in the 1980s, the private and public schemes for promoting and supporting the creation of new firms and the management of small companies, as well as pro-enterprise education, multiplied nationally and locally.

In Mexico, the movement was launched, after the external debt crisis of 1982 and the nationalization of the banking system of the same year, by the groups of business people most inimical to the PRI political regime, by way of a massive campaign of entrepreneurship education started in the educational institutions these business people influenced, like the prestigious ITESM, which they supported financially. Other schools and universities soon followed ITESM's promotion of entrepreneurship. At the same time, some public champions of the movement began to diffuse the idea of entrepreneurship in popular media. Finally, the government, in a marked switch of policies, relying on foreign knowledge channelled through a United Nations agency, also started to promote entrepreneurship through several public agencies.

The theme of the entrepreneurship movement in Mexico is self-employment or micro-firms. The dominance of this theme comes from the convergence of a number of factors: the lack of academic resources in the country capable of disseminating a more sophisticated version of entrepreneurship; the urgency for new sources of employment; and ideological causes: for entrepreneurship as micro-firms is a perfect popular and populist 'idea force' for legitimating a more active social, economic, and political role for civil society versus the statism of the PRI regime.

In Spain, after the grave economic crises resulting from the increases in energy prices, most of the educational, social, and political manifestations of the entrepreneurship movement that appeared in Mexico and Britain can also be found. However, in spite of the socially positive evaluation that free enterprise and the world of business gained in the 1980s, as a result of the booming economy, the movement has no single dominant theme and its social visibility is not as important as in the other two countries. This may be attributed to the absence of a social group (politicians or business people or academics) deeply committed to the diffusion and institutionalization of the idea of entrepreneurship, and with important organizational and cultural resources.

Discussion

Three points deserve especial emphasis in the final discussion of the data gathered for this research. The first is the very fact that the data support the hypothesis held. Most recent sociological works on the generation, transmission and consumption of knowledge, from social technologies to ideologies, propose that the causes for its popularization are not endogenous to their conceptual value (the intellectual market hypothesis). Diffusion and institutionalization of ideas require the interplay of several social processes: triggering economic and political events, and the actions of social actors – producers, carriers, advocates, audiences, and consumers of ideas – made possible by their resources (for instance, cultural legitimacy and organizational resources). Since these factors vary in each country, the popularization of ideas should have different contents and levels of intensity. From very different quarters, the neo-institutional school of organizational theory also supports this perspective.

This research has applied this loose theoretical model to the popularization of a management idea: entrepreneurship in the 1980s. Applying the sociological literature on knowledge and ideologies to a management idea is justified by the analogy of business knowledge and ideologies. The bases for this analogy are functional (both ideologies and management knowledge are aimed at simplifying and making sense of the countless data enacted by the social and organizational world and at facilitating action on it) as well as structural (both can be conceived of as packages, internally built as *bricolages*, including everything from descriptive and analytical to prescriptive and normative ingredients).

For the case of entrepreneurship, the model has been especially appropriate because entrepreneurship is perhaps one of the most ideological business ideas: it is highly motivational, with a weakly defined academic content, and with strong social, political and macroeconomic connotations. This makes it more malleable in the hands of those agents interested in its diffusion and institutionalization – and, therefore, more revealing of the connections between business knowledge and societal contexts.

The reasons for the differences in timing, content and intensity of the entrepreneurship movement found among the three countries studied may be explained by the principal hypothesis held in the research. If the positions, dispositions, and cultural and organizational resources of the actors affected by and interested in business knowledge and ideas are critical for their diffusion and institutionalization, the different timing, intensity, and thematic content that the movement has in different countries would correspond to the differences in the situation that those actors and resources have in each of them. As DiMaggio (1988) has said, summarizing the main argument of the neo-institutional school of organizational theory:

> Put simply, the argument . . . is that institutionalization is a product of the political efforts of actors to accomplish their ends; and that the success of an institutionalization project and the form that the resulting institution takes depend upon the relative power of the actors who support, oppose, or otherwise strive to influence it.

Even when there is a lack of dominant theme and social visibility of the entrepreneurship movement, as in the Spanish case, it may be explained precisely by the absence of a social group, with strong organizational and cultural resources, committed to the diffusion and institutionalization of the idea of entrepreneurship. For instance, Spanish, business people, given the favourable economic environment and the absence of menacing ideological aggressions that might have pushed them to a social intervention, ended by almost completely inhibiting themselves from taking any steps similar to those adopted by their counterparts in Mexico and Britain. But even if they had decided upon that course, they would have found important difficulties: their influence, for instance, on business schools is not as direct and strong as in Mexico.

And political groups were not promoting the movement in Spain either. Although during the 1980s the Socialist Party in power enforced straightforward monetarist and liberal policies, it neither promoted liberal ideas and enthusiastically celebrated capitalism, nor diffused an ideological and political discourse legitimating its policies (the main justification of these policies for the Socialists being merely technocratic). While one of the main assumptions of the conservative revolution in the US and Britain was that ideas matter, in Spain there has not been a well-organized, openly liberal, and conservative ideological offensive in which entrepreneurship would have been one of the centre pieces. In Spain, then, the lack of a resourceful social actor explains the lack of intensity and content definition of the entrepreneurship movement when compared with that in Britain and Mexico.

In sum, for a social idea to reach the unusual visibility and importance entrepreneurship gained in Mexico and Britian it needs the decisive action of social groups, motivated by exceptional circumstances and opportunities. But it needs more than that. The second point we would like to underline in this discussion is that it also requires the availability and the academic, political, or ideological maturity of an idea that fits the situation, the time and the needs of the social groups.

The reasons for entrepreneurship being the object of such success in the 1980s has to do with its elective affinities with social ideologies on the rise, and with its great advantages and appeal as a key ideological component of the liberal economic crusade of the last decade. Prominent among them is that, paradoxically, entrepreneurship does not look ideological, does not appear at first glance to be political or partisan, since it is based on the individual's right to launch private economic activities: it is, in sum, a pre-political and indisputable issue. Also, it is pure and has no vices, since entrepreneurship gets perverted only when it ceases to be so, that is, when it converts itself into bureaucratic management.

This representativeness by entrepreneurship of the capitalist spirit derives from its being both ontogenetic and philogenetic (each new or small firm is assumed to reproduce in itself the virtues of the whole capitalist system, regenerating it); and from entrepreneurship's populism and egalitarianism, since, as is proposed for instance in the micro-firm version of the entrepreneurship movement in Mexico, everyone could be an entrepreneur.

Moreover, the main cause of entrepreneurship's appeal has probably to do also with the very intensity of the tensions and anxieties derived from entrepreneurial activities, which is also true of business behaviour in general – which makes of entrepreneurs and managers social groups with a very high natural demand for ideologies. If by channelling anxieties into admiration towards and identification with socially positive figures and themes, then ideologies, as the so-called relative deprivation approach (Wuthnow 1987) and Geertz's (1973) strain theory suggest, serve to placate the tensions of those fulfilling difficult tasks in situations of crisis or in unpredictable environments. The mythical figure of successful entrepreneurs – loners, fighters, sufferers, uncompromising, successful – as well as the narratives of their struggle for success are ideal for triggering the emotional identification of business people. By showing that it is possible to make it, these characters and narrations lower their anxieties as well as motivate them to keep trying.

A final point that we consider necessary to emphasize in order to explain the exceptional success of entrepreneurship in the 1980s, across countries located at different levels of development, is the international circulation of management knowledge. The spread of entrepreneurship in Mexico and Spain would not have been possible without the reception of academic materials and social and ideological inputs diffused from other societies that are traditional exporters of management knowledge, especially the USA.

As indicated in the previous pages, in business education the influence of knowledge originated in other countries, the United States in most cases, has been paramount. In Mexico and Spain it has been and still is an indispensable condition. But, very importantly, it has to be emphasized that the initiative for this diffusion has come from the receiving pole of the transmission. It has not been the centre of the US business education system or even the promoters of conservative ideologies – such as think-tanks located in the United States – which systematically pushed the entrepreneurship movement across national borders. There have been local actors at the periphery, following the dynamics discussed in this chapter, who either imported entrepreneurship courses, publications, government measures, and social ideas, or went to the United States to literally buy knowledge materials and carry them to their countries.

This is also true regarding the actions promoting entrepreneurship carried out by the governments. In the cases of Mexico and Spain a good number of these actions had the support of international agencies. And although there is no doubt that these international institutions provided much to the movement, from knowledge materials to political force, the first steps and connections were established following initiatives of the receptor countries.

Administrative knowledge is for practice. Cohen and March (1986), however, have cautioned that for business knowledge to impact on practices it needs to be perceived as socially reputed. These authors posited that for formal administrative knowledge to serve as a reputational basis for administrative action it needs to be integrated with other types of knowledge and with ideologies, and be socially legitimated (for instance, by prestigious institutions of business education or business media). Whatever their importance, the dynamics – in this research called pro-cesses of diffusion and institutionalization – leading to the popularization and reputation of management ideas have not elicited so much empirical research.

This research has shown how entrepreneurial ideas have spread and have adopted a content that depends very much on economic and political triggering events, social carriers, institutional resources, and cultural affinities, all of them external to the evolution of formal management knowledge itself. In doing so it suggests that, most probably, Cohen and March's warning about the importance of social processes of legitimation of business ideas is quite well founded. That is, one cannot understand the production, diffusion and consumption of business knowledge without taking into account the politics of the actors generating, transmitting and applying management ideas.

This chapter has focused on the macro-politics behind the success of one of the most ideological business ideas, entrepreneurship. But the politics of business knowledge also operate at a more micro, organizational level. As Eccles and Nohria (1992) have pointed out, most fads in business ideas are used as legitimators of managerial actions aimed at organizational change. While this chapter has established the politics of the most macro and ideological business ideas, much fruitful research may be done by focusing on the micro-politics of the use of business knowledge in organizational life.

Notes

This chapter summarizes some aspects of the unpublished doctoral dissertation of the author: 'The international diffusion and institutionalization of the new entrepreneurship movement: a study in the sociology of organizational knowledge'. Department of Sociology, Harvard University, 1991.

1 This chapter does not discuss the relationship between the spread of pro-entrepreneurship ideas and the actual creation of new firms or intrapreneurial activities. It should be mentioned that several authors have proposed that economic conditions have been much more important for the revival of entrepreneurial activities than the success of new ideological trends and the spread of entrepreneurial knowledge (Curran and Burrows 1986; Whitley 1989b). Whitley, for instance, poses five structural or non-ideological causes for the revival of small business in Europe: 'the decline of manufacturing employment and the growth of the service sector; second, the rise in unemployment since the early 1970s; third, income growth in the 1960s and 1970s leading to changing market structures for consumer goods; fourth, technological changes reducing the minimum efficient size of plants; and, fifth, a move by many large firms to disintegrate their activities and rely on subcontractors to a greater extent.' Whitely concludes that 'the increasing significance of small businesses in many European countries since the mid 1970s is as much a result of change in large firms' policies and practices as a consequence of an upsurge of "entrepreneurship" in Europe'.

References

Abrahamson, E. (1991) 'Managerial Fads and Fashions', *Academy of Management*, 16(3).
Bannock, G. and Peacock, A. (1989) *Governments and Small Business*. London: Paul Chapman.
Barley, S., Meyer, G. and Gash, D. (1988) 'Cultures of Culture: Academics, Practitioners and the Pragmatics of Normative Control', *Aministrative Science Quarterly*, 33(1).
Bendix, R. (1974) *Work and Authority in Industry*. Berkeley, CA: University of California Press.
Berger, P., Berger, B. and Kellner, H. (1974) *The Homeless Mind: Modernization and Consciousness*. New York: Vintage Books.
Boudon, R. (1986) *L'Idéologie ou l'origine des idées reçues*. France: Fayard.
Bourricaud, F. (1980) *Le Bricolage idéologique: essai sur les intellectuels et les passions démocratiques*. Paris: Presses Universitaires de France.
Bourricaud, F. (1986) *Le Retour de la droite*. France: Calmann-Lévy.
Cohen, M. and March, J. (1986) *Leadership and Ambiguity*. Boston, MA: Harvard Business School Press.
Cole, R. (1985) 'The Macropolitics of Organizational Change: a Comparative Analysis of the Spread of Small Group Activities', *Administrative Science Quarterly*, 30.
Curran, J. and Burrows, R. (1986) 'The Sociology of Petit Capitalism: a Trends Report', *Sociology*, 20(2).

Curran, J. and Stanworth, J. (1982) 'The Small Firm in Britain – Past, Present and Future', *European Small Business Journal*, 1(1).

DiMaggio, P. (1988) 'Interest and Agency in Institutional Theory', in L. Zucker (ed.), *Institutional Patterns and Organizations: Culture and Environments*. Cambridge, MA: Ballinger.

Eccles, R. and Nohria, N. (1992) *Beyond the Hype: Rediscovering the Essence of Management*. Boston, MA: Harvard Business School Press.

Gallagher, C. and Doyle, J. (1986) 'Job Generation Research: a Reply to Storey and Johnson', *International Small Business Journal*, 4(4).

Geertz, C. (1973) *The Interpretation of Cultures*. New York: Basic Books.

Hackman, R. (1985) 'Doing Research That Makes a Difference', in E.E. Lawler (ed.), *Doing Research That is Useful for Theory and Practice*. San Francisco: Jossey-Bass.

Hall, P. (1986) *Governing the Economy: the Politics of State Intervention in Britain and France*. New York: Oxford University Press.

Mohr, L. (1982) *Explaining Organizational Behavior: the Limits and Possibilities of Theory and Research*. San Francisco: Jossey-Bass.

Rainnie, A. (1985) 'Small Firms, Big Problems: the Political Economy of Small Business', *Capital and Class*, 35.

Stevenson, H. and Sahlman, W. (1986) 'Importance of Entrepreneurship in Economic Development', in R. Hisrich (ed.), *Entrepreneurship, Intrapreneurship, and Venture Capital: the Foundation of Economic Renaissance*. Lexington, MA: Lexington Books.

Useem, M. (1984) *The Inner Circle: Large Corporations and the Rise of Business Political Activity in the US and UK*. Oxford: Oxford University Press.

Whitley, R. (1989a) 'On the Nature of Managerial Tasks and Skills: their Distinguishing Characteristics and Organization', *Journal of Management Studies*, 26(3).

Whitley, R. (1989b) 'The Revival of Small Business in Europe'. Working Paper, Manchester Business School.

Wuthnow, R. (1987) *Meaning and Moral Order: Explorations in Cultural Analysis*. Berkeley, CA: University of California Press.

Wuthnow, R. (1989) *Communities of Discourse*. Cambridge, MA: Harvard University Press.

6

Excellence at Large: Power, Knowledge and Organizational Forms in Mexican Universities

Eduardo Ibarra-Colado

Organization Studies and the Transformation of Universities

'Discipline' cannot be identified either with an institution or with an apparatus. It's a kind of power, a modality to exercise it, which involves a set of tools, techniques, procedures, application levels, goals; it is a 'physics' or an 'anatomy' of power, a technology.

Michel Foucault, *Discipline and Punish*

Universities are undergoing a period of profound transition that redefines discursive strategies, relations of power and organizational forms. This process of change has been a generalized one, and many researchers have observed common tendencies derived from comparative analyses carried out in various countries (Brunner 1990; Center for Higher Education Policy 1992; Courard 1993; Neave 1988; Trow 1989). This transformation of universities gains greater relevance in the context of globalization, as it is through their processes that knowledge acquires strategic importance as a lever of economic development.

While it is difficult to deny the existence of such general trends, if we limit ourselves simply to observing them, this would conceal the complexity of local realities. One cannot use these general 'truths' as an aprioristic matrix of explanation for every local reality. The intention of this chapter is to overcome such reductionism; from the perspective being developed here, organization studies acquire their greatest relevance when they focus on the uniqueness of events, when they produce meticulous knowledge of difference and detail rather than an understanding of universals (Foucault 1977b).

Transformation processes in higher education are evident in the redeployment of neo-liberal discourse, deeply disturbing for existing state forms, redefining their functions and the characteristics, dimensions and organizational structures of their apparatus, as well as the profile of their officials (Ibarra and Montaño 1992; Morgenstern 1989). Recently there has been an emergence of a new 'possessive individualism', one of whose discursive strategies at an organizational level has been the successful 'excellence' literature. Through such strategies of excellence is facilitated the emergence of differentiation mechanisms that reshape social reality in new terms, where the regulation and exclusion of phenomena are based on strict evaluation processes.

A distinctive *fin de siècle* trait has emerged in the evaluation of performance. Performativity is now everywhere: from the bedroom to the boardoom, from the classroom to the factory floor, there is a heightened focus on performance and its evaluation. An increase in social contrasts, together with a further division of the spaces in which each individual is located regarding individual performance, result from this new performativity. Not only is this evident in the grading, ranking and comparison of prowess between individuals. Organization implications also become apparent. Organizationally, new relations of power, beyond apparent and well-conceived intentions, accompany those flexible organizational forms that strengthen differentiation. At one level, these have contributed to a debate concerning 'postmodern' organizations (Clegg 1990; Gergen 1992; Parker 1992; Power 1990).

The analysis of Mexican universities presented here contributes to the organizational debate concerning these so-called 'postmodern realities'. Notwithstanding the importance of an emphasis on the study of successful economic realities in East Asian countries, it is necessary to research other social environments. We should join this debate in Mexico, not only because Mexican local reality might exemplify a 'barely industrialized postmodernism' but because, as a late entrant to modern realities, Mexico's historical shape displays great contrasts and historical remnants as well as the possibility of postmodern niches (Clegg 1992: 146). The structure of hybrid cultures, not widely analysed to date, acquires a singular importance from this perspective (García 1995). It is within such realities that postmodern niches will more easily emerge, as they do not have to worry about great social contrasts because these have been part of the scenery for so long. Where postmodernism is under construction, there may first be the modernist state to dismantle; where it was virtually unbuilt, so much the better, so much the easier. Yet it is worth mentioning that, despite this, it is in these late entrants to the world constituted by modern realities that the most severe social ruptures can occur, as premodernity jostles with modernity and both recoil from the shock of the new in the context of the already old.

The de-differentiation processes that postmodernism instigates, as new disciplinary practices may be more subtle and effective in these late modern realities. The establishment of postmodern niches organized as flexible and participating forms that receive awards for their performance and productivity, on the one hand, allows for the consolidation of extensive masses of deprived people, organized under highly hierarchical and centralized forms, on the other. This process, far from granting us a fairer and more balanced future, promises the strengthening of a hybrid modernism, a kind of 'late hypermodernism' that could eventually collapse due to such deep inequalities (Willmott 1992). Postmodern tendencies, then, are no Whiggish roller-coaster to progressive futures, as Clegg (1990) has been at pains to develop.

The conjoint emergence of masses and niches promises a new order that identifies and individualizes through awards and punishments, expressing power relations and mobilization of knowledge oriented to the emergence of new organizational forms, as it simultaneously hones the old prison houses of bondage. The strategic nature of this detail, the mechanisms and technologies of power (Clegg 1989: 150–6; Garduño et al. 1989; Ibarra 1993a), comprise a triad of organizational transformations composed through power, knowledge and organizational forms.

The analysis of recent transformations in Mexican universities allows one to address the ideas outlined, through considering the transition process the sector is undergoing. Transformations lead to new relations, shaped from differentiation mechanisms in which rewards and punishments become more clearly specified. The structure of these new differentiation technologies, in the context of the redefinition of state–university relations, and the state discourse about education, will be the frame for this analysis.

Transitions in State–University Relations

The future of the university institution in Mexico has already arrived, because the changes seen in the five year period 1989–93 characterize a model from which, even with a project of resistance, it seems unlikely that we will escape. The set of modifications that the university faces conceals its relevance through the disarrangement ('rearrangement' would not do the change justice) of the functionality and of the forms by which the institutions themselves relate to the state and the society, through reciprocal links and conditions.

Today, we face a new discursive strategy and new organizational forms that outline a highly differentiated system. The exaltation of individual performance and the establishment of differentiating mechanisms, of either exclusion or inclusion, mark the route of 'excellence' in Mexican universities, the route of their modernization. From this perspective, it is necessary to understand that we face a transformation totally different in nature to those witnessed in the past, where reform projects hardly went beyond a simple game of rhetoric. Unlike yesterday, change now lies in the normalization of new power relations and, with them, of new disciplinary mechanisms and organizational forms that substantially modify the nature of university and academic work. Its future imposes a new structure at different levels, capable of granting a new order that illustrates the characteristics and possibilities of the system, and those of each of its institutions and individuals. Through a differentiation strategy, the aim is to build a comprehensive chart of higher education and science and technology in Mexico, identifying regions, institutions, programmes, and individuals.

This process will result in new economies, for example, a deeper knowledge of what we have or greater speed in institutional change; but we also find negative aspects, for example, quality taken as quantity, simulation of work, and construction of fictitious institutional scenarios. Thus, the future of Mexican universities is already being written with the pen of differentiation.

However, to reach this point, it is convenient to outline a series of shifts that have taken place. In the last two decades and a half, we have witnessed a gradual modification of the emphasis of governmental discourse, leading to new language games. The 'equality of opportunities' of the 1970s that accompanied the expansion of the higher education system has given way to the exaltation of individual fulfilment, always acknowledging virtues inherent to administrative rationalization. Likewise, the state's approach to the conduct of higher education develops a surveillance system that strives to guarantee more direct control of the institutions and their academics: a financing policy that incorporates restrictions and conditions that today acquire their full sense when anchored to evaluation. Finally, at a salary level the 'law of the three stages' has prevailed: in the last quarter-century, academics have tasted the sweetness of salary stability and the bitterness of lengthy deterioration, and today experience what we may refer to as the bittersweet taste of gradual and selective recovery, through some extraordinary incomes earned in competition. In Table 6.1 we present a characterization of the changes observed during this long period, presenting the axes for government policies and their institutional change.

To summarize, the university in Mexico is located today in the context of structural changes that assume the redefinition of the terms of its relations with the state and civil society, the modification of its organizational forms, and the emergence of new social individuals, located in the limited spaces of the institutions, who can be clearly identified through specific differentiation processes. To understand such changes better, let us analyse the strategic mechanisms of such differentiation processes (Ibarra 1993a; 1993b).

Excellence Discourse, or the Seductions of Individual Success

Changes in Mexican universities based themselves explicitly on the excellence discourse, whose origins trace to 1982, when Peters and Waterman shocked the business and administrative world with the publication of their book *In Search of Excellence.*[1] This book distinguished itself for highlighting the indetermination, the heterogeneity and the ambivalence that business faced at the end of the century. In addition, not only did it face paradoxes and ambiguities; it also proposed new ways of dealing with them, through the collaboration of members of the organization. Empowerment became the 1980s canalization of the rhetoric of participation and democracy that had characterized the late 1960s and early 1970s. The need to shape corporate cultures in which the individual could participate, while maintaining a 'practical autonomy', organizationally constructed and supported in an informal environment, received emphasis. From now on, the enterprise must concern itself with providing workers with an identity that orients their thoughts, beliefs and values. The canalization of participation meant, effectively, the colonization of the workforce in a new bondage of willing service rather than sullen submission.

According to these authors, the effective control of the enterprise depends on the ability of top management to build a scenario in which the individual can acquire a figurative sense of themselves as autonomous subjects, devoid of any sense of anxiety and insecurity. This figurative sense bases itself on the exaltation of individualism, on enterprising ability, and on the initiative and leadership that every worker supposedly, presumably and unknowingly carries in their contract but dares not to discover. So, when all responsibility rests on individual performance, the enterprise is not to blame for failures, even though it was responsible for defining the limits to initiatives and participation. Under this context, failures will always belong to the individual, and successes to the organization.

Although this proposal's translation into higher education is not precise, it is undeniable that its dissemination in this site recaptures some of its essential elements: we live in such times that excellence silently disseminates through various and diverse social spaces, in the era of *excellence at large*. The repeated presence of the excellence discourse shows the strength of language as a tool to shape behaviour (Foucault 1981). It is a discursive strategy that glorifies the goodness of individual performance to justify, almost imperceptibly, the exclusion of the great contingents. The acknowledgement of merit allows for the justification of differences and contrasts; the projected message indicates that those excluded are to blame for their own exclusion. Their permanent reinforcement necessarily passes through the exaltation of the skill of the few who have qualified, placing them as models to follow.

This new discursive practice also has an impact on evaluation mechanisms and on organizational forms. In the former, it orients a specific idea of what quality and excellence are; everything that does not fit this definition, this simple fact excludes. It concentrates on surveillance, measurement and recording mechanisms that respond to this specific idea.

Furthermore, the application of standards that permit the evaluation of the institutional and individual performance and its differentiation, with the mere presence of their indexes and indicators, comprises the myth of the objectivity of numbers and its endorsement in 'scientifically established'

Table 6.1　*Governmental policies and institutional changes, 1970–1994*

Sphere	1970–78	1979–88	1989–94
Strategic sector			
Discursive strategy	The *equality of opportunities discourse* positions itself as a paradigm to support the expansion of the higher education system of the country	The *planning discourse* takes its place to face the necessary restructuring of a system that grew anarchically	The *excellence discourse* positions itself as a paradigm to set forth a set of policies that intend to clearly differentiate a disorderly system. Its apparent intention is to increase the quality in each of its sectors
State regulation	Practically non-existent in higher education. Initially created in science and technology, through the creation of the National Council of Science and Technology (CONACYT) in 1970. Expansion of the higher education system, thanks to the creation of new universities and technological institutes, oriented by new organizational forms based on departmental structures and on functional and administrative decentralization	Surveillance from a distance based on seldom applied planning exercises, partly due to the great budgetary constraints of this period. Relative contraction of the higher education system: reduction of demand in relative terms, decrease in curricula and scholarships for postgraduate studies in the country and overseas	Direct surveillance through the establishment of a set of mechanisms structured from evaluation. Its reward and punishment system lies in the extraordinary financing sphere, in contested incomes and certification. Reordering the national higher education system and the science and technology system in the framework of a dual and unclear structure that will respond to differentiated policies
Financing policy	The public origin of financing is indisputable and its amounts are determined under a political logic that is loosely coupled to decisions of economic policy	Provision of resources regardless of any surveillance and evaluation procedure. Such allocation was based on the consideration of student demand and on faculty growth. In the framework of the austerity policy of government (1982–8), the resources in real terms for education and science and technology were reduced. This element explains the unnecessary contraction of a system that has been largely neglected	Provision of resources linked to the evaluation processes taking into consideration two essential mechanisms: (a) ordinary and determined subsidy that responds to strategic decisions of economic policy, taking into account the amount provided the previous year, as well as compensations derived from the annual inflation rate, from wage and salary increases and from punctual support for institutional growth and the quality thrust;

Wage and salary policy	Bilateral negotiation between university authorities and unions, in the framework of collective work contracts	Wage and salary restraint through the establishment of a wage ceiling and through homologated salary policies by reranking approvals	Wage and salary restraint through the establishment of a wage ceiling and through dehomologation salary policies. These policies suppose extraordinary incomes in competition determined by evaluation processes of productivity and performance of the academic staff
			(b) extraordinary resources in competition, linked to evaluation processes in charge of the pertinence, speed and success of the institutional change
General regulation (legal means)	Without relevant changes	Important modifications to ensure a greater state coordination of higher education; a greater autonomy of the university authorities over the unions, concentrating decisions about access, promotion and permanence of the academic staff as a whole. Also a new labour legislation that obstructed the establishment of a single national union	No changes, except the provisions of the Third Constitutional Article that clearly established that higher education is not free
Institutional sector Institutional change	Institutions move freely regarding the dynamics that their own communities impose on them, leading to the emergence of different institutional experiences deeply permeated by political projects	Consolidation of specific institutional projects, modifications according to the institution itself and first confrontations between the government and the institutions with non-shared political projects	Institutional change is a central demand of the modernization programme and the state surveyed it, conditioning the provision of additional resources. This project is oriented to the consolidation of a bureaucratic model of organization that achieves high efficiency levels, facilitating the generation of flexible organized niches, structured from institutional mechanisms of differentiation

Table 6.1 *continued*

Sphere	1970–78	1979–88	1989–94
Financial structure	Its composition is basically governmental and is provided in the absence of alternative financing policies	Its composition is basically governmental and is provided in the absence of alternative financing policies. In addition, it presents a severe lack of balance because, in most of the cases, 90 per cent of the resources granted are allocated to the payment of wages and salaries	Policy implementation to support the diversification of financing oriented to the fulfilment of sponsored agreements, to the sale of services and to the periodic increase of students' tuition
Labour relations	Not well structured, related to the institutional problems. Emergence and consolidation of the trade union movement oriented to the constitution of a single national union	Confrontation of the trade union movement avoiding the creation of a single national union. Weakening of unions with their restricted participation in the processes of access, promotion and permanence of academic staff and with the institutional backing of the wage ceiling policy	Preservation of the essential traits of the previous period and implementation of the salary dehomologation project regarding the institutional project. This institutional differentiation, expressed in the type of programmes implemented (their demands, amounts and timings), seeks increased competitive ability of the institution in an academic market that is in formation
Institutional regulations (legal means)	Casuistic	Few changes and introduction of particular regulations. In many cases, preservation of a functioning structure based on custom and everyday practices	Revision of the institutional regulations so that they are consistent with the new model and to avoid legal obstacles that may delay the proposed changes and reforms. Structuring and formalization of standards and procedures that clarify the institutional order

quantitative models. The myth survives repeated questioning. Objectivity in evaluation, as long as it can be conceived beyond hermeneutics, escapes from the determination of formalized indexes and indicators that, in reality, belong to power and discipline technologies structured from differentiation rules. In this sense, *through the definition of its specific forms, evaluation has already taken action, even before its implementation* (Foucault 1977a; Rendón and Montaño 1983). It might be worth reiterating that in creating such indexes and indicators, rendering benefits to certain actions and discouraging others, the government is influencing directly the nature, contents and organization of academic work.

New discursive practices facilitate the cohabitation of highly centralized and hierarchical organizational forms with more flexible and participating organizational forms, characteristic of 'excellence groups'. In this sense, we face a discursive strategy that permits the normalization of inequality and contrasts, inhibiting the critical capacity of people. It is highly specific in its operations. Excellence symbols create and place limits on certain realities, building a shared meaning that gains its strength in the hope that those who are outside can enter, and in the intimidation imposed on those who are inside for fear of being excluded.

In its more specific terms, the symbolism related to this discursive game allows for the exaltation of a model endowed with more recent and flexible organizational forms, disqualifying from the outset all institutional experience not oriented in that direction. In Mexico, symbolism related to the departmental structure (Clark 1983), in contrast to the school, faculty and research centre structures, takes naturally as if it were the flag of a new discourse flown as the masthead of change. Moreover, the discursive practices that have gained importance in the field of higher education, those language games that find their battle horses in quality, excellence and deregulation, tend to reinforce the apparent advantages of a model that in fact has been hardly analysed. The set of knowledge about modernization has placed those organizational forms that define the new university in the 'throne of truth': the *modern university* must be held accountable for the definition and fulfilment of its own institutional project, that is, of its mission and strategies, of a conceptual set that grants it its identity and that distinguishes it from the rest; it must adopt a flexible structure of a departmental type and function in a decentralized way in functional and administrative terms; it must adopt planning systems that protect its gradual growth and enable its stabilization; it must sustain the quality of its substantive functions in the objective and periodic evaluation of its various institutional spheres and of each of its community sectors, depending on evaluation bodies clearly established with unequivocal regulations; it must diversify its financing sources as a means to increase its autonomy, placing the responsibility for the costs of their own education on its students; it must link itself with society and industry and have a great adaptation ability before the rapid changes imposed by its context; in short, according to our own terms, the modern university must be a university based on differentiation from surveillance mechanisms sustained on rewards and punishments, which will eventually lead to the establishment of excellence niches, integrated by individuals with high performance and merits.[2]

Evaluation and Differentiation Standards or the New Governmental Gaze

In this context, no surprise attaches to the fact that the Mexican Government has shifted the emphasis of planning toward evaluation. The importance granted to the latter expresses a new governmental attitude towards higher education and science and technology, which abandons the 'surveillance from a distance' of previous times to implement a set of mechanisms that ensure the direct conveyance of the system and its differentiation.

This displacement comprises a change of strategy that finds its fundamental element of action in the control of the nature, contents and organization of university work. This element is fundamental to achieve a greater link between university, industry, and society, and to eliminate those perceived vices and inefficiencies that hamper it. It also involves the intention of achieving a greater clarity of the profile of the higher education system at a national level, and in particular, of each one of its institutions. In the acknowledgement of the institutional differences, of their specific traits, we find the expression of its intention to give flexibility to a national system that requires a greater coordination.

Thus, the evaluation of performance establishes a specific gaze that acknowledges, marks and situates each institution in its precise place. This incisive gaze will always be ready to record all changes in institutional performance, either to reinforce or to modify the place previously granted to it.

In this context we should place the ample evaluation strategy of the National Commission of Evaluation (CONAEVA), whose aim is to look in detail at the characteristics of the system, to induce institutions to see within themselves, and to ensure that expert eyes from outside see into their interior. Here, expert gazes include evaluation of research projects, postgraduate programmes, national scientific reviews, faculties and departments, researchers, students and professionals. Their differentiation standards express their exclusionary nature in the results observed in the Allowances of Resources to Science, the Excellence Postgraduates Poll, the Mexican Scientific Reviews Poll, the National System of Researchers, the Indicative National Examination before the master's degree and the General Examination of Professional Quality. Assuredly, these multiple gazes must provide the knowledge that ordains and modifies institutions and individuals, producing new realities under the scenario of excellence.

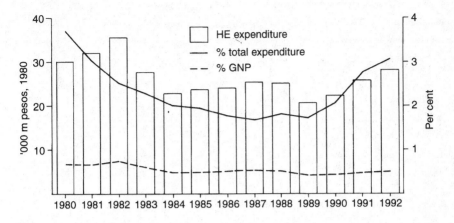

Figure 6.1 *Federal expenditure on higher education and its contribution to total expenditure and GNP, 1980–1992 (Fifth Government Report, 1993: implicit deflator GNP; National Accounts System, INEGI)*

Financing Policy or the Rewards for Excellence

To be effective, the accompaniment of a precise gaze must be likewise precise consequences. It is useless to oversee if this does not entail consequences. Thus, the evaluation of institutions gains its strength as a control mechanism if linked to finance policy, which in this framework claims its necessary flexibility.

After enduring a decade of financial constraints without mediations, financial policy set its foundations in the decision to grant the universities an ordinary subsidy that, according to the rhythm of economic recovery, can guarantee its continuous operation. According to official data, public expenditure in higher education recorded between 1989 and 1993 an increase of 47 per cent in real terms. However, as we can see in Figure 6.1, such growth has not yet compensated the expenditure level reached in 1982, measured in real terms. The present administration (1988–94) avoided negative 'growth' of resources to higher education institutions but never reversed accumulated losses.

Nevertheless, this policy also contemplates a new element for its flexibility: through the creation of the Higher Education Modernization Fund (FOMES), the allocation of extraordinary resources for institutions depends on the results obtained in the evaluation processes. These resources are channelled to carry out specific projects. Under this logic, the government is willing to grant supplementary support, where demonstration exists of the quality and the feasibility of the institutional project by 'objective indicators', that is, as long as they ensure the change in their organizational forms or show their impact in the academic-administrative improvement of the institution. Thus, from now on, the government no longer considers direct subsidy for the universities as a privileged way to

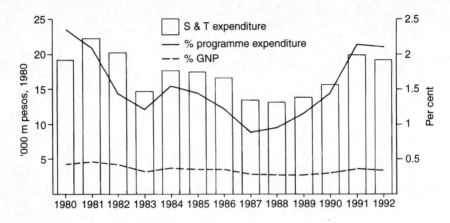

Figure 6.2   *Federal expenditure on science and technology and its contribution to programme expenditure and GNP, 1980–1992 (Fifth Government Report 1993: implicit deflator GNP; National Accounts System, INEGI)*

achieve the financial recovery of the institutions. Instead, we find extraordinary governmental financing and institutional capacity through the diversification of its income sources.

The financial treatment provided to higher education complements that granted to science and technology, placed as a strategic centre for sustaining the economic recovery of the country. The evident differentiation of these two sectors, easily confirmed, demonstrates itself in a greater recovery of expenditures in science and technology. As can be seen in Figure 6.2, this has registered an accumulated increase of 58.5 per cent in real terms in comparison to 1988, without yet attaining the level recorded in 1981 (Alzati 1993). The incorporation of extraordinary financing gained in competition, and the differentiation of policies, mechanisms and financing means between higher education and science and technology, achieves flexibility and enhances governmental ability to manage the system, without upsetting discipline in public expenditure.

Salary Policy or the Apparent Virtues of Dehomologation

The strategic circle of governmental action becomes completed by salary policy towards the academic staff of universities. It is one that considers differentiation mechanisms to achieve a closer surveillance of professors and researchers and a more precise institutional orientation of their work. As in the case of financing, there is a new stage of greater flexibility where the policy of salary restraint (which existed in practice since the first years of the 1980s) now finds its justification in an extraordinary incomes policy.

From the beginning, the present administration faced the dilemma of low academic salaries. One difficulty in thinking about it was the salary ceiling policy. Recent policy responded to the guidelines of economic policy, adopted with a scrupulous discipline. It was difficult to find solutions to the problem of low academic salaries. Salary dehomologation represented the regime's master key, making flexibility its policy, one that would offer extraordinary incomes in competition. Such competition concerned individual performance and productivity, also dependent on the availability of resources. This solution, although partial, avoided the high economic costs of a direct general increase in salaries and evaded negotiation with the trade unions, as it did not consider such incomes legally as salary. Again, flexibility appears as a strategic orientation.[3]

Among the mechanisms that have made dehomologation possible, we find the creation of the Merit Pay Programme for Academic Performance in February 1990 and the Merit Pay Programme for the Teaching Career of the Academic Staff of Higher Education Institutions in June 1992. These programmes, found within the administration of each institution, with different modalities according to their specific characteristics and their institutional project, aid the functioning of differentiation at this level.[4] The declared objective of these programmes was to reward permanence, quality in performance and full-time dedication, thus supporting the salary recovery of some academic staff in relation to their individual perform-ance.

The mechanisms have as a background the creation in 1984 of the National System of Researchers, a governmental programme oriented to reward economically the top researchers in the country and which has been strengthened, in the five-year period considered here, with an increase in the amounts for grants it provides and with an increase in the number of its members. This scenario is completed by the existence of institutional bonus programmes, increasingly implemented since 1989. Like the others, such programmes intend to reward dedication and productivity, to support differentiation and to foster intra- and inter-institutional competition.

This new salary policy translates into an accelerated increase in the incomes of the academics incorporated in these programmes and who managed to stay in them, a small contingent indeed. If we consider as a reference point the case of the Autonomous Metropolitan University (UAM), in just three years and five months academic income increased substantially (Figure 6.3). So, for example, in the case of the highest category in the academic rank, corresponding to Professor C, the monthly income went from 1,993 new pesos (US$604.74) in February 1990 to 11,452 new pesos (US$3,473.62) in June 1993.[5] This amounts to an accumulated increase of 474.4 per cent. To these incomes, we must add the National Research System Grant and the additional incomes obtained through the institutional bonus programmes, so that Professor C in the end has a maximum monthly income of 16,418 new pesos (US$4,979.87, i.e. US$67,228.28 per year).

One result of this salary policy is to modify deeply the composition of academic income: now it can depend on up to six different sources. With

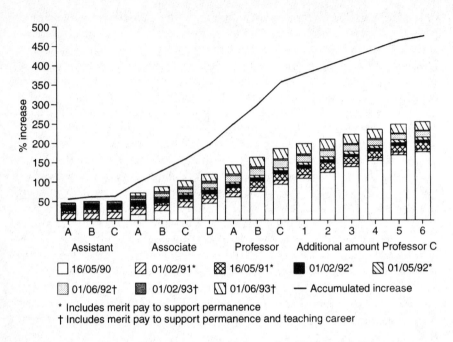

Figure 6.3 *Income evolution of the academic staff at UAM, including institutional bonuses, February 1990 to June 1993*

this, the weight of the basic salary – according to academic rank – displaces to other types of income under competitive processes of selection. In the extreme situation, that is, in those few cases where the whole of the additional income contemplated in the dehomologation programmes obtains, the basic rank salary can represent only 23.2 per cent of the professor's income; the other 76.8 per cent is subject to periodic evaluation processes that question the economic stability of the academic staff, often generating work simulation, stress and anxiety.

In addition, this process has meant a vast variety of incomes within the same category and level, considering the academic rank (Figure 6.4). Again, in the case of Professor C at UAM, the salary range comprises a minimum income of 3,804 new pesos (US$1,153.78) and a maximum of 16,418 new pesos (US$4,979.87). In between these two extremes, it is possible to find more than 288 different income combinations, determined from the sources that integrate them. So, the *personalized salary* has suddenly become a reality of our late hypermodernism.

Even though, at first glance, the increase in academic income might seem extraordinary, it is necessary to establish two points. First, it must be noted that those who have access to these additional incomes are few. The most optimistic institutional estimates have generally located them as 30 per cent of the total full-time and permanent academic staff.[6] Second, despite all these additional incomes, academics have not yet recovered the

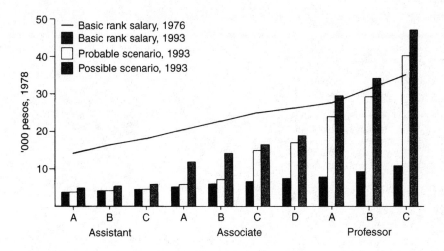

Figure 6.4   *Income range at UAM by category and level, and comparison of academic staff incomes in real terms, 1976–1993 (deflator INPC, June 1993)*

salary level they had in 1976. As can be seen in Figure 6.4, the only exception corresponds to the maximum category of the academic rank, which slightly exceeds the salary level it had two decades back, but now under conditions of instability and competitiveness hard to imagine then. Thus, in spite of the possible advantages of such a payment strategy, totally registered in the scheme of the economic policy pursued by the government, its effects are beyond doubt. These have become apparent in the form of increased dissatisfaction, stress and anxiety, simulation of work, persistence of the brain-drain problem, as well as the high hidden costs of its implementation under a highly bureaucratic certification and evaluation scheme.

Do these initial consequences worsen the human cost of the Mexican universities, typical in the 1980s, instead of putting a brake to it?

Mexican Universities, their Masses and their Niches

Surveillance and punishment seem to be replacing the structural axes in the new formation of Mexican universities. Disciplinary power, its mechanisms and technologies, are outlining a greatly differentiated university system in Mexico, one characterized by the establishment of masses and niches. This arrangement of the institutions and the individuals as subject to new, more subtle and penetrating gazes, seems to outline the routes of excellence, that is, the paths of exclusion, the steps to oblivion.

Taking into account the evidence presented, consider an initial characterization of the scenario of universities in Mexico by the end of the century, under the assumption that the parameters do not suffer substan-

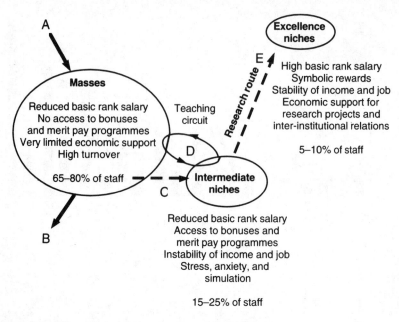

Figure 6.5   *The university, its masses and its niches:
the routes to excellence*

tial modification. Such a scenario assumes the gradual convergence of three highly differentiated academic contingents.

The Masses

A great contingent of academics would be primarily devoted to teaching activities through temporary contracts and with heavy workloads in the classroom as they work simultaneously in various education institutions. This group has a very low basic rank salary and would be at the margins of the dehomologation programmes. Its size would amount to 65–80 per cent of the academic staff nation-wide. A high turnover of personnel, owing to the need to receive additional incomes, dependent on professional opportunities outside of teaching, is likely. Thus, this great *academic army* would go from one institution to another and would pass from its teaching activity to other professional activities, establishing its strongest links outside the university. This first route assumes continuous circulation A ⟷ B depicted in Figure 6.5.

The Intermediate Niches

From the great contingent made up by the masses, there would be a much smaller contingent that had the intention of establishing an academic career in the long term. This smaller group comprises academics with two clearly differentiated orientations: on the one hand, academics that focus their higher efforts in teaching activities, distinguishing themselves by their ability in the teaching process and by their ability to elaborate materials and books that support this instruction; on the other hand, academics mainly oriented towards research, showing high levels of quality and productivity in their work. As in the previous case, this group would receive a reduced basic rank salary, although it would participate in the dehomologation programmes, a fact that could increase its income three-fold or fourfold. This group would account for 15–25 per cent of the full-time academic staff nation-wide, with important variations from one institution to another.

The first group, the one oriented towards teaching, would have few possibilities for going beyond this intermediate position, as the dehomo-logation programmes tend to show an inclination for research activities. Thus, its mobilization route would characterize a teaching circuit D in Figure 6.5. The members of the other group, so long as they are able to show their qualifications as researchers and participate in the groups consolidated in their disciplines, would have the possibility to transit eventually through the *excellence route* C $\rightarrow$ E, a route on which apparently a return ticket would not be considered.

The Niches of Excellence

A very small group of full-time academics would be devoted to research activities that enjoy a high appreciation from their institution and from the academic communities where they move, at both national and international levels. In fact, these small highly institutionalized research groups ensure the reputation of their universities; also, they are responsible for the direction of postgraduate and research programmes with governmental support, and for direction of scientific reviews evaluated as excellence reviews. In addition, the constituents of these niches will occupy the evaluation spaces, ensuring their permanence and establishing the profile of their generational expansion. So, the gaze that evaluates these extensive masses, perhaps secure in their illusions about the exercise, locates itself in the unattainable redoubt of excellence.

On the other hand, the payment of the members of these excellence groups will be significant, providing income, job stability and social assurance for retirement. Moreover, they will benefit from very good working conditions, with sufficient governmental funds to support the fulfilment of their research projects, having institutional support expressed in the flexibility of their organizational forms, structured on the margins of those bureaucratic standards that could hamper the mobility of their constituents or the timely exercise of assigned funds. The excellence niches would represent 5–10 per cent of the full-time academic staff nation-wide, showing important variations at the institutional level.

Conclusion

The universities in Mexico are undergoing radical changes. These are neither a Mexican phenomenon alone nor part of some global necessity. They are an effect of the adoption of quite specific discursive, financial, salary and evaluation policies. Gradually they are taking shape through a new model that originated from the excellence discourse. Its contradictions express the power relations that are creating more complex disciplinary mechanisms that limit, order and regulate its scenarios through new exclusion standards, through more subtle and violent differentiation procedures.

The evidence seems to indicate that the creation of excellence niches is being sought beyond the confusing multitudes, to provide them with a new order. To include, it is necessary to exclude; to grant privileges, it is necessary to degrade; to reward, it is necessary to punish: and all this in a continuous process of acknowledgement, of location, of classification that disciplines and regulates. The search for excellence demands the preservation of mediocrity as an essential condition.

This new functionality, its economies and its negative traits, have been outlined in this chapter, showing that organization studies of local institutional realities are necessary to search deeper than managerially and organizationally apparent rhetoric to understand the different elements that make up the traits of modernity and their postmodern contradictions in realities such as Mexico.

Que sera, sera: not as fatalism but because the future is such thanks to its indetermination. Even though Mexican universities are undergoing the changes outlined, it is necessary to accept that the last word remains unuttered. There is no doubt that the excellence offered to us by modernity today is a synonym of exclusion; it entails high risks that might foster the emergence of a social force capable of breaking, at any time, the springs of differentiation. In this sense, could we establish that, in our late hyper-modernism, excellence at large might be understood as a resistance against itself?

What occurs in Mexico is not unique. Nor is it the preserve of a less developed economy, in that splendid euphemism. It is a part of a trend that sees discursive strategies for constituting management, in this case of the tertiary sector, disseminated widely if not universally. Excellence began in a fevered response on the part of American management educators to the success of Japan as number one. It achieved global marketing success. Like aerobics or jogging, it is, for its moment, pervasive. Like an urban myth, we all half-believe everyone seeks excellence. While this chapter addresses itself to one empirical instance of the excellence phenomenon, more concerted comparative work is required. What are the strategies of excellence in other countries, other sectors; what are the similarities, the differences, the strategies of control and the strategies of resistance?

Notes

I would like to acknowledge helpful discussions with the members of the Organizational Analysis and Higher Education Seminar at Autonomous Metropolitan University and with the colleagues who participated in the section Organizational/Managerial Ideas and Social Science of the 11th EGOS Colloquium (Paris, July 1993). They helped me clarify my thoughts on some of the issues discussed in earlier drafts of this chapter. In addition, I would like to thank Stewart Clegg and Salvador Porras for the editorial work that they did on an earlier copy of this chapter. The responsibility for the outcome, of course, is entirely my own.

1 This managerial proposal has been inscribed in other books, such as *A Passion for Excellence* (Austin and Peters 1985) and *The Renewal Factor* (Waterman 1987). The excessive optimism of the excellence literature has been abandoned gradually. This change of direction is illustrated in Peters's two most recent books, *Thriving on Chaos* (1989) and *Liberation Management* (1992). Among the few critical approximations to the excellence literature we find the book *Le Coût de l'excellence* (Aubert and De Gaulejac 1991). Likewise, Willmott (1992) has put forward interesting clues that mention the need to analyse in more detail and depth the role of organizational/managerial ideas in the framework of power relations and the new organizational forms.

2 The papers by Brunner (1990: 77–132, 161–77; 1993), CEPAL/UNESCO (1992: 125–98), Guevara (1992: 78–86), Coombs (1991), the New Universities Project of the Higher Education and Scientific Research Department at the Public Education Ministry (Delvalle 1990; SESIC/SEP 1989; Vargas 1989; White 1990), Todd and Gago (1990: 121–54) and UNESCO/CRESALC (CRESALC 1992: 77–91) are important examples of the recent literature that is aware of this discursive exaltation. Even though all these texts are not necessarily located along the same argumentation lines and they do not propose unique models or the same organizational formulas, all of them agree on the need for change based on quality. They observe benefits in more flexible organizational forms, such as the departmental one, to face the uncertainty. They express their conviction about the advantages of evaluation processes. They agree on the need to diversify the financing forces and highlight the necessary and unbreakable link of higher education institutions with those of industry and society. The specific results of these discursive strategies, that have assimilated many of the conceptual elements of the corporate culture literature, the excellence literature and the strategic planning literature, are now evident in the orientation of the institutional change of the universities (Ibarra 1993c), in the model of the newly created University of Quintana Roo (SEP 1991), and in the diffusion of a new administrative knowledge that provides new concepts and tools for university management (Sanyal 1992). The contrast regarding this trend in search of excellence in the universities can be appreciated in Ibarra (1993b).

3 During the first five years of the regime (1989–93), the wage ceiling has been established at 10, 12, 17, 13 and 5 per cent respectively, giving in some cases a low salary reranking. The inflationary indexes always exceeded such percentages, locating from 1989 to 1993 at 19.7, 29.9, 18.8, 11.9 and 8.1 per cent.

4 Even when the merit pay programmes are the same in all the public universities, the federal government has permitted some institutions to manage them with high degrees of discretion. This institutional differentiation complies with a very precise function that has not often been observed: giving preferential treatment to some institutions raises a barrier to clear analysis of the negative traits of the policies advanced, re-creating mirages to which some can aspire and for which others will fight because they feel mistreated. The analysis of the negative traits of these policies of dehomologation is displaced by the reflected demand for the generalization of the programmes, amounts and opportunities of the institution that provides them on more favourable conditions. Let us make one comparison that clarifies this idea: in this logic, the academic is like the poor person that no longer asks the reasons for his poverty but still demands, although he will remain poor, access to the services of the welfare state.

5 The conversion to dollars was made using as baseline the exchange rate on 18 October

1993 (US$1=N$3.297). Take into account that the Mexican peso still has a slight slide against the dollar, affecting adversely the wage and salary rates. The daily sliding rate of the peso against the US dollar was established as N$0.0004 in retail sales (Salinas 1993: 55). This rate was modified by the severe economical and political crisis that Mexico experienced throughout 1994. See OECD (1995: 1–50).

6 According to the most recent data for UAM, only 15.3 per cent of the full-time academic staff obtained the institutional bonuses (306 out of 2,000) and 28.8 per cent the merit pay for permanence (579 of 2,013). We observed similar percentages in other institutions in which the number of awarded merit payments has depended frequently on the budgetary authorized resources (Ibarra 1993c).

References

Alzati, F. (1993) 'Scientific Development, Technological Modernization, and the State', in J.L. Boldú and J.R. de la Fuente (eds), *Science Policy in Developing Countries: the Case of Mexico*. Mexico: Fondo de Cultura Económica. pp. 194–202.

Aubert, N. and de Gaulejac, V. (1991) *Le Coût de l'excellence (The Excellence Cost)*. Paris: Seuil.

Austin, N. and Peters, T.J. (1985) *A Passion for Excellence*. New York: Fontana.

Brunner, J.J. (1990) *Educación superior en América Latina: cambios y desafíos (Higher Education in Latin America: Changes and Challenges)*. Chile: Fondo de Cultura Económica.

Brunner, J.J. (1993) 'Evaluación y financiamiento de la educación superior en América Latina: bases para un nuevo contrato' ('Evaluation and Financing of Higher Education in Latin America: Bases for a New Contract'), in H. Courard (ed.), *Políticas comparadas de educación superior en América Latina*. Chile: FLACSO. pp. 45–86.

Center for Higher Education Policy (1992) 'International Perspectives on Trends and Issues in Higher Education Policy'. Manuscript, Bertelsmann Foundation, The Netherlands.

CEPAL/UNESCO (1992) *Educación y conocimiento: eje de la transformación productiva con equidad (Education and Knowledge: Axis of the Productive Transformation with Equality)*. Chile: Naciones Unidas.

Clark, B.R. (1983) *The Higher Education System: Academic Organization in Cross-National Perspective*. Berkeley, CA: University of California Press.

Clegg, S.R. (1989) *Frameworks of Power*. London: Sage.

Clegg, S.R. (1990) *Modern Organizations: Organization Studies in the Postmodern World*. London: Sage.

Clegg, S.R. (1992) '¿De las culturas antiguas a la fatuidad posmoderna?' ('From the Ancient Cultures to the Postmodern Fatuity?'), *Gestión y Política Pública*, 1(1): 103–53.

Coombs, P.H. (ed.) (1991) *Strategy to Improve the Quality of Higher Education in Mexico. Report for the Secretary of the Public Education Ministry by the International Council for the Development of Education*. Mexico: Fondo de Cultura Económica.

Courard, H. (ed.) (1993) *Políticas comparadas de educación superior en América Latina (Polities Compared in Latin American Higher Education)*. Chile: FLACSO.

CRESALC (1992) *Reunión internacional de reflexión sobre los nuevos roles de la educación superior a nivel mundial: el caso de América Latina y el Caribe (International Meeting on the Reflection of the New Roles of Higher Education Worldwide: the Case of Latin America and the Caribbean)*. Mexico: ANUIES.

Delvalle, J. (1990) *Proyecto nuevas universidades. Personalidad, organización y gobierno de la nueva universidad (New Universities Project. Personality, Organization and Governing of the New University)*. Mexico: SEP.

Foucault, M. (1977a) *Discipline and Punish: the Birth of the Prison*. Harmondsworth: Penguin.

Foucault, M. (1977b) 'Nietzsche, Genealogy, History', in D. Bouchard (ed.), *Michel Foucault: Language, Counter-Memory, Practice*. Oxford: Blackwell.

Foucault, M. (1981) 'The Order of Discourse', in R. Young (ed.), *Untying the Text*. London: Routledge and Kegan Paul.

García, N. (1995) *Hybrid Cultures: Strategies for Entering and Leaving Modernity*. Minnesota: University of Minnesota Press.

Garduño, G., Ibarra, E. and Montaño, L. (1989) 'Tríptico del poder' ('Triptych of Power'), *Casa del Tiempo*, 9(89): 75–9.

Gergen, K.J. (1992) 'Organization Theory in the Postmodern Era', in M. Reed and M. Hughes (eds), *Rethinking Organization: New Directions in Organization Theory and Analysis*. London: Sage. pp. 207–26.

Guevara, G. (ed.) (1992) *La catástrofe silenciosa (The Silent Catastrophe)*. Mexico: Fondo de Cultura Económica.

Ibarra, E. (1993a) 'Foucault, entre el poder y la organización' ('Foucault, between Power and Organization'), in G. Martínez (ed.), *Mercados y regulación*. Mexico: Universidad Autónoma Metropolitana. pp. 11–32.

Ibarra, E. (ed.) (1993b) *La Universidad ante el espejo de la Excelencia: enjuegos organizacionales (The University before the Excellence Mirror: Organizational Elements)*. Mexico: UAM-I.

Ibarra, E. (1993c) 'La UAM, políticas gubernamentales y cambio institucional' ('UAM, Government Policies and Institutional Change'). Manuscript, Universidad Autónoma Metropolitana, Mexico.

Ibarra, E. and Montaño, L. (1992) 'Teoría de la organización y administración pública: insuficiencias, simplezas y desafíos de una maltrecha relación' ('Organization Theory and Public Administration: Insufficiencies, Simplicities and Challenges of a Battered Relation'), *Gestión y Política Pública*, 1(1): 49–75.

Morgenstern, S. (1989) 'Crisis de acumulación y respuesta educativa de la nueva derecha' ('Accumulation Crisis and Education Response of the New Right'), *Universidad Futura*, 1(2): 49–57.

Neave, G. (1988) 'Higher Education under the State Evaluation: Trends in Western Europe', *European Journal of Education*, 23(1–2).

OECD (1995) *OECD Economic Surveys: Mexico*. Paris: OECD.

Parker, M. (1992) 'Post-Modern Organizations or Postmodern Organization Theory?', *Organization Studies*, 13(1): 1–17.

Peters, T.J. (1989) *Thriving on Chaos*. London: Pan.

Peters, T.J. (1992) *Liberation Management*. California: Alfred A. Knopf.

Peters, T.J. and Waterman, R.H. (1982) *In Search of Excellence*. New York: Harper and Row.

Power, M. (1990) 'Modernism, Postmodernism and Organization', in J. Hassard and D. Pym (eds), *The Theory and Philosophy of Organizations: Critical Issues and New Perspectives*. London: Routledge. pp. 109–24.

Rendón, M. and Montaño, L. (1983) 'Sistema, modelo e ideología: notas para un análisis del poder en las organizaciones' ('System, Model and Ideology: Notes for an Analysis of Organizational Power'), *Iztapalapa*, 4(9): 225–36.

Salinas, C. (1993) *Quinto Informe de Gobierno, 1993. Anexo estadístico (Fifth Government Report, 1993. Statistical Addendum)*. Mexico: Presidencia de la República.

Sanyal, B.C. (1992) *Improving the Managerial Effectiveness of Higher Education Institutions: State of the Art*. Paris: UNESCO.

SEP (1991) *Creación de la Universidad de Quintana Roo (Creation of the Quintana Roo University)*. Mexico: SEP (Public Education Ministry).

SESIC/SEP (1989) *Proyecto sobre nuevas universidades (New Universities Project)*. Mexico: SESIC/SEP (Higher Education and Scientific Research Department/Public Education Ministry).

Todd, L.E. and Gago, A. (1990) *Visión de la universidad mexicana, 1990 (Vision of the Mexican University, 1990)*. Mexico: Castillo.

Trow, M. (1989) 'A Comparison between the Perspectives of Higher Education Policies in the United Kingdom and in the United States', *Oxford Review of Education*, 14(1): 81–96.

Vargas, E.A. (1989) *Project Report: the New/Experimental University*. Mexico: SEP.

Waterman, R.H. (1987) *The Renewal Factor*. New York: Fontana.

White, A. (1990) *Proyecto nuevas universidades. Una propuesta inicial para una estructura financiera universitaria (New Universities Project. An Initial Proposal for a University Financial Structure).* Mexico: SEP.

Willmott, H. (1992) 'Postmodernism and Excellence: the De-differentiation of Economy and Culture', *Journal of Organizational Change and Management,* 5(1): 58–68.

7

From Cultural Imperialism to Independence: Francophone Resistance to Anglo-American Definitions of Management Knowledge in Québec

Jean-François Chanlat

After the Second World War the Western countries experienced, until the mid 1970s, a period of prosperity unprecedented in modern history. Since that golden age, those societies have known more difficult times. These difficulties reached their peak in the 1990s with the persistence and growth of unemployment faced in most of the industrialized world (Reich 1992; Julien 1993).

These periods of our recent history have also been the stage for a big development in management sciences and, more generally, a process of institutionalization of managerial ideas in many social spheres (Mintzberg 1989). This deep interest in management and the development of its sub-disciplines has prompted studies in many parts of the world (Whitley 1984; Morgan 1986; Audet and Malouin 1986; Déry 1988, 1992; Martinet 1990). Up to now, among the published works on this subject, few if any have studied the evolution of managerial ideas in the Québec business school system. This chapter presents some of the elements in that field.

The province of Québec, like all other parts of the Western world, has had its share of prosperity and social difficulties over the last thirty years. But its socio-cultural particularism, combined with its geographical location, gives Québec an interesting originality at the socio-anthropological level. That is why I am interested, as a sociologist, professor, researcher and consultant in the management field working in that state-province, to see how managerial ideas have changed since the beginning of the 1960s and how the socio-historical experience of Québec, as a majority francophone province in Canada, has influenced this evolution. When I say managerial ideas, I refer exclusively to particular sub-fields – management, organization theory and organizational behaviour – which are the historical core of management curricula. For this reason, I have not included strategy, which is today a managerial discipline in itself (M. Côte 1992; Allaire and Firsirotu 1993).

My chapter will be divided into three sections; each section corresponds to a distinct period in the history of managerial thought. The first section focuses on the 1960s, years during which Québec discovered American management. The second section concerns the 1970s; this period corresponds to the French translation era of American management. The third and final section presents the 1980s, which saw the emergence and development of management *à la québécoise* in general, and in particular of an original current of thought based on knowledge of human and social sciences and observation of the concrete reality of Québec business firms.

The Discovery of American Management in the 1960s

The 1960s were, in Québec, characterized by deep social change. The arrival of the Liberal Party in 1960, supported by all segments of Québec society, meant the end of the political hegemony of l'Union Nationale, a conservative party in power since the war (Linteau et al. 1986). Criticisms by intellectuals, journalists, union representatives, even religious figures, organized in the 1950s, saw their fulfilment in this political change (Roy 1976). What the historians called *la révolution tranquille* (the quiet revolution) was under way (*La Presse* 1975). The government, backed by all the progressive social elements and inspired by a 'catch-up' ideology, launched great reforms in many areas of social policy: education, public administration, health, culture and so on (Rioux 1968). The most important was education policy. Having been educated by a system deeply influenced and controlled by the Catholic Church, Québecers wanted to build a modern public system. The well-known Parent Report led the way for these reforms in the field of education (1963–6) and the Ministry of Education was created in 1964. This new institution became the principal agent of the changes which took place in those times. In 1968, the government created the CEGEPs, a college network between the high school and university levels, in which students could study a general curriculum leading to university or a professional education in preparation for employment. Within this new professional curriculum there was an 'administrative technique' option.

In 1968, the government created the network of the University of Québec in order to give access to university programmes in every region. Before that, only the great cities offered such possibilities. So, campuses were created in Trois-Rivières, Rimouski, Chicoutimi, Hull and Rouyn-Noranda. Moreover, a campus was established in downtown Montréal for reinforcing the French network in Québec's major city. At that time there was only one French university, l'Université de Montréal, but two English-speaking institutions, McGill and Sir George Williams (the latter subsequently became Concordia University when it merged with Loyola College) (Linteau et al. 1986). In the 1960s Montréal was still the pre-eminent metropolis of Canada, but Toronto was already challenging this position.

All these important changes were inspired by certain key ideas: the right to be educated, accessibility, integration, free tuition, and curriculum modernization (Gérin-Lajoie 1989). According to the reformers, without these reforms Québec's economic development would always be subordinate to English-Canadian or foreign interests (Saint-Germain 1973; Linteau et al. 1986). Education was seen by francophones as the first move towards control of their own society, and as necessary to bridge the gap between the English and French parts of Canada.

Among other great refoms inspired by the same spirit, we can mention the creation of a modern provincial state apparatus and the full nationalization of the main resource of hydro-power, controlled mostly at that time by English and American investors. (In fact the latter was a second step: there had been a first nationalization in 1944 but that only applied to the Montréal area (Linteau et al. 1986).) This political gesture was to become a symbol of the reappropriation of the economic sphere by the francophones (Chanlat et al. 1984). Thus, between 1960 and 1980, many state corporations were created for the same reasons in different sections: SOQUEM (mining), SOQUIP (petroleum), SIDBEC (steelworks), SGF (finance), and so on (Gagnon 1994).

So Québec's modernization had been set in motion. The social elite of the 1960s wanted to adapt the provincial structures to the mood and outlook of the continent, even of the world. The success of the Universal Exhibition in 1967 in Montréal, followed by the Olympic Games of 1976, vividly illustrated this collective desire (Linteau et al. 1986). In the 1960s there also took shape a modern infrastructure of expressways, arts centres, and sports stadiums. The architecture of Montréal changed rapidly. Skyscrapers and modern buildings gave a more American flavour to this former Victorian city (Marsan 1983).

This quest for administrative efficiency and social modernization was driven by the more ambitious project of the recapture of the economy, largely controlled by foreign or English-Canadian interests (Saint-Germain 1973; Sales 1979; Niosi 1980). Since the turn of the century, this idea had been supported by numerous intellectuals, journalists, politicians, union representatives and even clergy. The creation of the oldest Canadian business school in 1907, l'École des Hautes Études Commerciales (HEC) in Montréal, was an early sign of this determination (Rumilly 1967; Paquet 1985; Sales 1985).

In such a period of change, it was natural for the existing French providers of commerce education to look to the experience of the United States. At that time, the USA was the most powerful and the richest country in the world (Julien 1968). The fascination with the American dream was real not only in Québec but also in many parts of the Western world (Servan-Schreiber 1967). Indeed, numerous were those who tried to understand the keys to this success. Management, as a new discipline, as a new technique, appeared to be a determining factor. We were in the years of the best and the brightest (Simon 1991). In the last fifteen years, in a similar way, the world believed that Japanese success was also deeply linked to its way of organizing things (Clegg 1990).

Québec in this context, and also as a North American state-province, developed a deep interest in the American managerial experience. In a succession of educational reforms, the existing schools and faculties of commerce transformed their programmes, and changed their degree titles. For example, at the undergraduate level, the traditional European title of 'licence' was abolished in favour of its American counterpart, the 'bachelor's degree'. The university system was reorganized on the American model (bachelor, master, PhD). The contents of education programmes in business were largely inspired by American curricula, notably in management and organizational behaviour. Books, manuals and articles read by students came, to a large extent, from the USA and were, of course, in English. Among the most popular works were those by Drucker, Blau and Scott, Etzioni, Schein, Lawrence and Lorsch, Thompson, Herzberg, Koontz and O'Donnell.

University teachers were increasingly educated in the USA. They rapidly gained a greater influence than their older colleagues, who were mostly educated in Europe (traditionally in the United Kingdom, France and Belgium). The American model was seen as being more modern and effective than the European, even if, at the same time, Québec was developing deep cultural relations with France. Consequently, the 1960s was the decade of the discovery of American management. This image of management was taught without real adaptation. Course titles, contents and literature were typically American. The American model of a professional school with university requirements (Simon 1991) was adopted and replaced the old European model (Rumilly 1967; Linteau et al. 1986; Langlois 1990). But in some programmes, in particular at HEC, the oldest and most influential business school in the province, economics, statistics, mathematics and accounting remained dominant in the new bachelor programme, notably during the first and second years. At the same time, formal teaching in management, organizational sociology and psychology was introduced into the programme in 1968.

The Translation Era of the 1970s

In Québec, the 1970s was the era of the rise of the social critics, great strikes in the public and private sectors, and 'nationalist' agitation (Linteau et al. 1986). The different governments of this period continued to follow modernization policies. They intervened in many spheres of social life, notably in the health sector: the 1974 great reform created a universal system of health and social services (Renaud 1977; Leseman 1981).

The growing public and para-public sectors, and the newly created public financial institutions, absorbed more and more young francophones. They offered them new job opportunities and new challenges (Bélanger and Fournier 1987). The professionalization of the public sphere had begun, but so too had social technocratization (Simard 1979; Godbout 1983).

In this period, the conflict with the central power, the federal state, and the cultural minority character of Québec in North America, fed nationalism in general and the French language defence policy in particular. The coming of the Parti Québécois into government in 1976 encouraged this tendency (Linteau et al. 1986).

In the management teaching area, the first publications in French appeared. The desire to provide students with more French literature pushed some business schools and faculty professors to translate and adapt American ideas into French. If we look closely at the most important publications of the period, in number and influence, we can readily observe the transfer of ideas and methods. In management, one book, a reader edited by Pierre Laurin (1972), is a very good illustration of this.

Widely used in both colleges and universities, this book, entitled *Management: Readings and Cases*, was organized like American books in the field. Inspired by the Harvard model (its editor had a DBA from Harvard), the volume had very few references in the social sciences and was largely rooted in the American way of thinking and doing. It was original because it was the first book of its kind written in French (see Table 7.1) and because it presented Québec cases, even though American examples were more numerous and half the book consisted of articles translated from the English. Very *normative*, this publication attempted to be a guide to good modern management. Research was totally absent, as in most of the books of this nature at that time. A few years later, there was another important publication on management by M. Crener and V. Monteil (1975). An introductory book, it sought to present management as a 'scientific' discipline using a systemic approach; it was less American orientated than the other publications of that time, but the authors' European origin may partly explain the more analytical orientation. Books in most management academic disciplines were to follow the same pattern, i.e. their form was largely influenced by American production knowledge.

In the organizational behaviour area we may observe the same phenomenon. The most popular books in this period were Québec adaptations of American volumes. Largely inspired by industrial psychology and the works of the human relations movement, these publications were also mostly descriptive and normative. They were based on very few original research studies (Hogue 1971; Bergeron et al. 1979) (see Table 7.2). Nevertheless, during this decade the management teaching system became institutionalized. Its content exploded into different sub-disciplines (marketing, production, finance, etc). New diplomas were created in most of Québec's institutions, in particular at the graduate levels, with the MBA at the beginning of the period and the MS and PhD in the later stages.

The movement towards management research emerged tentatively. For example, HEC created a research department in 1977. In 1976 was launched the most important review in the field today: *Gestion*, which was

Comparative cultural recipes

Table 7.1 *Management publications*

	Le Management: textes et cas P. Laurin (1972)	*Principes de management* M. Crener and B. Monteil (1975)	*Le Manager et la gestion* M. Boisvert (1980)	*La Direction des entreprises: concepts et applications* R. Miller (ed.) (1985)	*Le Management entre tradition et renouvellement* O. Aktouf (1989)
Number printed	NA	3,060	NA	NA	10,000
Total references	158	260	296	574	540
Social and human sciences references	8	34	39	58	184
Ratio of social and human sciences to total references	5.06%	13.07%	13.17%	10.10%	34.07%
Main disciplines referenced	Sociology (6)	Sociology (15) Economy (7) Psychology (5) History (5)	Sociology (27) Economy (8) Political sciences (4)	Sociology (20) Economy (15)	Sociology (61) Economy (30) Psychology (27) Anthropology (15) Biology-physics (15) Philosophy (15) History (8)

Table 7.2   *Organizational behaviour publications*

	Les Relations humaines dans l'entreprise J.P. Hogue (1971)	Les Aspects humains de l'organisation J.L. Bergeron et al. (1979)	L'Homme et l'organisation J.P. Hogue (1980)	Individu, groupe et organisation N. Côté et al. (1986)	L'Individu dans l'organisation J.P. Chanlat (ed.) (1990)
Number printed	10,000	43,700	6,000	30,000	5,000
Total references	19	265	130	822	~1,500
Social and human sciences references	5	38	25	126	~1,100
Ratio of social and human sciences to total references	26.5%	14.3%	19.2%	15.3%	~75%
Main disciplines referenced	Psychology (4) History (1)	Psychology (31) Sociology (5)	Psychology (20) Sociology (9)	Psychology (41) Sociology (34) Anthropology (8) Social psychology (29)	Sociology History Anthropology Psychology Philosophy Linguistics
Number of pages	187	337	333	440	776

Table 7.4   *Summary of the recent history of management thought in Québec*

at that time the twin sister of its French counterpart, *La Revue française de gestion*. Inspired also by the *Harvard Business Review, Gestion* aimed to become the definitive journal for managers, students and professors in management. Its content reflected the preoccupations of that time: it provided a French-language review for Québec and the francophone communities at large (Laurin and Barraux 1976). Today, its high circulation in the francophone world indicates that its original goal has been largely achieved.

During this period there was a relative decline of the fundamental disciplines (economics and mathematics) in most of the management programmes, as room was made for the new courses produced by management fragmentation. The programmes and the courses, in most cases, gave little space to the human and social sciences in the bachelor curriculum. The exceptions were at HEC and the McGill Faculty of Commerce: students had more compulsory courses of that type at HEC, and more optional courses at McGill and HEC, than in other provincial programmes. Eventually, criticism began to appear in some institutions. At McGill, Mintzberg's (1973) classic study of managers provoked a revision of the nature of managerial work, and at HEC a group led by several professors tried to build an alternative to classical management. The translation of American management increasingly echoed the singularity of the Québec experience. There was a progressive evolution towards what we can today term the 'School of Montréal', which is a differentiated, unconventional way of looking at organizations and management. That school integrates, more than any other current in management, the notion that people should prevail over organizations. Organizations come to be seen as a means for people's fulfilment, and not the opposite.

The Development of a Managerial Critique and the Emergence of a Management *à la Québécoise* in the 1980s

The 1980s began with a referendum on sovereignty in 1980 and with the re-election of the Parti Québécois. These two events illustrated the will and the desire on the part of a great number of Québecers to build a sovereign state in a reorganized Canada. Although the referendum was lost, the national question has remained a fundamental issue to the present day. More recently, the failure of the Meech Lake accord, and the rejection of the Charlotteton agreement, show how this question is complex and continuing. The results of the referendum in Autumn 1995 illustrated once again that this issue continues to be of great social importance. Nationalistic fever is fed by a strong cultural affirmation and some interesting developments in the economic sphere. The past policies and great reforms of the 1960s and 1970s instituted a modern state apparatus and universal social services (Gagnon 1994). The creation of public financial institutions, in particular the growth of the Caisse de dépôt et placement,[1] founded in 1964, offered many private firms the possibility of development (Fournier

1979; Bélanger and Fournier 1987). The great public investments, notably in the hydro-electricty network, created opportunities for Québec companies and particularly engineering firms (Parent 1983; Niosi and Faucher 1987).

It is during this period that francophone firms became multinational, in particular in the transportation, paper and pulp, telecommunications, printing and engineering industries (Niosi 1983; Parent 1983; Bélanger and Fournier 1987). At the same time the Québec economy became controlled by majority francophone interests (Vaillancourt and Carpentier 1989; Moreau 1992). More and more evident became a Québec model, 'Québec Inc.', which associated unions, government, cooperative movements and the private sector in the development of socio-economic policies (Fraser 1987; Dupuis 1995; Noël 1995); the Caisse de dépôt et placement, the largest pension and investment fund in Canada, was the flagship of this model (Pelletier 1989). On board were all the major groups: unions, cooperative movements, private interests and the state (Bélanger and Fournier 1987).

The fiscal crisis of the state, the hard recession of 1981–2, and the decline of the popularity of the Parti Québécois all helped to return the Liberal Party to power in 1985. Then, as everywhere else, the era of deregulation, privatization and rationalization hit Québec. Business firms became cult objects. Francophone entrepreneurs became the new idols of the economic success. Business publications were numerous and popular. Economic and business coverage in the media attained great importance. Many people from the francophone middle and upper classes learnt to play the stock market. Encouraged by government legislation, businesses, viewed over many decades as instruments of foreign domination and exploitation, became accepted.

This myth of free enterprise, the creator of wealth, was not confined to Québec, of course. The fiscal crisis of the state and the failure of collective planning promoted the revival of liberal values and politics in many industrialized countries. As in the USA and the UK, for example, Canada and Québec, in a less extreme manner, developed a new discourse. The state and the public sector were required to function like private firms (CPSE 1986).

During this period, especially in the mid 1980s, the business teaching system was in a state of euphoria. Students became more and more numerous (Table 7.3). Management became very popular among college students and in society at large. In 1990, 27.1 per cent of Québec bachelor students came from administrative sciences programmes (Conseil des Universités 1992). The schools and the faculties recruited new professors. Publications and research budgets were growing. Management became the key to employment and professional careers and replaced the social sciences, which were the disciplines *par excellence* in the 1960s and 1970s (Fournier et al. 1985). Québec became *the* management province in Canada, with one-third of its students in this discipline. A similar

Table 7.3   *Student enrolment in Québec's business schools*

Year	Total HEC	Total UQAM	Bachelor HEC (day and evening)	Bachelor UQAM Management Sciences Section	Laval University Faculty of Administrative Sciences	Sherbrooke University Faculty of Management
1967–8	5,387	379	1,063	379	NA	NA
1980–1	7,156	5,921	2,325	3,284	NA	NA
1985–6	8,506	11,656	2,294	5,461	NA	NA
1991–2	9,100	12,439	3,007	4,777	1,922	592

phenomenon was evident elsewhere in the industrialized world (Rousseaux 1988; Porter and McKibbin 1988; Sainsaulieu 1990).

The emergence of the so-called Québec model and the popularity of management education did, of course, affect the type and nature of the programmes. More and more people, not only in management departments, sought to study these phenomena (Bélanger and Lévesque 1994; Dupuis 1995) and in particular the Québec experience (Aktouf et al. 1992). During this period there developed an original current, in particular at HEC, inspired by Europeans, largely critical, and based on the human and social sciences: this current was based on a renewal of managerial thinking. Several colloquia and publications illustrated the dynamism of this movement.

The first event took place in Montréal in 1980. Entitled 'Les Sciences de la vie et la gestion' (Life Sciences and Management), this colloquium brought together some of the best-known researchers in the human sciences (biology, psychology, linguistics, anthropology, ethnology, etc).[2] Held at HEC, the purpose of this colloquium was to interact with great scholars to see how their disciplines could help the management professors to understand organizational phenomena as human processes.

The proceedings of this colloquium were published in 1985. Entitled *La Rupture entre l'entreprise et les hommes* and edited by A. Chanlat and M. Dufour (1985), this publication aimed to put forward a new vision, more humanist and less commercial than most of the perspectives in this field. Prior to this work, another book written by A. Chanlet et al. (1984) presented an analysis of the largest company in Québec, Hydro-Québec; it was also the first multi-disciplinary approach to management, and it contained numerous references to the social and human sciences.

Omar Aktouf (1983), A. Chanlat's first PhD student, authored one of the first critical works on management in the French-speaking world. Based on multi-disciplinary knowledge and on ethnographical observation of two breweries, one in Montréal and one in Algiers, his thesis showed how human reality was lived concretely in these two organizations. In showing the suffering of the workers in both companies, this research, carried out by a managerial scholar and not by a sociologist of work, criticized the normative and optimistic vision of the classical management works. The thesis prompted numerous articles in French. Several years later, Omar Aktouf (1989) published a book on management which offered an alternative to traditional thinking in this domain. This book has had great success among students and professional managers, and has been translated into English and Spanish. Its success seemed to show that such questioning was not far from the daily life of many people.

In 1986, two other colloquia were held at HEC. The first, initiated by L. Lapierre, aimed to take a fresh look at leadership through psychoanalytic studies, notably the work of a Harvard scholar, Zaleznick, and a former McGill professor, M. Kets de Vries. Entitled 'Imaginary and Leadership', this meeting tried to establish a link between the psychic life of managers, as viewed by psychoanalysis, and their management styles and behaviours. This important colloquium, headed by the most important scholars in the field, played an important role in developing the international network 'Psychoanalysis and Organizations'. A little later, HEC hosted the annual symposium of this scientific society (1988). The colloquium papers have since been published (Lapierre 1992; 1993).

The second symposium, organized by A. Chanlat, brought together professors and practicians from different parts of the world, mainly Europe, Latin America, Africa and Canada. This colloquium aimed to question the teaching of management around the world and to show the intellectual and human void in these programmes.

This meeting was important for various reasons: first, it continued the action launched in 1980; second, it enlarged the network of participants; and, third, it set up a true intellectual network, a kind of invisible college, ready to respond to new events. The meeting was a great success, enabling some Québec professors, and particularly HEC professors, to become better known abroad and to observe how their concerns were shared by their foreign counterparts.

In 1988 there was an important colloquium about women managers' issues, organized by a HEC research group, entitled 'Women, Management and Business Firms'. This event brought together a group of francophone researchers to examine the situation of Québec women executives. This event was also a great success and more than 300 people attended. It demonstrated the popularity and dynamism of research on women's issues (Harel-Giasson and Robichaud 1988). It was linked closely to the rise of women in management but also to the popularity of management studies among the female student population. In most of the bachelor programmes, statistics show (Langlois 1990) that women are now in the majority.

At the end of the decade, a new book appeared on organizational behaviour. Edited and inspired by J.F. Chanlat, this volume contained contributions by thirty-six researchers from seven countries. One-third of the contributors were from HEC. The book was published in August 1990 and was officially launched in September 1990 during an international colloquium.

This new colloquium, organized by J.F. Chanlat, R. Déry and L. Lapierre, was a forum for all the book's collaborators. The three-day event was organized according to the structure of the book. Most of the contributors participated and 200 guests from universities and the professions attended. Participants came from all parts of the world, and some were English speaking. Strongly based on the human sciences, the book and the colloquium offered a new vision of human behaviour in organizations. By considering human beings as subjects in acts, as persons in situations, this perspective sought to escape from too simplistic and behaviourist a view of human action. It focused on forgotten dimensions such as language and speech, space and time, psychic life, symbolic imagery, and work psychodynamics.

The impact of the book and the colloquium illustrated the growing interest in academical and professional spheres in less conventional visions. In fact, the book has been translated into Portuguese (Chanlat 1992); a Spanish version is in discussion; and the argument has been published in English (Chanlat 1994a).

This activity has been reflected in the programmes and courses at HEC; in particular, the books in this current have become the manuals on several courses. Other institutions and professors have taken similar steps. The master's and PhD programmes attract students who want to think differently. In the Québec network, the HEC group has become an intellectual focal point; it is also recognized as such internationally, notably in Latin America, Africa and Europe. As for English Canada and the USA, the picture is very different. The group rarely publishes in English, and so this dynamism, to my knowledge, is not so well known. But this is an illustration of the historic cleavage between the francophone and the Anglo-American world (Chanlat 1994b). Fortunately, this gap is gradually diminishing through the efforts of international networks, notably EGOS, SCOS, and SASE, and the openness of some review procedures.

In this effort to reconsider management in the light of the human and social sciences, other Québec researchers, particularly sociologists, sought a better understanding of the so-called Québec model (Dupuis 1995). In their works, in most cases sociological, they attempted to describe the singularity of the Québec organizational system (Bélanger and Lévesque 1992b; 1994) or what R. Whitley (1992) called business systems. This interest in business was reinforced by the legitimacy acquired by this subject among Québec's departments of sociology. After a long period of ignorance, even in some cases of rejection, it became legitimate for firms to be studied by sociologists (Bélanger and Lévesque 1992a). The theoretical radical criticism was replaced by work in the field (Chanlat 1994b) and by analysis of the new managerial strategies (Hamel et al. 1984; Dalpé 1984). This growing interest offered management teaching much interesting research and a better knowledge of the socio-economic reality of the province (Bélanger and Fournier 1987; Bélanger and Lévesque 1994), it also provided a basis for discussion of the Québec Inc. model itself (Dupuis 1995).

In the faculties and schools of business, there was also a tendency to put more emphasis on entrepreneurship issues and to ameliorate the knowledge of the environment (Joyal and Bhérer 1987; Toulouse 1979; Filion 1991).

As the appearance of what we call today the dual nature of society was, to some extent, enacted in these new managerial strategies based on financial goals, work flexibility and computerization of work (Gorz 1988; Lever-Tracy 1988; Reich 1992) the study of these managerial strategies in Québec became fundamental to examining how society could maintain coherence (Bélanger and Lévesque 1992b) as economic thought grew more abstract and formal (Paquet 1985) and social cleavage in Québec remained a social reality (Conseil des Affaires Sociales 1989).

During this period the management field also saw the great success of Mintzberg, a McGill professor. The popularity of his ideas was characterized by the massive utilization of his books on management courses, and the adoption of his typology of organization by professors, consultants and managers. Mintzberg's work became, in Québec as in many other parts of the world, a central and very influential reference point. His criticism of management educators countered some of the critics of his French-speaking colleagues, and contributed to giving Montréal its own flavour. In more academic circles, a key role was played by the work of D. Miller, who is a full researcher at HEC and was a visiting one at McGill.

In this period, the francophone sphere also witnessed the appearance of organization theory. A book published in 1985 by M. Boisvert, an HEC professor, with the collaboration of R. Déry, introduced the organizational perspective in management. The founder of a work study group, Boisvert wanted to give management a new scientific basis, particularly in founding his position on research and a socio-technical approach. Consequently, his work was very different from its 1970s counterparts. Widely used in many introductory courses at different levels (college and university), this book replaced the normative and descriptive texts for several years. There was also the publication of two important readers in organizational analysis, which gave francophone students access to the classics (Séguin and Chanlat 1983; Chanlat and Séguin 1987). Finally, we can note the beginning of epistemological thinking in the administrative sciences (Audet and Malouin 1986; Déry 1988; 1992).

The 1980s were also the time of the great popularity of some American publications about excellence and corporate culture (Peters and Waterman 1982; Deal and Kennedy 1982). This movement was particularly strong among consultants. Descriptive and normative, these books offered professionals guides for action. Very American-oriented, they continued the normative managerial tradition. In Québec, these books had a large readership until the second half of the decade. Many enterprises and organizations used the term 'excellence' in their advertising slogans. Many professional colloquia were organized to boost excellence ideas. But by the end of the 1980s, people had become more aware of the limitations of these publications and their simplistic vision, and even of the cost of this management style (Aubert and de Gaulejac 1991). As we know, reality is more complex than theoretical schemes produced by consultants. The management world seeks universal prescriptions but often discovers to its cost that it cannot reduce organizational singularities to a general approach (Friedberg 1993). A minimum of reflection and critical distance is necessary to understand organizational and human complexities. Field lessons become a necessity.

So, the 1980s were *les années folles* for management teaching in general and for the production of managerial knowledge in Québec in particular. After a decade of translating American thought, there was a renewal of managerial thinking in organization theory, management and organizational behaviour. Based on work in the human and social sciences and on the observation of concrete actions in organizations, this renewal was deeply embedded in a more general questioning of the technocratic orientation of our societies (Chanlat and Dufour 1985; Mintzberg 1989; Aktouf 1989; Chanlat 1990; Pitcher 1992; Saul 1995).

This movement of renewal, in giving an important role to fundamental human sciences and concrete observations, influenced programmes and courses, particularly at HEC. But we can also see its impact in the revised editions of organizational behaviour works of the 1970s, in which social science references became more numerous than before (N. Côté et al. 1986). To some extent it altered the selection of professors. Sociologists, communication specialists, psychologists, anthropologists and political scientists became more numerous in business schools and faculties. The firm became a multidisciplinary object of research. Each discipline provided an element. Only knowledge of this plurality could give a better representation of the nature of an organization (Morgan 1986). This fervour explains the popularity of Morgan's (1986) book *Images of Organizations* and its translation into French at the end of the decade (Morgan 1989). Morgan, a York University professor, arrived in a field where the multiparadigmatic vision was particularly popular. This francophonization of Morgan was the work of Michel Audet, a Laval University professor in Québec City, who has also translated the work of Giddens into French, and Richard Déry, an HEC professor.[3]

This movement is opposed, to a large extent, to the universalistic, normative and American vision of management so widespread in our field (Mills, Helms and Hatfield 1995). Looking for a new miracle recipe is not the object of this movement. The goal is a better understanding of human actions in organizations. If this understanding improves the quality of working life and organizational performance, that is, of course, a welcome consequence. In other words, instead of bringing an intellectual toolkit, universalistic and normative, to improve human efficiency, this movement tries to understand the singularity of each organizational universe and to open the doors to some forgotten dimensions (Chanlat 1990).

This humanistic current, relatively influential in some spheres of teaching and professional areas, is not dominant. Alongside it, there are more classical visions of management inspired by American works (Miller 1985). Less dominant than before, this more orthodox conception still plays an important role. We can find it in many works and several teaching programmes. Nevertheless, the arrival of professors with PhDs modified the equation. This academization of business school professors offers a better reception to new ideas if they are embedded in a strong social and human sciences background. But it could also lead to a new empirical abstraction criticized by many (Porter and McKibbin 1988; Aktouf 1989; Mintzberg 1989), or to American recognition if people choose to play by the rules of the American scientific game, largely oriented to American issues. Such recognition is of doubtful value in view of the limited role played by foreigners in that area (Daft and Lewin 1990). So, if a Québec professor wants to be known in the States, he has to do the same kind of research. It is obvious that the emergent current, assuming it knows what the American business professors produce, is not oriented to the rules of the American business teaching field. The socio-cultural specificity of Québec (its language, its history, its mode of social organizing) prevents the research and the professors in this field being completely absorbed by American rules (Chanlat 1994b). Some Canadian and Québec English-speaking colleagues seem to share the same views on these issues (Mintzberg 1989; Pitcher 1992; Mills, Helms and Hatfield 1995; Saul 1995), as do other researchers around the world (d'Iribarne 1989; Morgan 1989; Clegg 1990; Daft and Lewin 1990; Hassard and Pym 1990; Sainsaulieu 1990; Whitley 1992; Friedberg 1993; Brunstein 1995).

Conclusions

In North America, the Québec experience in managerial thought has been a consequence of its own originality. From the 1960s to the beginning of the 1990s, each decade has been characterized by a particular dominant profile: the 1960s as an American period; the 1970s as a translation era; and the 1980s as a time of building an indigenous model (Table 7.4). This distinct profile has been closely linked to the social transformation and upheaval, in the province (Linteau et al. 1986; Langlois 1990) but also to the strong penetration of the social and human sciences into the management curriculum. In other words, the movement was a response to an Anglo-American definition of management knowledge based on daily experience and concrete studies. This movement is not very different from movements observed elsewhere in the world. It reminds us that any management knowledge is always embedded in its own society's dynamics and practices (d'Iribarne 1989; Clegg 1990; Whitley 1992). If the 1980s were the decade of the building of intellectual and social differences in

Table 7.4   *Summary of the recent history of management thought in Québec*

Main characteristics	1960s The discovery of American management	1970s The translation era	1980s The emergence of a management à la québécoise
Management teaching	Modification and Americanization of business programmes Most literature in English More professors educated in the USA	Creation of graduate studies Emergence of business research French adaptation of American literature Foundation of the main review	Popularity of business studies among students Growth of faculty staff Development of research and publications Rising of an original current
State	Great social reforms Modernization of state apparatus 'Quiet revolution'	Continuity in reform policies Work conflict in the public sector Arrival of a nationalist party (1976) Francization policy (Bill 101)	Crisis of the welfare state Comeback of neo-liberal ideas, deregulation, privatization, rationalization Constitutional crisis
Society	Change in values Social movements (unions, nationalistic groups) Beginning of affirmation of the cultural singularity of Québec (poetry, literature, theatre, cinema, etc.)	Rise of feminist movement Union struggles in private and public sectors Continuation of policy of affirmation of French identity Accessibility to education	Economical values become legitimate Rise of individualism Excellence ideology Internationalization Dualization
Economy	Economy controlled by American and Anglo-Canadian interests Economy based on natural resources Montréal main pole of Canadian headquarters Nationalization of hydro-power Great infrastructure works English main language at work Few French Québécers among the power elite	Development of francophone private firms (engineering, transportation, printing, paper) Creation and development of state-owned enterprises Role of cooperative movement (saving, credit union, agriculture) Montréal loses her Canadian metropolis status Emergence of a francophone financial sector Francization policy	Economy controlled mostly by francophone interests Multinationalization of francophone business firms (transportation, engineering, printing, paper, telecommunications) Francophone financial sector Rise of unemployment Singularity of development model 'Quebec Inc.'

management studies and practices, the beginning of the 1990s seems to show a great movement towards internationalization, both in the schools and in society, the NAFTA Agreement being a very illustrative example, in which this singularity will be challenged by foreign competition, notably the USA and the future relationship with the federal state (Moreau 1992).

Notes

The author wishes to thank Louis-Jacques Filion, Jean-Pierre Dupuis, Allain Joly and Danny Miller for their comments on a first draft. As usual, they are not responsible for the final content.

1 The Caisse de dépôt et placement is a public institution which receives and manages all the funds from different social programmes (health, pensions, etc.). The model was inspired by the French Caisse de dépôt et consignation (Fournier 1979).

2 Among these were the biologists H. Atlan and H. Laborit, the psychoanalysts Elliot Jaques and Mertens de Villmar, the ethnologist G. Condominas, the linguist and formal logician J.B. Grise, and the ethologist P. Hopkins.

3 We can say francophonization because Morgan's French version is a real adaptation, notably in the references. A team of professors from HEC and Laval contributed, where relevant, the most important francophone references, with the kind agreement of the author (Morgan 1989).

References

Aktouf, O. (1983) 'Une approche d'observation participante et intellectuelle des systèmes de représentation dans les rapports de travail'. Thèse de doctorat, École des HEC, Montréal.
Aktouf, O. (1989) *Le Management entre tradition et renouvellement*. Montréal: Gaëtan Morin.
Aktouf, O., Bédard, R. and Chanlat, A. (1992) 'Management, éthique catholique et esprit du capitalisme: l'exemple québécois', *Sociologie du travail*, 34(1): 83–98.
Allaire, Y. and Firsirotu, M. (1993) *L'Entreprise stratégique: penser la stratégie*. Montréal: Gaëtan Morin.
Aubert, N. and de Gaulejac, V. (1991) *Le Coût de l'excellence*. Paris: Le Seuil.
Audet, M. and Malouin, J.C. (eds) (1986) *La Production des connaissances scientifiques de l'administration*. Québec: Presses de l'Université Laval.
Bélanger, P. and Lévesque, B. (1992a) 'Éléments théoriques pour une sociologie de l'entreprise', *Cahiers de recherche sociologique*, 18(19): 55–92.
Bélanger, P. and Lévesque, B. (1992b) 'Transformation des entreprises: approches théoriques et études de cas', *Cahiers de recherche sociologique*, 18(19): 11–23.
Bélanger, P. and Lévesque, B. (1994) 'La Modernité par les particularismes – le modile québécois de developpement économique', in F.R. Ouellette and C. Bariteau (eds), *Eutre tradition et universalisme*. Québec: IQRC. pp. 79–96.
Bélanger, Y. and Fournier, P. (1987) *L'Entreprise québécoise: développement historique et dynamique contemporaine*. Montréal: HMH Hurtubise.
Bergeron, J.L. et al. (1979) *Les Aspects humains de l'organisation*. Montréal: Gaëtan Morin.
Boisvert, M. (1980) *Le Manager et la gestion*. Montréal: Agence d'Arc.
Boisvert, M. with Déry, R. (1985) *L'Organisation et la décision*. Montréal: Agence d'Arc.
Brunstein, I. (ed.) (1995) *Human Resources Management in Western Europe*, Berlin: de Gruyter.
Chanlat, A., Bolduc, A. and Larouche, D. (1984) *Gestion et culture d'entreprise: le cheminement d'Hydro-Québec*. Montréal: Québec/Amérique.
Chanlat, A. and Dufour, M. (1985) *La Rupture entre l'entreprise et les hommes: le point de vue des sciences de la vie*. Montréal, Paris: Québec/Amérique.

Chanlat, J.-F. (ed.) (1990) *L'Individu dans l'organisation: les dimensions oubliées*. Québec, Paris: Presses de l'Université Laval.

Chanlat, J.-F. (ed.) (1992) *Individuo na Organizaçao*. São Paulo: Atlas.

Chanlat, J.-F. (1994a) 'Toward an Anthropology of Organizations', in J. Hassard and M. Parker (eds), *New Perspectives on Organization Theory*. London: Routledge. pp. 156–89.

Chanlat, J.-F. (1994b) 'Francophone Organizational Analysis (1950–1990): an Overview', *Organization Studies*, 15(1): 47–80.

Chanlat, J.-F. and Séguin, F. (1987) *L'analyse des organisations, Tome II: les composantes de organisation*. Montréal: Gaëtan Morin.

Clegg, S. (1990) *Modern Organization*. London: Sage.

Conseil des Affaires Sociales (1989) *Deux Québec dans un*. Montréal: Gaëtan Morin.

Conseil des Universités (1992) *Rapport sur les perspectives et le défi du premier cycle universitaire québécois*. Québec.

Côté, M. (ed.) (1992) *La Gestion stratégique d'entreprise: concepts et cas*. Montréal: Gaëtan Morin.

Côté, N., Abravanel, H., Jacques, J. and Bélanger, L. (1986) *Individu, groupe et organisation*. Montreal: Gaëtan Morin.

CPSE (1986) *Rapport du comité sur la privatisation des sociétés d'État*. Québec.

Crener, M. and Monteil, B. (1975) *Principes de management*. Montréal: Presses Universitaires du Québec.

Daft, R.L. and Lewin, A.Y. (1990) 'Can Organization Studies Begin to Break Out of the Normal Science Straitjacket? An Editorial Essay', *Organization Science*, 1(1): 1–9.

Dalpé, R. (1984) (La Situation technologique de bombardier', *Recherches sociographiques*, 25(2): 167–87.

Deal, T.E. and Kennedy, A. (1982) *Corporate Cultures: the Rites and Rituals of Corporate Life*. Reading, MA: Addison-Wesley.

Déry, R. (1988) 'L'épistemologie des sciences de l'organisation: le procès discursif de la problematique de la décision: une étude de cas à partir de la Revue Administrative Science Quarterly', Québec, Université Laval: Faculté des sciences de l'administration.

Déry, R. (1992) 'Enjeux et controverses épistémologiques dans le champ des sciences de l'administration', *Revue canadienne des sciences administratives*, 9(1): 1–12.

d'Iribarne, P. (1989) *La Logique de l'honneur*. Paris: Le Seuil.

Dupuis, J.P. (ed.) (1995) *Le Modèle québecois de developpement économique*. Cap-Rouge: Les Presses inter-universitaires.

Filion, L.J. (1991) *Vision et relations: clefs du succès de l'entrepreneur*. Montréal: Les Éditions de l'entrepreneur.

Fournier, M., Trépanier, M. and Girard, S. (1985) 'La Sociologie dans tous ses états', *Recherches sociographiques*, 24(3): 417–43.

Fournier, P. (1979) *Les Sociétés d'état et les objectifs économiques du Québec: une évaluation préliminaire*. Québec: Éditeur officiel du Québec.

Fraser, M. (1987) *Québec Inc.: les Québécois prennent d'assaut le monde des affaires*. Montréal: Les Éditions de l'Homme.

Friedberg, G.E. (1993) *Le Pouvoir et la règle*. Paris: Le Seuil.

Gagnon, A. (ed.) (1994) *Québec: État et Societé*. Montréal: Québec-Amérique.

Gérin-Lajoie, P. (1989) *Combat de révolutionnaire tranquille*. Montréal: Éditions CEC.

Godbout, J. (1983) *La Participation contre la démocratie*. Montréal: Saint-Martin.

Gorz, A. (1988) *Les Métamorphoses du travail*. Paris: Galilée.

Hamel, J., Houle, G. and Sabourin, P. (1984) 'Stratégies économiques et développement industriel: l'émergence de Forano', *Recherches sociographiques*, 25(2): 189–209.

Harel-Giasson, F. and Robichaud, J. (1988) *Tout savoir sur les femmes cadres d'ici*. Montréal: Les Presses HEC.

Hassard, J. and Pym, D. (1990) *The Theory and Philosophy of Organization: Critical Issues and New Perspectives*. London: Routledge.

Hogue, J.P. (1971) *Les Relations humaines dans l'enterprise*. Montréal: Éditions Commerce Beauchemin.

Hogue, J.P. (1980) *L'Homme et l'organisation*. Montréal: Éditions Commerce Beauchemin.
Joyal, A. and Bhérer, H. (1987) *Les Entreprises alternatives*. Montréal: Saint-Martin.
Julien, C. (1968) *L'Empire américain*. Paris: Livre de poche.
Julien, C. (1993) 'Ces élites qui règnent sur des masses de chômeurs', *Le Monde diplomatique*, avril: 1, 8–9.
La Presse (1975) 'Une certaine révolution tranquille', Montréal.
Langlois, S. (ed.) (1990) *La Société québécoise en tendances 1960–1990*. Montréal: IQRC.
Lapierre, L. (1992) *Imaginaire et leadership, Tome I*. Montréal: Québec-Amérique.
Lapierre, L. (1993) *Imaginaire et leadership, Tome II*. Montréal: Québec-Amérique.
Laurin, P. (1972) *Le Management, textes et cas*. Montréal: McGraw-Hill.
Laurin, P. and Barraux, J. (1976) 'Éditorial', *Gestion*, 1(1): 3.
Leseman, F. (1981) *Du pain et des services*. Montréal: Saint-Martin.
Lever-Tracy, C. (1988) 'The Flexibility Debate: Part-Time Work', *Labour and Industry*, 2(2): 210–41.
Linteau, P.A., Durocher, R., Robert, J.C. and Ricard, F. (1986) *Le Québec depuis 1930*. Montréal: Boréal.
Marsan, J.C. (1983) *Montréal: une esquisse du futur*. Institut québécois de recherche sur la culture.
Martinet, A.C. (ed.) (1990) *Épistémologie et sciences de gestion*. Paris: Économica.
Miller, R. (ed.) (1985) *La Direction des entreprises: concepts et applications*. Montréal: McGraw-Hill.
Mills, A., and Helms Hatfield, J.C. (1995) 'From imperialism to globalization: internationalization and the management text. A review of selected US texts', paper presented at the 6th APROS International Colloquium, December 1995, Cuernavaca, Mexico.
Mintzberg, H. (1973) *The Nature of Managerial Work*. New York: Harper and Row.
Mintzberg, H. (1989) *Mintzberg on Management: Inside Our Strange World of Organizations*. New York: Free Press.
Moreau, F. (1992) 'La Résistible Ascension de la bourgeoisie québécoise', in G. Daigle (ed.), *Ce Québec en jeu: comprendre les grands défis*. Montréal: PUM.
Morgan, G. (1986) *Images of Organizations*. San Francisco: Sage.
Morgan, G. (1989) *Images de l'organisation*. Québec: PUL.
Niosi, J. (1980) *La Bourgeoisie canadienne*. Montréal: Boréal Express.
Niosi, J. (1983) 'La Multinationalisation des firmes canadiennes-françaises', *Recherches sociographiques*, 24(1): 53–73.
Niosi, J. and Faucher, P. (1987) 'Les Marchés publics comme instruments de développement industriel: le cas d'Hydro-Québec', *Recherches sociographiques*, 28(1): 9–28.
Noël, A. (1995) 'Québec inc: Veni! Vidi! Vici?', in J.P. Dupuis (ed.), *Le Modèle québécois de développement économique*. Cap-Rouge: Les Presses inter-universitaires. pp. 67–93.
Paquet, G. (1985) 'Le Fruit dont l'ombre est la saveur: réflexions aventureuses sur la pensée économique au Québec', *Recherches sociographiques*, 26(3): 365–96.
Parent, R. (1983) 'Les Multinationales québécoises de l'ingénierie', *Recherches sociographiques*, 24(1): 75–94.
Pelletier, M. (1989) *La Machine à milliards*. Montréal: Québec-Amérique.
Peters, T. and Waterman, R. (1982) *In Search of Excellence: Lessons from America's Best-Run Companies*. New York: Harper and Row.
Pitcher, Patricia C. (1992) 'Character and the Nature of Strategic Leadership: Artists, Craftsmen and Technocrats'. Thèse de doctorat. McGill University.
Porter, L. and McKibbin, L.E. (1988) *Management, Education and Development*. New York: McGraw-Hill.
Reich, R.B. (1992) *The Work of Nations*. New York: Vantage Books.
Renaud, M. (1977) 'Réforme ou illusion? Une analyse des interventions de l'état québécois dans le domaine de la santé', *Sociologie et Société*, 9(1): 127–52.
Rioux, M. (1968) 'Sur l'évolution des idéologies au Québec', *Revue de l'Institut de sociologie*, 1: 95–124.
Rousseaux, N. (1988) 'Le Culte de l'entreprise', *Autrement*, septembre, Paris.

Roy, J.L. (1976) *La Marche des Québécois, le temps des ruptures (1945–1960)*. Montréal: Leméac.

Rumilly, R. (1967) *Histoire de l'École des Hautes Études Commerciales*. Montréal: Fides.

Sainsaulieu, R. (1990) *L'Entreprise, une affaire de société*. Paris: Fondation nationale des sciences politiques.

Saint-Germain, P. (1973) *Une économie à libérer*. Montréal: PUM.

Sales, A. (1979) *La Bourgeoisie industrielle au Québec*. Montréal: PUM.

Sales, A. (1985) 'La Construction sociale de l'économie québécoise', *Recherches sociographiques*, 26(3): 319–60.

Saul, J. (1995) *The Unconscious Civilization*. Toronto: Canadian Broadcasting Corporation.

Séguin, F. and Chanlat, J.F. (1983) *L'analyse des organisations, Tome I, les thèories de l'organisation*. Montréal: Gaëtan Mozin.

Servan-Schreiber, J. (1967) *Le Défi américain*. Paris: Livre de poche.

Simard, J.J. (1979) *La Longue Marche des technocrates*. Montréal: Saint-Martin.

Simon, H. (1991) *Models of My Life*. New York: Basic Books.

Toulouse, J.M. (1979) *L'Entrepreneurship au Québec*. Montréal: HMH.

Vaillancourt, F. and Carpentier, J. (1989) *Le Contrôle de l'économie du Québec: la place des francophones en 1987 et son évolution depuis 1961*. Montréal and Québec: Centre de recherche et développement économique, Conseil de la langue française.

Whitley, R. (1984) 'The Fragmented State of Management Studies: Reasons and Consequences', *Journal of Management Studies*, 21(3): 331–48.

Whitley, R. (1992) *The European Business Systems*. London: Sage.

8

Interrogating Reframing: Evaluating Metaphor-based Analyses of Organizations

Ian Palmer and Richard Dunford

The use of images, metaphors and multiple perspectives in organization and management theory has grown over the past decade. Morgan (1980) argued that machine and organism metaphors dominate orthodox organization theory, and that a range of other metaphors inform alternative organizational paradigms. This was followed in the mid 1980s by influential texts by Bolman and Deal (1984) and Morgan (1986) which argued that the utilization of multiple frames or images provides an enhanced ability to analyse organizational phenomena. More recently the concept of 'reframing' has been used to characterize this approach (Morgan 1988; Lundberg 1990; Bolman and Deal 1991; Frost et al. 1991; Marx and Hamilton 1991).

The increasing dissemination of multiple perspective analyses has been accompanied by a number of debates and critiques (e.g. Pinder and Bourgeois 1982; Bourgeois and Pinder 1983; Morgan 1983; Tinker 1986; Reed 1990; Tsoukas 1991). However, none has provided a comprehensive analysis of the contribution of reframing to managerial theory and practice. This chapter therefore sets out to identify key elements necessary for such an analysis.[1] Specifically, it is argued that the contribution of reframing needs to be assessed at different analytical levels. First, at an empirical level attention needs to be directed to the extent to which managers perceive reframing to be useful. Second, any attempt to assess managerial responses to reframing raises a number of methodological issues which need to be addressed. Third, at a theoretical level, the internal consistency underlying the claims made about reframing is in need of investigation. Fourth, the assumptions underpinning reframing as a theory need to be interrogated in the light of the wider theoretical debates about the production of knowledge.

The structure of this chapter therefore mirrors Whetten's (1988) distinction between a contribution *of* theory and a contribution *to* theory (cited in

Gioia and Pitre 1990). The first and second sections of our chapter, the empirical and methodological discussions, analyse reframing's perceived contribution to managerial practice. The third and fourth sections, which focus on the internal logic of the theory and its theoretical underpinnings, explore the contribution of reframing to organization and management theory.

Do Managers Perceive Reframing as Useful?

A range of claims have been made about the benefits of using reframing. These include the following: making situations more manageable (Bolman and Deal 1991: 37); increasing managerial effectiveness (Morgan 1986: 12); empowering managers (Bolman and Deal 1991: 17); enhancing their communication abilities (1991: 18); fostering creativity (Morgan 1986: 337); facilitating change (Bolman and Deal 1991: 309), contributing to 'both personal freedom and organizational prosperity' (1991: 18).

Despite the growth of interest in reframing techniques and their application to management education, there has been little assessment of the extent to which managers perceive the claimed benefits of reframing. An exception to this is provided by Dunford and Palmer (1995) who found a high level of support for the approach, with 98 per cent of respondents rating it as helpful or very helpful in understanding organizations, 78 per cent believing that they now analysed situations differently than prior to exposure to the multiple-perspectives approach, and 89 per cent believing that it gave them a competitive advantage inside their organization.

Following Bolman and Deal (1991), Dunford and Palmer (1995) utilized the four-frame schema: structural, human resource, political and cultural. They found that the relative reliance on the structural frame declines markedly after exposure to a multiple-perspectives approach, while cultural and political frames increase in importance. One explanation for this is that the structural frame may be the dominant or 'official' organizational discourse, and, therefore, is the one most likely to change once people are exposed to a multiple perspectives approach. Indeed it may be through a multiple perspectives approach that legitimacy is accorded to political interpretations of organizational actions.

The study also revealed that the connection between analysis of situations, actions and outcomes is complicated by the perception of constraints. Exactly 50 per cent of the sample said they had been in situations which they had been able to analyse using multiple perspectives, but where they felt constrained from taking subsequent action. They perceived both structural and political factors as serving to constrain their actions. This combination of factors is probably not surprising, given the difficulty of distinguishing between effects due to positions of authority and effects resulting from the formal power often accorded to such positions. Such an overlap can be identified in the literature on power (e.g. Morgan 1986).

With regard to the claims of reframing noted above, Dunford and Palmer (1995) found there was support for all of these, although a paired *t*-test indicated that there was a significant difference ($p<0.001$) between the support for the claims about 'manageability', 'effectiveness', 'communication' and 'creativity' and the support for the claims about 'empowerment' and 'freedom and prosperity'. The lower level of support given to the claim about empowerment accords with the finding that a large proportion of their respondents did not perceive that reframing could eliminate constraints derived from political or structural sources. Whilst advocates of reframing see it as a vital management skill, the lower level of support for the 'freedom and prosperity' claim indicates that practitioners have a somewhat more guarded assessment of the extent to which reframing will be useful in overcoming all management and organizational problems with which they are confronted.

In summary, Dunford and Palmer (1995) conclude that managers are generally positive in their evaluation of the contribution to managing of a multiple perspectives approach. The latter is seen by these managers as enabling better cognition of organizational issues and recognition of a wider array of actions available to them to take when confronted with organizational problems.[2]

Methodological Issues in Assessing Perceptions of Reframing

A number of methodological issues emerge in an assessment of perceptions of reframing: five key ones will be explored below.

A first issue relates to whether managers claim to utilize reframing, but do not actually do so in their day-to-day practices. This question reflects the now classic distinction which Argyris and Schon (1974) make between espoused theories and theories-in-use. Their espoused view may reflect a desire to be seen as conforming to 'good practice'. However, even if made in good faith, statements by managers must not be taken unproblematically as descriptions of practice because the ability to reframe may require the existence of certain transformational conditions. For example, Westenholz (1993: 54) argues that reframing is likely to require: (i) the existence of a forum where carriers of different frames can meet and discuss; (ii) the presence of people who have already proven able to reframe; and (iii) unexpected actions that disrupt existing interpretations. Westenholz (1993) views reframing as involving the replacement of one frame by another rather than multi-frame thinking. This different usage of the term 'reframing' means that her results are not directly applicable to the concerns of this chapter. However, they do highlight the point that insufficient attention has been given to the conditions under which managers adopt multi-frame thinking. The lack of information on this process adds to the difficulty of assessing claims to be using reframing.

A second issue concerns whether benefits can always be clearly articulated. For example, competency may be enhanced without individuals being aware or conscious of this occurring. Reframing may produce subtle but pervasive effects on an individual's personal style of management of which he or she is unaware. Even where there is a general consciousness of benefits this may not extend to being able to identify specific events where reframing affected action.

A third issue relates to the question of whether individual factors act as intervening variables in determining the ability to reframe. In a detailed review of research on cognitive structure, Streufert and Nogami (1989) note that a number of reliable and valid tests exist that enable individuals to be able to be characterized in terms of their 'cognitive complexity'. Cognitive complexity refers to 'the number of bipolar dimensions that are used to conceptualize, organize, and understand the perceived world' (1989: 106). High cognitive complexity implies that multiple dimensions are considered; low cognitive complexity that only one or few are considered. While this literature makes no direct reference to reframing, the possible implications are too significant to ignore. Specifically, the ability to reframe may be more a function of an individual's 'cognitive style' than of the degree of exposure to the concept of reframing.[3]

A fourth issue relates to whether or not the perceived benefits of reframing continue over time. That is, are such benefits the result of its newness, with consequent diminishing effects over time, or does reframing contribute to a more fundamental and enduring insight into organizational problems? There is an absence of longitudinal studies addressing the continuing impact of reframing on managerial actions.

A fifth issue deals with the question of whether enhancing individual management skills through exposure to reframing will automatically lead to greater organizational effectiveness. Advocates of reframing tend to assume a direct link between these two issues but this link needs to be questioned. Reframing may enhance the former, but without necessarily impacting directly upon the latter. For example, whilst some claim that management training will impact positively upon organizational effectiveness (Whetten and Cameron 1991: 13–14), others (Mohr 1992) argue that organizational effectiveness is contingent upon too many variables to be able to establish the causal effect of one particular variable (such as management training). This suggests that there is a need to evaluate the effectiveness of reframing on two levels; firstly, in terms of whether it enhances day-to-day skills of the manager, and secondly, in terms of whether the actions arising from the exercise of these new skills lead to greater organizational effectiveness.[4]

Issues Internal to the Logic of Reframing

Acceptance of the concept of reframing does not preclude a number of problems associated with its usage. Four different issues are addressed below which concern areas of theoretical ambiguity within the reframing literature.

The first issue is whether what is important is the utility of particular frames or multiple-frame thinking *per se*. Whilst Bolman and Deal (1991) argue for the relevance of the structural, human resource, political and symbolic frames, others suggest that it may be useful instead to 'think of organizations as clouds rather than structures, songs rather than systems' (Gergen 1992: 207). A focus on particular frames implies that certain frames are somehow 'better' at capturing organizational reality than others. The alternative view is that the use of metaphor is advantageous primarily because it encourages creative and lateral thinking, that is, any multiple-perspective approach undermines the restriction of options that goes with the dominance of a single metaphor.

The second issue concerns an ambiguity in the usage of reframing. In Dunford and Palmer's (1995) study, respondents were split almost equally between (a) those who treated reframing as a contingency theory, in which the appropriate frame for analysing the problem was determined by the nature of the situation/problem in question, and (b) those who saw reframing as requiring the application of multiple frames to any given situation. This division reflects an ambiguity in Bolman and Deal's arguments, on the one hand that 'for different times and different situations, one perspective may be more important than others' (1991: 325) and, on the other, that 'all organizations contain multiple realities' (1991: 322). A question therefore remains as to whether the dominance of any one metaphor in an analysis of an organizational situation is a reflection of the nature of that situation or, as Martin (1992) asserts, is a product of the inclination and predisposition of the analyst.

A third issue involves the extent to which there is a direct relationship between reframing and the production of new outcomes. While the act of reframing may result in new recommendations for action, organizational constraints may prevent action being implemented successfully, if at all. Being able to see a situation in a new light may alert one to a whole range of new possibilities but, without the appropriate support and resources to successfully implement these new ideas, the situation may remain substantially unaltered. In the reframing literature there is an absence of discussion whereby analysis of a situation is linked to subsequent achievement of a desired future state.

A fourth issue concerns an underlying assumption that organizational actors will approach organizational situations and actions in a conscious, calculative manner if exposed to reframing. That is, they will take deliberate steps to apply a multi-frame analysis to any organizational situation with which they are confronted, and then implement action which they regard as having the greatest prospect of success. Whilst a role for 'intuition and artistry' (Bolman and Deal 1991: 325) is acknowledged as important, reframing nevertheless assumes a mechanistic connection between analysis and action.

These four issues address points which have yet to be clarified *within* the reframing literature. Whilst advocates of reframing point to the value of the approach, some unresolved issues remain in how it is to be used.

How Valid is Metaphorical Knowledge?

Whereas the previous section addressed issues internal to the logic of reframing, this section locates reframing within the broader context of debates about the nature of theory.[5] The four main areas of debate where metaphorical analysis has been addressed are: ontology, epistemology, idealism/materialism and commensurability/incommensurability.

Ontological Debate

Ontology debates concern whether social reality is only a cognitive construct having no existence independent of the names, concepts and labels which purport to describe it (nominalist/subjective position), or whether social reality has an existence independent of and external to individuals (a realist/objectivist position) (Burrell and Morgan 1979: 4). This debate is reproduced in the literature on metaphors and frames. Is reality only that which is produced through metaphor, or is reality something which exists independent of metaphorical descriptions of it?

Morgan takes a subjectivist position, arguing that organization theory is based upon a range of metaphors and to this extent 'it is an essentially subjective enterprise concerned with the production of one-sided analyses of organizational life' (1980: 612). The implication is that multiple metaphors or frames are needed in order to avoid 'excessive commitment to favoured points of view' (1980: 612).

For those who favour a realist position, two different avenues are pursued. First, criticism is directed to subjectivist assumptions, that ultimately they lead to relativism or solipsism and 'the idea of a social reality existing independently of subjective perceptions and interpretations melts into thin air' (Reed 1990: 36). This position is also mirrored in some recent criticisms of postmodernist theory. For example, Norris is critical of postmodernism for promoting the idea that reality 'is a purely discursive phenomenon, a product of the various codes, conventions, language games or signifying systems which provide the only means of interpreting experience' (1992: 16).

Norris (1990; 1992) argues a realist position but not that of the naive realist. Indeed, it is his contention that postmodernists set up a straw person by equating the realist stance with the view that objective truth is ascertainable through directly measurable 'facts'. He argues that 'one can defend a critical-realist position on principles that involve no such naive ontological commitment' (1992: 42). Norris cites Solomon's (1988) notion of 'potentialist realism' which assesses the inherent probabilities associated with the emergence of a particular sequence of actions. Adopting this position means that explanations of why particular sequences of actions emerge need to be couched in terms of 'our knowledge of the broader regularities that characterize human experience in general' (Norris 1992: 57). This position leads to a rejection of postmodernist assumptions that reality cannot be separated from the linguistic, rhetorical or narrative modes which represent it. In making this point is should be recognized, however, that there are divergent views as to what constitute the central tenets of postmodernist thought, including its stance on realism (see, for example, Marsden 1993).

At the same time, it should not be assumed that reframing is unambiguously a postmodernist stance on organizations. Yet this is clearly the position argued by Reed (1990) in his attack on Morgan's work which he sees as involving an unfortunate transformation from 'paradigm warrior to postmodernist guru'. Reframing retains modernist assumptions regarding meta-narrative and the authority of the author (Martin 1992: 193). With respect to the former, reframing involves a strong sense of the application of multiple frames/images producing an overall 'better picture'. For Bolman and Deal reframing provides a superior ability to 'generate creative responses' (1991: 4). Similarly, each frame is seen as providing 'glimpses of the truth' (1991: 12) with 'the depth and complexity of organizational life' (1991: 16) only being appreciated through applying multiple frames. That is, the reframing perspective retains a sense of there being an underlying reality which the aggregation of frames is able to more accurately portray. By comparison, postmodernism is 'disdainful of metatheories' (Martin 1992: 193) since it rejects the metatheoretical assumption that it is possible to synthesize something 'closer to the truth' from diverse perspectives. With respect to the authority of the author, reframing presents itself as a technique that enhances the skills of the user with regard to organizational analysis. It therefore remains modernist in the sense that it implies that the individual reframer, by not being locked into a fixed frame, will be a neutral analyst of the organizational situation. Postmodernism rejects the notion of the neutral position and sees the authority that is attached to authorship as consolidating the view that 'the truth' has been revealed (Foucault 1977: 113–38).

The second avenue, pursued by some authors outside of the organizational and management field, is to recognize the value of using metaphors to capture an independently occurring reality. The problem they cite is that simple metaphors and analogies do not sufficiently capture the complexity of particular situations and to this extent are dangerous by themselves. They therefore advocate two 'antidotes'. One is by clarifying the ways in which particular analogies 'fail or mislead or are incomplete' (Spiro et al. 1989: 499) so that the pitfalls of different analogies are known in advance. The other involves multiple and complex analogies being integrated into a 'composite image that has selective instantiations of the correct and useful information found in each analogy but suppresses the inappropriate information' (1989: 515). The idea that analogies or metaphors are 'correct' in parts, and 'incorrect' in others, is predicated upon a reality independent of the concepts used to describe it. Spiro et al. (1989: 525–7) suggests eight different functions of multiple analogies: supplementation (with new analogy), correction (with new analogy), alteration (of an earlier analogy), enhancement (of an earlier analogy), magnification (or elaboration), perspective shift, competition and sequential collocation. Each of these functions is aimed at providing a clearer enunciation of an underlying reality.

To summarize, a key theoretical issue which emerges is whether multiple perspectives are used to capture an objectively given reality, or rather to enact different, multiple realities. It is now clear that the ambiguity identified above in Bolman and Deal's usage of reframing reflects this deeper unresolved ontological issue.

Epistemological Debate

Epistemological debates concern arguments about how knowledge is produced. Whereas adherents to positivist assumptions seek knowledge about organizations by looking for patterns of enduring actions and their underlying causes, those who adopt anti-positivist assumptions maintain that organizational knowledge can be obtained by subjectivist processes of understanding 'the frame of reference of the participant in action' (Burrell and Morgan 1979: 5).

In the search for scientifically valid knowledge the positivist camp seeks to use literal language and to avoid the use of metaphors:

> to the extent that it is possible, administrative science must strive to control figurative terms in the development of formal hypotheses and theory. The point at which a trope loses its heuristic value and starts to mislead research and theory construction is difficult to determine. Therefore it is important to formulate concepts in literal terms that are rooted in observable *organizational* phenomena as soon as possible during the development of ideas into theory. (Pinder and Bourgeois 1982: 647)

From this positivist view, the goal of the social scientist should be the elimination of the use of metaphors. In a soft version of this, Bourgeois and Pinder (1983) put forward a slightly different position, one they term 'constructive empiricism'. They maintain that there is a single reality 'but there is no way of knowing whether or how our perceptions correspond to it' (1983: 610). They reject the idea of the literal truth of a theory, but maintain that objectivity exists within groups who construct the world in particular ways. However, for them, theoretical clarity can only be obtained ultimately through the use of literal language.

Anti-positivists reject the assumption that they should search for an absolute truth (Lakoff and Johnson 1980) and instead search for 'truths' which are constructed subjectively in different social frameworks of understanding. This is what Weick (1989: 516) refers to as sense-making, a methodology based upon a process of imaginative understanding (see also Lakoff and Johnson 1980: 193; Morgan 1980: 612). The need to recognize the important ways in which metaphors are an integral part of our conceptual system, and therefore of our construction of reality (Lakoff and Johnson, 1980; Weick 1989), is associated with the endeavour to remove the 'chastity belt of science' (Jackson and Carter 1991: 125) and the positivist search for 'truth'. This means that it is not possible to eliminate metaphors since both live and dead metaphors underpin what is often purported to be literal meaning (Morgan 1983; Lakoff and Johnson 1980). For Sternberg (1990: 5) the more important task for scientists is for them to reflect upon how the knowledge they construct is based upon a range of underlying metaphors. From this perspective there should be an acceptance of the integral basis of metaphors in the construction of knowledge; the search for a literal language constitutes an approach which will 'over-concretize' (Morgan 1980: 612) social reality.

Emerging Directions There are three epistemological directions which emerge from this debate. One has already been noted in the discussion of ontology. This is the position that there is a knowable world and that knowledge of it can be acquired using multiple metaphors. Consequently, from this perspective, we need to search for the 'correct' metaphors and analogies which reveal this reality (Collins and Burstein 1989: 562; Spiro et al. 1989: 525–7).

A second direction attempts to collapse the duality between metaphorical and literal language by arguing that the use of multiple metaphors or frames is legitimate, but only as an initial part of the process of knowledge production. Language – and therefore metaphors – are recognized as being 'both descriptive and constitutive' (Tsoukas 1991: 567) of reality. Metaphors are good at capturing the 'flow of experience' (1991: 571) and can therefore be used to provide initial insights into the topic at hand. Literal language, however, is good at abstracting and segmenting knowledge and, in what appears to be a second stage of knowledge construction, literal language takes over to reveal the 'real mechanisms and identities' (Tsoukas 1991: 572, citing Pinder and Bourgeois 1982). Metaphors serve to provide possible hypotheses which are then tested for their literal, causative value. The 'seed of literal language may exist within metaphorical language, but in order for it to grow and develop . . . the nurture and care of the scientist are required' (1991: 582). Ultimately, this approach still rests upon the assumption that it is possible to have a literal, scientific language – something which is rejected by non-positivists.

The third approach draws upon postmodernist assumptions and follows Lyotard's dictum that 'language is not meant for telling the truth' (1977: 96, cited in Jackson and Carter 1991: 125). The use of multiple frames and metaphors is 'essential to human understanding and as a mechanism for creating new meaning and new realities' (Lakoff and Johnson 1980: 196). Scientists should, therefore, accept that 'contradictory knowledges' (Morgan 1983: 606) may be generated and that analyses are sufficient if they are of 'interest, inform [and] provoke' (Aldrich 1992: 38). Norris is critical of such an approach for assuming that ' "truth" and "reality" are obsolete ideas' (1992: 31). Further, he argues that 'we have reached a point where theory has effectively turned against itself generating a form of extreme epistemological skepticism which reduces everything . . . to a dead level of suasive or rhetorical effect where consensus-values are the last (indeed the only) court of appeal' (1990: 4).

To summarize, the key epistemological issue which emerges is whether multiple frames and metaphors impede the orderly, cumulative production of knowledge or whether they are, in fact, integral to the production of any knowledge – including positivist, scientific knowledge.

Idealism/Materialism Debate

A third area of debate surrounding the use of metaphors and multiple perspectives concerns the extent to which they enable or constrain human actions. The debate here is cast between those who argue that multiple frames liberate since they provide alternative cognitive schemes or mind-sets, and those who argue that the use of multiple frameworks can fall into voluntarism, thereby neglecting the material underpinnings of organizations and society.

With respect to the former view, Gioia and Pitre (1990: 584) claim that the field of organization theory has advanced to the stage where multi-paradigmatic thinking has gained recognition as a way of avoiding too narrow a view of organizational reality. If a particular metaphor comes into prominence this is assumed to be because of the compelling nature of its advocates' arguments (1990: 598).

Against such a view is the argument that diversity can lead to 'political voluntarism' when there is a lack of appreciation of 'the ideological roots of metaphor' (Tinker 1986: 364). The charge levelled at multi-frame thinking is that it treats metaphors as being socially unstructured and assumes 'that the world is infinitely pliable to be molded at human will so that "anything goes" ' (Tsoukas 1992: 644; see also Norris 1992: 130). The problem with this position is that it fails to appreciate the ways in which social inequality and power can affect the emergence and dissemination of particular metaphors (cf. Tinker 1986: 368). As a result, false consciousness, mis-perceptions and misunderstandings are products of such thinking (Reed 1990: 39). Whilst not all metaphors fall prey to this problem, the 'promiscuous use of metaphor' (Tinker 1986: 267) will lead to an inad-equate understanding of social reality.

Each side of this debate accuses the other of conservatism. On one side is the view that adherence to particular perspectives will result in either dogmatic opportunism (Morgan 1990: 14) or, more seriously, a denial of other cognitive realities – a position which can be both 'politically and socially dangerous' (Lakoff and Johnson 1980: 159). Accepting the legitimacy of a plurality of perspectives avoids the 'imperialism' of orthodox approaches (Jackson and Carter 1991). On the other side is the view that conservatism can result from maintaining the legitimacy of using a plurality of metaphors since this ignores the impact of institutionalized power (Tinker, 1986: 368; Reed 1990: 39–40).

To summarize, concern at the material origins of metaphors does not necessarily imply a dismissal of the use of multiple frames or metaphors; rather it may involve a plea to use only 'politically correct' ones. The argument against this is that since reality is not known in advance of the concepts used to construct it, then limiting the use of certain frames or metaphors is only a short step away from political authoritarianism. These positions are further sharpened in the following debate.

Commensurability/Incommensurability Debate

The acceptance that there are multiple perspectives, each having core metaphors associated with them (Aldrich 1992: 17), has posed questions concerning their use in practice. One position is that different perspectives are 'incommensurable' (Burrell and Morgan 1979; Jackson and Carter 1991) as their core assumptions are fundamentally different. An alternative position is that organizational analysis should move beyond single perspective research since using a range of perspectives and paradigms will enable the elucidation of a wider variety of insights and explanations (Morgan 1980; 1990). A multiple perspectives approach will enable composite pictures of organizational issues to emerge.

A different approach is the search for a synthesis among competing frames. The soft version of this is based upon the view that epistemological boundaries are permeable at the edges – what Gioia and Pitre refer to as the 'transition zones' (1990: 592). Whilst maintaining the view that a fundamental synthesis of perspectives cannot occur and that organizations can be conceived of simultaneously through different images, they suggest that some bridges can be constructed across paradigms so that insights might be incorporated into one picture. The hard version denies the value of subjectivism and cognitive relativism and seeks to identify 'the shared criteria through which different schools of thought or research groups [assess] one another's work' (Reed 1990: 39).

In summary, a key practical issue which emerges out of this debate in terms of how managers use reframing is how multiple mappings are merged. If it is assumed 'that people frequently construct their understandings of systems by multiple mappings, [then] theories will have to specify how conflicts are resolved about what properties to map from each analogy' (Collins and Burstein 1989: 559). Clearly there is the expectation that multiple mappings will liberate managerial perceptions and actions, but the method whereby they merge, synthesize or separate the perceived benefits of different mappings remains an area to be explored theoretically.

Discussion

It is our contention that to date the assessment of reframing, and metaphorical analysis more generally, has failed to adequately distinguish the different levels at which this needs to be addressed. A major contribution of the chapter has been to identify four different levels of analysis which are needed in a comprehensive assessment of reframing.

The first level identified is the utility which managers attach to reframing. The importance of this issue lies in the fact that the marketplace for these ideas does not just comprise organizational theorists. That organizational theorists may be dismissive of an approach to organizational analysis bears no necessary relationship to the way those ideas will be received by managers, a point already debated some time ago in the *Harvard Business Review* (March–April 1984). Evidence suggests that reframing has a strong attraction to managers and supports the value of further research into the broader question of what attracts managers to particular theories of organization.

The second level involves determining what impact reframing has had on organizational analyses and actions. Whilst advocates of reframing make a number of claims about the virtues of reframing, a range of methodological issues have been identified in this chapter which remain to be addressed in any empirical substantiation of such claims.

The third level addresses issues relating to the internal consistency and theoretical logic of the reframing literature: that is, does reframing contain an internally coherent set of statements about its characteristics? This chapter has identified a number of ambiguities that have been glossed over within the reframing literature, but which substantially affect what reframing actually means.

The fourth level takes a broader view of reframing by locating it within debates on the place of metaphorical analysis in the production of knowledge. What this reveals is a vigorous debate as to the significance of the contribution of metaphors to the development of knowledge.

Finally, recognition of the different levels at which reframing can be assessed has a twofold importance. First, it acts as a means for identifying the level or levels of intervention of existing debate on reframing. Second, it provides a heuristic device for identifying the range of issues which a comprehensive assessment of the value of reframing will need to address.

Notes

1 Given the close correspondence of reframing with the concepts of images, metaphors, multiple perspectives and paradigms (see Burrell and Morgan 1979; Morgan 1980; 1986; 1988; Bolman and Deal 1984; 1991) the discussion which follows will be inclusive of these interrelated terms. Nevertheless, we are aware that these concepts are not always used in the same way by different organizational theorists. We are therefore sympathetic to attempts to delimit the usage of such terms, for example Lundberg's (1990: 12) exhortation to 'use the terms "perspective" and "reframe" instead of the now overused and often misused "paradigm" and the more current but less precise "metaphor" '.

2 Dunford and Palmer (1995) do not address what it is about reframing that managers find attractive. This issue is part of a broader question concerning what it is that attracts managers to particular management 'recipes'.

3 Cognitive complexity should not be treated as fixed across both space and time. For example, there are research findings which suggest both that an individual's cognitive complexity need not be constant in all domains and that some individuals are able to increase their cognitive complexity through training (Streufert and Nogami 1989: 120).

4 The research on cognitive complexity 'clearly points to more effective functioning of the cognitively complex individual, at least in advanced e.g. managerial, positions' (Streufert and Nogami 1989: 122). This area of research, cited earlier as a potentially important link with reframing, may provide additional insights into how the link between reframing and individual effectiveness might be assessed.

5 See also Palmer and Dunford (1996) for further discussion and development of the debates referred to in this section.

References

Aldrich, H.E. (1992) 'Incommensurable Paradigms? Vital Signs from Three Perspectives', in M. Reed and M. Hughes (eds), *Rethinking Organization: New Directions in Organization Theory and Analysis*. London: Sage. pp. 16–45.

Argyris, C. and Schon, D.A. (1974) *Theory in Practice: Increasing Professional Effectiveness*. San Francisco: Jossey-Bass.

Bolman, L.G. and Deal, T.E. (1984) *Modern Approaches to Understanding and Managing Organizations*. San Francisco: Jossey-Bass.

Bolman, L.G. and Deal, T.E. (1991) *Reframing Organizations: Artistry, Choice and Leadership*. San Francisco: Jossey-Bass.

Bourgeois, V.W. and Pinder, C.C. (1983) 'Constrasting Philosophical Perspectives in Administrative Science: a Reply to Morgan', *Administrative Science Quarterly*, 28: 608–13.

Burrell, G. and Morgan, G. (1979) *Sociological Paradigms and Organisational Analysis*. Aldershot: Gower.

Collins, A. and Burstein, M. (1989) 'Afterword: a framework for a Theory of Comparison and Mapping', in S. Vosniadou and A. Ortony (eds), *Similarity and Analogical Reasoning*. Cambridge: Cambridge University Press. pp. 546–65.

Dunford, R. and Palmer, I. (1995) 'Claims about Frames: Practitioners' Assessment of the Utility of Reframing', *Journal of Management Education* 19(1): 96–105.

Foucault, M. (1977) *Language, Counter-Memory, Practice*. Ithaca, NY: Cornell University Press.

Frost, P.J., Moore, L.F., Louis, M.R., Lundberg, C.C. and Martin, J. (eds) (1991) *Reframing Organizational Culture*. Newbury Park, CA: Sage.

Gergen, K.J. (1992) 'Organization Theory in the Postmodern Era', in M. Reed and M. Hughes (eds), *Rethinking Organization*. London: Sage. pp. 207–26.

Gioia, D.A. and Pitre, E. (1990) 'Multiparadigm Perspectives on Theory Building', *Academy of Management Review*, 15(4): 584–602.

Jackson, N. and Carter, P. (1991) 'In Defence of Paradigm Incommensurability', *Organization Studies*, 12(1): 109–27.

Lakoff, G. and Johnson, M. (1980) *Metaphors We Live By*. Chicago: University of Chicago Press.

Lundberg, C.C. (1990) 'Towards Mapping the Communication Targets of Organisational Change', *Journal of Organizational Change Management*, 3: 6–13.

Lyotard, J.F. (1977) 'The Unconscious as *mise-en-scène*', in M. Benamou and C. Caramello (eds), *Performance in Postmodern Culture*. Madison, WI: Coda Press. pp. 87–98.

Marsden, R. (1993) 'The Politics of Organizational Analysis', *Organization Studies*, 14(1): 93–124.

Martin, J. (1992) *Cultures in Organizations: Three Perspectives*. New York: Oxford University Press.

Marx: R.D. and Hamilton, E.E. (1991) 'Beyond Skill Building: a Multiple Perspectives View of Personnel', *Issues and Trends in Business and Economics*, III: 1–4.

Mohr, L.B. (1992) *Explaining Organizational Behavior: the Limits and Possibilities of Theory and Research*. San Francisco: Jossey-Bass.
Morgan, G. (1980) 'Paradigms, Metaphors, and Puzzle Solving in Organization Theory', *Administrative Science Quarterly*, 25(4): 605–22.
Morgan, G. (1983) 'More on Metaphor: Why We Cannot Control Tropes in Administrative Science', *Administrative Science Quarterly*, 28: 601–7.
Morgan, G. (1986) *Images of Organization*. Beverly Hills, CA: Sage.
Morgan, G. (1988) *Riding the Waves of Change: Developing Managerial Competencies for a Turbulent World*. San Francisco: Jossey-Bass.
Morgan, G. (1990) 'Paradigm Diversity in Organizational Research', in J. Hassard and D. Pym (eds), *The Theory and Philosophy of Organizations: Critical Issues and New Perspectives*. London: Routledge. pp. 13–29.
Norris, C. (1990) *What's Wrong with Postmodernism*. London: Harvester Wheatsheaf.
Norris, C. (1992) *Uncritical Theory*. London; Lawrence and Wishart.
Palmer, I. and Dunford, R. (1996) 'Conflicting Uses of Metaphors: Reconceptualizing Their Use in the Field of Organizational Change', *Academy of Management Review*, 21(3).
Pinder, C.C. and Bourgeois, V.W. (1982) 'Controlling Tropes in Administrative Science', *Administrative Science Quarterly*, 27: 641–52.
Reed, M. (1990) 'From Paradigms to Images: the Paradigm Warrior Turns Post-Modernist Guru', *Personnel Review*, 19(3): 35–40.
Solomon, J.F. (1988) *Discourse and Reference in the Nuclear Age*. Norman, OK: University of Oklahoma Press.
Spiro, R.J., Feltovich, P.J., Coulson, R.L. and Anderson, D.K. (1989) 'Multiple Analogies for Complex Concepts: Antidotes for Analogy-Induced Misconception in Advanced Knowledge Acquisition', in S. Vosniadou and A. Ortony (eds), *Similarity and Analogical Reasoning*. Cambridge: Cambridge University Press. pp. 488–531.
Sternberg, R.J. (1990) *Metaphors of Mind: Conceptions of the Nature of Intelligence*. Cambridge: Cambridge University Press.
Streufert, S. and Nogami, G.Y. (1989) 'Cognitive Style and Complexity: Implication for I/O Psychology', in C.L. Cooper and I. Robertson (eds), *International Review of Industrial and Organizational Psychology*. New York: Wiley. pp. 93–143.
Tinker, T. (1986) 'Metaphors or Reification: Are Radical Humanists Really Libertarian Anarchists?', *Journal of Management Studies*, 23(4): 363–84.
Tsoukas, H. (1991) 'The Missing Link: a Transformational View of Metaphors in Organizational Science', *Academy of Management Review*, 16(3): 566–85.
Tsoukas, H. (1992) 'Postmodernism, Reflexive Rationalism and Organizational Studies: a Reply to Martin Parker', *Organizational Studies*, 13(4): 643–9.
Weick, K. (1989) 'Theory Construction as Disciplined Imagination', *Academy of Management Review*, 14(4): 516–31.
Westenholz, A. (1993) 'Paradoxical Thinking and Change in the Frames of Reference', *Organization Studies*, 14(4): 37–58.
Whetten, D.A. (1988) 'Theory Building in Organizational and Management Sciences'. Paper presented at the meeting of the Academy of Management, Anaheim, CA, August.
Whetten, D.A. and Cameron, K.S. (1991) *Developing Management Skills* (2nd edn). New York: Harper Collins.

9

Managing Sceptically: a Critique of Organizational Fashion

Harvie Ramsay

The proclamation of the management panacea is nothing new, as aficionados of human relations writings in the Mayovian or Maslovian traditions could readily confirm. The sales pitch has grown more clamorous and hyperbolic in recent times, though; the packaging more sophisticated, the dismissal of past models more scathing and complete, the tone more edgy, the pace of the product cycle more frantic.

Perhaps this view might be dismissed as merely the effects of time dilation on an academic generation who have joined the ranks of those who have 'seen it all before'. But the recognition of fad and fashion, and of their deleterious potential, has begun to be acknowledged even in the circles of management writings themselves. Thus the main professional organization for personnel specialists in the UK, the Institute of Personnel and Development, list 'fads and fashions' over the years 1969–94 (suggesting a steady increase in the numbers after 1990 especially) in a major recent review (1994: 31). Eccles and Nohria, in a text targeted on this problem and entitled *Beyond the Hype*, speak of 'this desperate quest for new approaches to management' (1992: 2), and address their words to 'the thoughtful manager' who has 'a healthy skepticism about the latest sure-fire solutions to what they realize are eternal problems' (1992: 10–11). Christopher Bartlett (1983), an influential analyst of international business management, enjoins companies to 'get off the reorganization merry-go-round', while for Stern (1994) 'executives cleave to business theories like alcoholics to their bottles. In both cases the treatment could make the affliction worse.' Writing in the widely read periodical of the British Management Association, *Management Today*, Ezzamel et al. (1993) warn their audience to 'be wary of new waves', while in another popular source Byrne (1986) prophesies 'one more panacea and we will all go nuts.'

Even the gurus themselves have begun to acknowledge fashion, though with varying depth of analysis. Thus although Tom Peters detects that everything is 'going fickle, ephemeral, fashion' (1993: 6), he celebrates this as a pathway to empowerment and decentralization. Kanter, on the other hand, is characteristically more cautious, acknowledging that many innovations have been correctly criticized by sceptics 'for being faddish, superficial, quick fixes with fragmented implementation' (1989: 354), though she still strives to see an evolutionary management process emerging through fashion and even failure. In similar vein, Pascale prefaces his own proposals for a more effective model of continuous change management with a brief analysis of how 'the consumption rate and shelf life of business fads' is 'an indicator of managerial panic' (1990: 18). He echoes most other commentators by detecting a rapid acceleration in the pace of gimmickry after 1980.

Unsurprisingly, however, the recognition of superficiality rarely goes further than an identification of a fault to be overcome with a more solid and sustained commitment to new methods, still bearing much resemblance to the flexibilization and teamishness which suffuses most of those fashionable ideas themselves. The problem is not the ideas, or even the structural constraints (which may be recognized but can be overcome), but the lack of proper implementation of basic truths by a management with thoroughgoing commitment to the desirable new order. Even Eccles and Nohria's insightful analysis of rhetoric in management leads at the end only to a somewhat plaintive call for a return to seeing management as action and process, not structure and design, and so seeing a need to continually manage situations in constructive ways – even using rhetoric! – instead of seeking formula solutions. The prescription, predictably, lacks the conviction and dilutes the eventual impact of the critical analysis.

The Need for Explanation

However, there may be some doubts as to whether a critical analysis of management fashion is required. Why should it not be sufficient merely to acknowledge the need to treat hype with caution and choose carefully from the available models on the market? The argument against this *laissez-faire* view is summarized in two steps below: firstly, the record of fads in operation; and secondly, the consequences of failure of a hyped technique.

Failure Outweighs Success

To judge by the volume of output on any of a long list of fashionable management ideas, they are a raging success. From vague gains in positive attitudes, motivation, loyalty and morale, to more concrete claims about productivity, reduced staff absenteeism and turnover, effortless technological change, quality and so forth, the most popular management outlets offer repeated accounts of success and transformation. Qualifications are few, and it seems at times as if the message could almost be written blind, leaving blanks for the particular technique, company and so on to be filled in later.

When a fad fades, however, so too does attention to it, in a way which follows the recipe book rather than the corrective reportage approach: that which has not worked no longer warrants attention, since the only relevant recipes to be printed are those which can claim to produce delicious results. Dismissive backward glances, intended only to contrast the tarnished past product with the latest shiny device, mark the typical limit of retrospective analysis. Yet even the archetypal guru text admits that 'the bones of these programs are scattered on America's low-productivity desert' (Peters and Waterman 1982: 241). Or similarly, in the words of another reviewer,[1] 'Tom Peters' ideas on excellence today become a blueprint on corporate failure tomorrow.'

Take the example of quality circles. This idea exploded onto the scene with remarkable velocity in the US and later the UK from the late 1970s. By the early 1980s, surveys were reporting consistently that about half of all organizations were claiming to operate QCs or equivalent bodies.[2] Yet by the end of that decade there was plentiful evidence of failure and decline,[3] such that one researcher who had tracked the performance of QCs over the decade was moved to describe the late 1980s as 'the tail end of the quality circle movement' (Hill 1991).

Similar historical careers may be charted for various task or work group focused initiatives – job enrichment schemes or semi-autonomous work groups during the 1970s, for instance (Ramsay 1985). More recently, the record of team briefing systems has come under scrutiny, and their effectiveness has been questioned (Marchington et al. 1992). If the claims for success of such employee involvement techniques seem to follow a predictable formula as suggested above, then the dossiers of failure are equally consistent, identifying a management search for quick fixes, a lack of resource backing, poor training and preparation, ill-advised crossing of unions, a lack of serious monitoring and auditing, and last but not least, middle management scepticism and resistance (Ramsay 1991).

Parallel criticisms are emerging for other areas of fashionable technique. One recent study found little positive support for delayering among 200 managers in a range of organizational settings, and in some even a quiet decision to re-layer without admitting it.[4] A study of change management, popular only after 1989 or so, found only one-third of companies even claimed marked progress on employee commitment, and many acknowledged difficulties in implementing culture or value shifts.[5] More sustained critiques have exposed the dubious nature of key evidence and claims in the massively influential text *The Machine that Changed the World* (Womack et al. 1990),[6] while others have unpicked the slackly woven threads of the once unchallenged excellence/strong-culture thesis developed by Peters and Waterman among others.[7] Perhaps most disturbing for the advocates of new management methods have been the high reported failure and discontentment rates for total quality management (TQM) and its successor, business process re-engineering (BPR),[8] distressing because these were the most complete, logically sustained and plausible proposals for organization reform yet to emerge.

In short, popular techniques are being heavily sold but poorly thought through, half-heartedly applied (but often with lip-service to unmitigated management commitment and a call for an attendant 'complete culture change' in the organization), and then frequently abandoned in disillusionment and possibly even an atmosphere of blame and recrimination. Yet the lessons from such failure rates can be drawn together and disseminated as guidelines and health warnings for would-be implementers. This remains true even though these failure rates are hard to specify (since 'failure' itself is not easily defined and, however delineated, is rarely publicly reported). The messages reporting reality might not be particularly exhilarating, but should carry a higher reliability (and performance outcome) index than their glossier counterparts. This provides one basis for an academic antidote to fashion, to which this chapter will return at its close.

Deficiences and Damage

The problem with taking a tolerant view of hype and fashion, especially in the light of the performance record reviewed above, is that the resulting impact of fashion generation has the potential to be systematically damaging in a number of ways. Change is disruptive by nature, though its restitution is enhanced performance and prospects. But an absence of solid returns, and so of real material improvement, deletes such compensation, since a return to the status quo ante is rarely an option; on the contrary, the sacrifices made (willingly or otherwise) by many organization members may be that much harder to suffer. Moreover, implementing a new approach can be very costly, and a lack of yield may thus actually damage competitiveness and survival chances of the organization, or at least force savings elsewhere, more often than not at the expense of the relatively powerless rather than of the fashion champions themselves.

Most damaging to trust relations, though, will be any exposure of a hidden management agenda for achieving concessions from staff under cover of adopting new and 'irresistable' methods, perhaps sweetened with lip-service to 'empowerment' or enhanced development prospects. Here 'labour process' cynicism gains purchase, fuelling the suspicion that for some managements greater intensification of effort is the only real aim, with each new method providing camouflage for reducing staff defences, even in the name of empowerment.[9] Where this analysis applies, the concepts of 'failure' and 'success' may be even harder to specify than otherwise.

Even if we leave aside this problem of defining the real processes involved, and take proposals for change as at least intended to be genuine, however flawed, the attempt to attribute blame for failure raises further problems, exacerbated by the propaganda image of techniques which implies that, as success is near universal, difficulties must be related to the exceptional obstructiveness or inadequacy of some of the parties involved locally. In the longer run, it may be that increasing numbers of organizational members become disillusioned by the repeating waves of top-down enthusiasm for new panaceas, thus learning to construct forms of passive resistance, or even active sabotage, to protect themselves.

Thus if impressions of a new order of the pace of change in fashions are correct, this problem is likely to be becoming cumulative (a likelihood arguably lent plausibility by the growing academic awareness of the issue). Resistance is likely to be most debilitating for implementation at the key node in the transmission line, in the middle management echelons, where past experience combined with lack of initiating authority will be particularly likely to breed scepticism, and where resources for resistance are likely to be greatest.

There is a further vicious turn to some of the circular processes here: as Watson (1994) exemplifies, managers may see the potential in some new ideas, but fear what actually happens when they are applied. In consequence, they may become sceptical by first instinct of all innovations but those which they themselves promote, thus collectively subjecting all proposals to the verdict of guilty of gimmickry until proven innocent.

Ultimately, these observations call for a detailed analysis of the mechanisms by which fashions get translated into organizations, and with what detailed consequences for various parties. Here it should be noted that there is no good reason to presume that the effects will be evenly spread across the organization's members, and there are solid grounds on reflection for expecting systematic differences of impact and response according to such factors as type of initiative, context of introduction, and a variety of individual variables including personality, attitude on various dimensions of commitment, career stage and present position of the individual (in both the formal and informal organization), and so forth. This forms part of the basis for a research agenda on the subject, to which we will return at the end of this chapter.

The Search for Explanation

The recognition of faddism is an important and welcome step, but affords little progress towards a response without a coherent explanation of the phenomenon. Indeed, the very emergence of an appreciation of fashions, rather than just innovations and advances in management practice, constitutes an interesting phenomenon inviting reflexive explanation in its own right.

Where an attempt at explanation is made, it is often a piecemeal one. Thus Pascale (1990) fixes his gaze on the post-war professionalization of management, which he believes led to a demand for a respectable presentation of their own activities, making them receptive to new theories. Guest (1992b) stresses the desire also for coherent and optimistic accounts of the management task and how to achieve it. Others turn their gaze somewhat casually on the rise of the consultancy industry, seeking constantly to justify itself, and also to repackage and redefine its products to renew old markets and open fresh ones.

Processual Accounts

From within a broadly managerialist framework, two recent attempts have been made to construct rather more sustained and plausible accounts. Gill and Whittle (1992) turn their attention on management by objectives, organizational development, and total quality management, observing a cyclical pattern of rise and fall in each case. They attempt to identify common features of the career of these concepts, in an attempt to account for this pattern. Their explanation privileges cultural and psychoanalytical factors, which they argue underlie more fully specified accounts of failure in new management techniques, whether of conception or of implementation. The cultural factors identified by the authors include an emerging anti-intellectualism on the part of practising managers, combined with a belief in grand strategy which emanates a touch of machismo, all these being impelled by the culture of consultancy. These combine to discourage objectivity, proper evaluation and monitoring, and stimulate the search for instant and universal 'turnkey' managerial products.

More fundamental still, in Gill and Whittle's view, is the identification of what they call an 'organizational life-cycle' for management ideas. This notion has some persuasive power, as will be discussed later, although it is hard to make the next step with them and see the organization as if it were an individual, going through birth, adolescent, mature and decline stages. The acceptance of this as metaphor is dispelled by their next move, characterizing executive groups as expressing certain types of psychodynamic cultures. Thus a fight/flight culture disposes management to grasp at panaceas through fear of competitors; a dependency culture initially accepts a guru as an unchallenged guide, but later sees this charismatic projection displaced by a Weberian decline into rules and regulations; while a pairing culture seeks utopian and grandiose ideas.

It is not the desire of this author to dismiss psychoanalytic factors as having no potential to help explain faddism in management. On the contrary, the focus on individual needs and reactions, and their aggregate and combined effect, affords an important micro-level contribution as suggested in the previous section. However, the translation of such an approach into metaphor and then supposed cultural type might be kindly described as partial, and more bluntly as arcane. It appears to grasp few of the organizational processes, let alone the wider pressures and contingencies, within its explanatory framework.

A rather more convincing account is provided by Huczynski (1993a; 1993b). Huczynski's broader project is an analysis of the history of management thought, where he is able to confirm the impression that there is much reproduction of themes and proposals over time, boiling down in his classification to just six families of management ideas (a classification which bears interesting comparison with the further reduction to just two by Barley and Kunda 1992, discussed below). His account of faddism focuses on the 1980s onwards, when he sees a new 'guru' school of thought emerging, rooted in an emerging 'entrepreneurial period' in business culture.

Whether the gurus are really a distinct school of thought, or just a recombination of earlier themes in more complex, interwoven and cohesive ways (which for the record is my own view), for our purposes here the relevant concern is the way in which Huczynski sets about analysing the accelerated and intensified rise and fall of fashions in this contemporary era. In the course of his explorations, Huczynski reviews a prodigious range of possible explanations, often pitched at quite different levels of causation.

Huczynski's major focus is upon the motivation of particular groups of actors, however: of managers (as customers for ideas and policies), and of consultants (as suppliers). He proceeds to a deconstruction of each. Managers are identified as having organizational, competition-driven, and individual reasons for seeking out new ideas to support. The organizational motives are identified as a response to declining company fortunes, the refreshing effect of novelty itself, and the provision of leverage for change by breaking down hidebound assumptions. Competitive reasons include managers' desires to do something (and to be seen to do something), to present a progressive company image, and to avoid competitors stealing a march with a new technique. At the individual level, personal career and status enhancement, and the search for a quick fix, are the main grounds identified. Consultants, meanwhile, are seen to be seeking externally to expand their market, and to do so with products whose obsolescence was planned, to ensure renewal of demand. They are aided in this by the need among hard-pressed managers for ready-made and already popular solutions. The promotion of packaged solutions is often powerfully reinforced by influential enthusiastic coverage in a few key sources – in *Management Today* and the *Financial Times* for the UK, for instance.

Huczynski's precise classifications here blur at the edges, and there is a lack of attention, for instance, to *which* managers will be drawn (and which deterred) by particular reasons, but the general account is both plausible and wide-ranging. The concentration on the personal and interactive responses has the particular strength of capturing much of the daily reality of this phenomenon, and so of process, though the working through of a processual account remains rather thin.

Structural Explanations

However, it remains open to question whether an explanation focusing exclusively on the outward and local manifestation of fashion generation and diffusion will prove adequate. In order to discern and then account for wider patterns of causation, a more systemic or structural approach seems necessary. Huczynski himself does signpost certain directions at this level also, firstly with reference to the intensifying competitive forces in capitalist economies, and secondly through use of Marglin's analysis of management's search for authority, through means to tackle symptoms rather than fundamental causes of conflict. This level of analysis remains underdeveloped, however.

In practice, most available structural explanations are realist in their approach, identifying and seeking to explain some kind of pattern to management innovations in technique, and so proceeding from the observation of the phenomena to the disclosure of their conditions of existence. Structural factors operate at the level of defining external constraint and influence, which are commonly seen to be manifested locally in conflicting demands, typically analysed as emanating from contradictions rather than mistakes or misunderstandings. An example here is Hyman's observation:

> Shifting fashions in labour management stem from [an] inherent contradiction: solutions to the problem of discipline aggravate the problem of consent, and vice versa. (1988: 52)

Such explanations are certainly suggestive, but without elaboration risk reducing the immediate context to a matter of detail or of homogenizing organizational settings, thus formularizing developments with little recognition of the importance of agency or process.

Another feature of many structural accounts is their emphasis on the cyclical undertow of surface oscillations. The cyclical pattern of employee relations policies has been noted in a number of accounts. Ramsay (1977) concentrates on worker participation initiatives, Cronin (1979) on strike waves, Jacoby (1990) on union growth and non-unionism, and Wright (1994) on job redesign and new production concepts, for instance.

The emphasis on the ideological propagation of participation at certain historical points in Ramsay's (1983) analysis is also used as a basis for rejecting the standard managerialist claim of an 'evolution' of managment thought, which provides one important plank in the critique of new management ideas as rhetoric rather than the progression of ideas which is the typical claim within each fashion. This critical view of evolutionist accounts is repeated in Barley and Kunda (1992), in a contribution which proceeds to depict 'surges' of managerial 'ideologies of control'. Their account discerns two types of emphasis in these surges, rationalist (emphasizing system and technique) and normative (stressing integration, authority and unitarism), which are argued to alternate. This intriguing proposition is diluted at the end of their contribution by the qualification that in practice rationalist thinking is probably always dominant, but normative factors receive more attention when issues in workforce motivation and control are higher on the agenda. It is certainly not easy to avoid this re-emphasis, since current fashions are not always easily classified within one camp of their dichotomy: TQM can present emphatic rationalist and culture-change emphases, for instance; while BPR or lean production proposals, though similarly Janus-faced, lean markedly more towards the rationalist view in a supposedly normative ideology era. The result of this restatement is to markedly weaken the force of the analysis, however, and to expose its overly generalizing, macro-level focus.

The best 'fit' in these historical analyses is consistently found to be with the putative 'long' or Kondratieff waves.[10] This, too, indicates that these accounts may not be well equipped to discern the dynamics of the fluctuations of fashion under consideration in this chapter. This does not render these approaches irrelevant to the question at hand, however: they may offer some insight into the reasons for the acceleration in the rate of generation of fads in management generally, and even explain some of the different emphases therein at different conjunctures (e.g. why TQM in particular was 'an idea whose time had come' in the early 1990s).[11] As an instrument they remain too blunt to tell us much more, though, just as they do not tell us *per se* about the reasons for differences between sectors or individual firms in the timing, pace, degree and nature of implementation of particular fashions.

Level-Headed Explanation

An attempt to offer a more organizational focus to analyses of cyclical accounts of fashions is found in a few analyses founded on case study methodology. Longitudinal accounts of industrial relations policy in BL and Cadbury (Whipp and Smith 1984) and in Chrysler (Baddon and Lockyer 1983) both reveal what the latter call 'microcycles' of employee involvement techniques and ideas within each company. This idea is reiterated in a more sustained fashion by Marchington et al. (1993), who trace 'waves' of participation initiatives in each of the companies they studied. These episodes of innovation, rise and decline are markedly shorter and more variable in length and timing than would be allowed by an explanation pitched exclusively at the social cycle or long wave level. The latter researchers aggressively claim that this level of analysis is more appropriate, at least from the 1980s onwards, to an understanding of managerial innovations aimed at involving employees (Ackers et al. 1992).

This claim actually highlights not the superiority of either level of analysis, but rather the futility of seeking explanation exclusively at any one level (Ramsay 1993). Indeed, it raises more questions than it answers, since the organizational level is in fact a meso-level if anything, between the micro-individualist focus on managers' and employees' perceptions and responses and the macro-structural account of contemporary and historical accounts of societal shifts in initiatives and ideologies of management. As such it, too, over-agglomerates and generalizes unwarrantedly, especially in the eyes of those inclined towards ethnomethodological or similar methods of observation and analysis.

Presuming that nihilism is not the desired academic response to these problems, the alternative is to seek to draw on the strengths of the different levels of analysis reviewed thus far. Strictly speaking, of course, we should seek to go beyond the confines of separate approaches to generate a single,

Figure 9.1   *Management fashions: levels of explanation*

integrated account, realizing the ambitions of structuration theory or similar, realist methods. To date, though, the social sciences have not achieved this equivalent of a unified field theory, though they have begun to address the problems.[12] For now, it is necessary to make do with a multi-layered approach which attempts to avoid asserting ontological profundity or automatic causal priority to any one level. A summary of some of the primary levels of analysis of management fashions which might be considered is indicated in Figure 9.1.

If we consider each of the levels described, it appears intuitively that during much of the 1980s there was a mutual reinforcement of pressures for finding solutions to challenges and crises at all points. This helps to explain the lack of restraint on the gathering pace of fashion generation in recent times. On the other hand, the accumulation of managerial scepticism, which it was suggested earlier is following from repeated waves of cultural revolution, will act as a braking force, but not necessarily a decisive one in so far as other levels of pressure are set to continue. The extent to which a number of levels of pressure have pushed change in the same direction also suggests the reason why causal explanations are so diverse, and why different versions can all appear plausible: because they are complementary, not conflicting, elements of the analysis.

An Illustration: Analysing the Role of Consultancy

The insights afforded by a willingness to open out from single levels of analysis may be exemplified with reference to a consideration of the role of the consultancy industry in the fashion cycle. Although the role of management consultants is most prominently located in Figure 9.1 at the level of organizational factors, it quickly becomes apparent on closer examination that this is a simplification. Instead, the issue of consultancy itself needs to be deconstructed at a number of levels.

On reflection this is unremarkable: consultancy is a phenomenon which can be discussed collectively as an impulse to fashion generation, but consultancies are also organizations, and these in turn are composed of individuals pursuing their own projects and seeking to make out in a pressured setting. Thus it is important to avoid reifying and homogenizing consultancy companies themselves. The policies and techniques promoted by these corporations have to be taken to the customer by employees, notwithstanding their high salaries and status, and the heavy responsibility vested by their employer in those staff.

Studies which examine the internal workings of consultancies as organizations are very rare, but glimpses suggest a need for personal survival by the consultant through extraordinarily long hours, working to tight schedules. In the course of one case study for a project on financial participation, this author was able to interview and use attitude surveys to explore a range of organizational issues in a medium-sized management consultancy, and the following impressions are drawn from that study,[13] confirmed and extended by disparate, often journalistic or fragmentary accounts. This is yet another area ripe for more sustained research – though problems of access should not be underestimated.

Typically, to manage in a limited time and in what may be a highly political environment, consultants may be forced to rely on corporate formulas combined with skilful gathering, collation and feeding back of knowledge and ideas garnered in the client organization itself. This may be further constrained by the need in effect to act as justifiers of policies already prefered by the senior client executive, paying the piper and expecting to call the tune. In this guise, a plausible reinforcement by a prestigious adviser, charging enough to be listened to,[14] is a catalyst for change which cannot be propelled with sufficient force by the champion from within. Yet this may coexist with a scathing dismissal of the capabilities of client managers: in the words of one consultant, 'We do not learn from clients. Their standards aren't high enough. We learn from other McKinsey partners.'[15]

Nonetheless, for the individual consultant, the independence and creativity such a job seems to offer may be fairly constrained. The work may be viewed as a high-paid 'burn' for a few years, which will also allow the individual to make contacts and await an invitation to join a client firm, and so move to a more stable position. For some individuals, this may lead to a relatively distanced and almost conflictual view of the employing company. In the author's own research, this seemed most likely to be sparked by poor performance pay and share option offers, reflecting rejection of management appraisal criteria. Though not widespread among the staff, any such responses are of course quite at odds with the typically highly unitarist organizational images and techniques which they are party to selling. There is a clear potential for role distancing in the job here, although this is a risky and exposed strategy given the customer's likely expectations.

Although peering inside consultancies reveals cracks in the monolithic image usually purveyed in the business press (or even more so in the trade union press for that matter: see e.g. LRD 1992), it is clear that in their external activities consultants are likely to find themselves fairly constrained to sell their employer's line. The effect is thus largely to confirm the pressures identified from the outside by Huczynski's attempt to express consultants' objectives as suppliers of fads. He reports a conscious planned obsolescence in techniques, for instance, with a two- to three-year life-cycle. As organizations, consultancies clearly have a vested interest akin to that of suppliers of automobiles or consumer durables: to offer replacements frequently enough to sustain their growth as firms, and attractive enough to appear worth ditching or adding to the old technique for. This draws us to consider the scale of the impact of these consultancies. The raw figures are startling enough, testament to the structural forces within the market economy which encourage such activities. Between 1970 and 1980, the revenue of management consultancies registered with the Management Consultants' Association doubled; from 1980 to 1987, it increased fivefold. In the UK, over the eleven years 1980–91 the number of consultants registered with the MCA more the quadrupled to 6,963, and their fees increased almost seventeenfold.[16] By the early 1990s, there were reckoned to be 100,000 consultants world-wide.[17] Growth figures in recent years for major players in the global consultancy game confirm the continuing acceleration in business from the late 1980s. Thus the largest company, Andersen Consulting, has been posting 9 per cent growth regularly (and as high as 19 per cent in the recession year of 1992). Second largest players, McKinsey, doubled revenue to $1.2 billion 1987 and 1993. Coopers and Lybrand, third globally (but second in Europe), saw revenues grow 107 per cent over the five years to 1993, and by then had 66,000 staff in 125 countries.[18]

In short, these are huge companies in their own right, and now wield an immense and international power in the discovery, development, packaging and sale of the latest techniques. Their scale, fees and growth indicate the acceleration of faddism itself, and suggest also the importance of their role therein. Hecht (1995) reports that in the previous eighteen months, ninety-four of the top one hundred British companies had used consultants, for instance. Like the interior world of consultants, their external activity remains largely unstudied. The evidence (including the recent report of the UK Government spending, in a public sector scandal, over £500 million without demonstrable gain) suggests that scrutiny is long overdue.[19] It also implies the importance of a comprehensive understanding of consultancy as one facet of the fashion plague.

Concluding Comments: Towards a Research Agenda

To draw together the implications of the foregoing, let us begin with the most active role which academics might play. The contribution of independent research in debunking the mythology of individual techniques and identifying the patterns of success and problems is already well established. The section above on the evidence of fad failure draws on a small sample of that literature. The need to fund more extensive and faster evaluation in this vein should be self-evident, given its potential benefit to practising managers as well as for academic journals and teaching. The dissemination of the resulting findings also needs to be massively improved, with a greater receptiveness shown by professional and managerial outlets than is presently the case.

Any trend towards the new right worship of market-driven and private-enterprise-sponsored research can only mitigate against this, given the real political constraints it places on researchers to heed the sensibilities of their paymasters. Criticism must also be directed at the tendency in many graduate business schools to treat guru and senior managerial pronouncements sycophantically and uncritically, since this approach has led academia to become a further part of rather than an answer to the problems under discussion here. The emergence of distanced and perceptive business-school-based analyses of the fashion phenomenon themselves point to progress in this arena.

Although the most important role for academic research is to expose and help to moderate the unproductive consequences of management fashions, there is also room for some detailed support for organizational policy in the faddist era. The relationship suggested earlier in this chapter between personality, career and other factors on the one hand, and the response to new techniques on the other, suggests a case for refinement and application of psychometric and other techniques to explore this area. The issue is emphatically interdisciplinary, between psychology and organizational or human resource management studies for instance. At the same time, the agenda should be not one of mere control, selecting or moulding employees to adapt to faddism, but one of building more effective organizational mechanisms for managing new techniques themselves (where scepticism should be not rooted out, but rather constructively harnessed to the prior evaluation and subsequent tracking of innovations, for instance).

At the level of explanation rather than application, further development of the analysis should begin to seek a more empirically based and cross-dimensional foundation, it is suggested. It is apparent, for instance, that

Table 9.1   *Types of organizational crisis*

Business context	Organizational performance	Labour/employee relationship
Price competition	Cost structure/level	Labour cost
Product quality/design competition	Financial performance	Productivity
Market shift/downturn	Restructuring	Discipline and control
Takeover threat	Organization coordination	Conflict/industrial relations
Legislation	Internal politics	Labour market
International events	Mangement succession	Commitment and motivation
	Managerial authority/ legitimacy	Morale
	Managerial skills: senior, middle/junior	Training system

fashions tend to be generated in certain locations, which become models or the foci of attention. The automobile industry and in more recent times the electronic sector seem to have been notably prominent here, suggesting that globalization and relatively integrated organization of companies may play a significant role. Within national economies, and the globalized economy more generally, certain types of organizations may thus be the incubators or test beds of new fads, these then being diffused through a variety of channels and with varying effect.

More generally, it should become possible to chart and consider more systematically the contingent factors in different settings. Thus speed of takeup and subsequent decline could be explored with reference to sectoral influences, competition levels, company profitability, size and structure and so forth. Another approach might use an analysis of the range, types and degrees of 'crisis' faced by different organizations. Table 9.1 offers one classification of the types of crisis organizations may face.[20]

Certain connections or clusters of crises on the different dimensions might be expected. Thus intensifying competition on price, and/or a downward shift in the market, would seem likely to set in motion financial crises and restructuring pressures, leading to an emphasis on employment costs, productivity, discipline and control, and perhaps provoking industrial relations problems. Greater perceived need for product quality and improved image might be expected to promote organizational changes and efforts to improve management coordination, and, provided the profit headroom is available, will encourage a more positive approach to employee contributions, stressing skill enhancement and training as part of an employee commitment programme. These two contrasting (almost ideal-type) scenarios are thus likely to provoke hard HRM, rationalizing, cost-reduction approaches on the one hand, or human resource developmental (HRD), soft HRM responses on the other. This typology might allow a less abstracted adaptation of the classification of management rhetorics and techniques proposed by Barley and Kunda.

In the broad sense used here, it should be noted, some kind of crisis may be an almost permanent feature of many organizations. It is the perception by the organizational gatekeepers of new methods which may be as important as any assessment of 'real' challenges, of course, Clearly, too, the type and intensity of crisis will affect the receptivity of potential fashion champions to different packaged solutions. The pattern of adoption might thus vary also with the other initiatives under way, e.g. whether its primary 'magic ingredient' is technological, production system, organizational process or human resource oriented. An investigation of all of these tentative patterns seems warranted.

To this research agenda may be added the exploration of internal processes of adoption or rejection, implementation, and assessment of outcomes. As was suggested above, here management variables, including those being examined by scholars interested in recruitment and selection, performance appraisal and forms of commitment, and the impact of different cultural variables, might be drawn on and developed. So too might studies of managerial micro-politics. The need for research in this area is thus profound, and the arguments here at best speculative in its absence, but the potential is hopefully evident.

Notes

1 Roger King in *The Times Higher Education Supplement* 11 August 1989.

2 The first Workplace Industrial Relations Survey, conducted in 1980, reported 63 per cent incidence among their sample; the CBI in 1981 suggested a figure of 55 per cent.

3 Even the CBI reported only 24 per cent incidence in their 1989 survey on involvement techniques, failing to comment that this figure was significantly half that reported in 1981 (see previous note).

4 Research by Linda Holbeach, reported in *Personnel Management* September 1994.

5 Kathryn Troy, *Change Management: an Overview of Current Initiatives*, Conference Board Europe, Brussels, 1994.

6 See e.g. Williams et al. (1992), Oliver and Hunter (1994), Berggren (1993).

7 See Silver (1987) and Guest (1992a) for general critiques and an account of the failure rate of the excellent paragons; Kotter and Heskett (1992) for a more detailed (and cautious) empirical questioning of aspects of the strong culture thesis.

8 On TQM see e.g. Wilkinson et al. (1992), Institute of Personnel Management (1993), James (1991). On BPR see Grint (1994), Willmott (1995).

9 See e.g. Elger and Smith (1994) on Japanization; Cunningham et al. (1994) on empowerment.

10 See Freeman (1984) and Tylecote (1992) for developed arguments in support of the existence of economic long wave analysis.

11 See e.g. John Gapper, 'An idea whose time has come', *Financial Times* 28 January 1991; Simon Holberton, 'An idea whose time has not only come but will prevail', *Financial Times* 20 March 91; Terry Burke and Frances Moss, 'Right place, right time, right stuff', *Times Higher Education Supplement* 6 April 1990.

12 The debate on macro/micro method is explored, for example, in Alexander et al. (1987), Ritzer (1990).

13 Baddon et al. (1989: especially Chapter 7).

14 'High fees protect us from not being taken seriously by the client', McKinsey manager quoted in Hecht (1995).

15 Quoted from a senior McKinsey consultant in *Forbes* magazine, as reproduced by Hecht (1995).

16 Figures cited in Labour Research Department (1988; 1992); fees are in actual, not constant prices, and so inflate the increase in real terms considerably.

17 *Consultant News*, cited (as 'recent' but without date) by Marquardt and Engel (1993: 60).

18 Figures from Evans (1994) for Andersen and Coopers and Lybrand; Hecht (1995) for McKinsey. See both sources for further information on the nature, operation and attitudes of the largest companies.

19 'Whitehall waste claimed in use of consultancy firms', in the *Financial Times*, 26 April 1994.

20 For a review of the literature on organizational crisis, which has been drawn on here, see Booth (1993). See also Cressey et al. (1985) for an earlier discussion of some of the types of labour-related crises organizations may face.

References

Ackers, P., Marchington, M., Wilkinson, A. and Goodman J. (1992) 'The Use of Cycles? Explaining Employee Involvement', *Industrial Relations Journal*, 23(4): 268–83.

Alexander, J.C., Giesen, B., Münch, R. and Smelser, N.J. (eds) (1987) *The Micro-Macro Link*. Berkeley, CA: University of California Press.

Baddon, L., Hunter, L., Hyman, J., Leopold, J. and Ramsay, H. (1989) *People's Capitalism? A Critical Analysis of Profit-Sharing and Employee Share Ownership*. London: Routledge.

Baddon, L. and Lockyer, C.J. (1983) 'Linwood: Forty Years of Marginalisation and Manipulation'. Mimeo, Department of Industrial Relations, University of Strathclyde.

Barley, S.R. and Kunda, G. (1992) 'Design and Devotion: Surges of Rational and Normative Ideologies of Control in Managerial Discourse', *Administrative Science Quarterly*, 37(3): 363–99.

Bartlett, C.A. (1983) 'MNCs: Get Off the Reorganization Merry-Go-Round', *Harvard Business Review*, 6(2) 138–46.

Berggren, C. (1993) 'Lean Production – the End of History?' *Work Employment and Society*, 7(2): 163–88.

Booth, S.A. (1993) *Crisis Mangement Strategy: Competition and Change in Modern Enterprise*. London: Routledge.

Byrne, J.A. (1986) 'Business Fads: What's In and What's Out', *Business Week*, 20 January: 40–7.

Cressey, P., Eldridge, J. and MacInnes, J. (1985) *Just Managing: Authority and Democracy in Industry*. Milton Keynes: Open University Press.

Cronin, J.E. (1979) *Industrial Conflict in Modern Britain*. London: Croom Helm.

Cunningham, I., Hyman, J. and Baldry, C. (1994) 'Empowerment: the Power to Do What?'. Paper presented to Conference on The Strategic Direction of Human Resource Management: Empowerment, Diversity and Control, Nottingham Business School, Nottingham Trent University, 14–15 December.

Eccles, R.G. and Nohria, N. (1992) *Beyond the Hype: Rediscovering the Essence of Management*. Boston: Harvard University Press.

Elger, T. and Smith, C. (1994) 'Global Japanization? Convergence and Competition in the Organization of the Labour Process', in T. Elger and C. Smith (eds), *Global Japanisation? The Transnational Transformation of the Labour Process*. London: Routledge. pp. 31–59.

Evans, R. (1994) 'The Consultancy Game', *International Management*, June: 20–3.

Ezzamel, M., Lilley, S. and Willmott, H. (1993) 'Be Wary of New Waves', *Management Today*, October.

Financial Times 'Whitehall waste claimed in use of consultancy firms', 26 April 1994.

Freeman, C. (1984) *Long Waves in the World Economy*. London: Pinter.

Gill, J. and Whittle, S. (1992) 'Management by Panacea: Accounting for Transience', *Journal of Management Studies*, 30(2): 281–95.

Grint, K. (1994) 'Reengineering History: Social Resonances and Business Process Reengineering', *Organization*, 1(1): pp. 179–201.

Guest, D. (1992a) 'Right Enough to be Dangerously Wrong: an Analysis of the *In Search of
Excellence* Phenomenon', in G. Salaman (ed.), *Human Resource Strategies*. London: Sage.
pp. 5–19.

Guest, D. (1992b) 'Human Resource Management in the UK', in B. Towers (ed.), *The
Handbook of Human Resource Management*. Oxford: Blackwell.

Hecht, F. (1995) 'The Firm Walks Tall', *Eurobusiness*, February: 30–4.

Hill, S. (1991) 'Why Quality Circles Failed but Total Quality Might Succeed', *British Journal
of Industrial Relations*, 29(4): 541–68.

Huczynski, A.A. (1993a) *Management Gurus: What Makes Them and How to Become One*.
London: Routledge.

Huczynski, A.A. (1993b) 'Explaining the Succession of Management Fads', *International
Journal of Human Resource Management*, 4(2): 443–63.

Hyman, R. (1988) 'Flexible Specialisation: Miracle or Myth?', in R. Hyman and W. Streeck
(eds), *New Technology and Industrial Relations*. Oxford: Blackwell.

Institute for Personnel and Development (1994) 'The Way We Were 1969–1994', *Personnel
Management*, mid December: 23–41.

Institute of Personnel Management (1993) *Quality*. London: IPM.

Jacoby, S.M. (1990) 'Norms and Cycles: the Dynamics of Nonunion Industrial Relations in
the United States, 1897–1987', in K.G. Abraham and R.B. McKersie (eds), *New
Developments in the Labor Market: towards a New Institutional Paradigm*. Cambridge,
MA: MIT Press.

James, G. (1991) 'Quality of Working Life and Total Quality Management'. ACAS Work
Research Unit Occasional Paper no. 50, London.

Kanter, R.M. (1989) *When Giants Learn to Dance*. London: Unwin.

Kotter, J.P. and Heskett, J.L. (1992) *Corporate Culture and Performance*. New York: Free
Press.

Labour Research Department (1988) *Management Consultants: Who They Are and How To
Deal With Them*. London: LRD.

Labour Research Department (1992) *Management Consultants and New Management
Techniques*. London: LRD.

Marchington, M., Goodman, J., Wilkinson, A. and Ackers, P. (1992) *New Developments in
Employee Involvement*. Department of Employment Research Series no. 2. London:
HMSO.

Marchington, M., Goodman, J., Wilkinson, A. and Ackers, P. (1993) 'The Influence of
Managerial Relations on Waves of Employee Involvement', *British Journal of Industrial
Relations*, December: 553–76.

Marglin, S.A. (1976) 'What do Bosses do?', in A. Gorz (ed.), *The Division of Labour*,
Brighton: Harvester Press.

Marquardt, M.J. and Engel, D.W. (1993) *Global Human Resource Development*. New York:
Prentice-Hall.

Oliver, N. and Hunter, G. (1994) 'The Financial Impact of Japanese Production Methods in
UK Companies'. Judge Institute of Management Studies Paper no. 24, Cambridge, July.

Pascale, R.T. (1990) *Managing on the Edge*. London: Penguin.

Peters, T.J.(1993) *Liberation Management*. London: Pan.

Peters, T.J. and Waterman, R,H, (1982) *In Search of Excellence: Lessons from America's
Best-Run Companies*. New York: Harper and Row.

Ramsay, H.E. (1977) 'Cycles of Control: Worker Participation in Sociological and Historical
Perspective', *Sociology*, 11(3): 481–506.

Ramsay, H.E. (1983) 'Evolution or Cycle? Labour–Management Relations in the 1980s', in
C. Crouch and F. Heller (eds), *First International Yearbook on Organisational Democracy*.
London: Wiley.

Ramsay, H.E. (1985) 'What is Participation for? A Critical Evaluation of Labour Process

Analyses of Job Reform', in D. Knights, H. Willmott and D. Collinson (eds), *Job Redesign: Critical Perspectives on the Labour Process*. London: Gower. pp. 52–80.

Ramsay, H.E. (1991) 'Reinventing the Wheel? A Review of the Development and Performance of Employee Involvement', *Human Resource Management Journal*, 1(4): 1–22.

Ramsay, H.E. (1993) 'Recycled Waste? Debating the Analysis of Worker Participation: a Reply to P. Ackers et al.', *Industrial Relations Journal*, 24(1): 76–80.

Ritzer, G. (1990) 'Micro–Macro Linkage in Sociological Theory: Applying a Metatheoretical Tool', in G. Ritzer (ed.), *Frontiers of Social Theory: the New Syntheses*. New York: Columbia University Press.

Silver, J. (1987) 'The Ideology of Excellence: Management and Neo-Conservatism', *Studies in Political Economy*, no. 24: 105–29.

Stern, S. (1994) 'Another Year, Another Theory', *International Management*, May: 42–3.

Tylecote, A. (1992) *The Long Wave in the World Economy: the Current Crisis in Historical Perspective*. London: Routledge.

Watson, T.J. (1994) 'Management "Flavours of the Month": their Role in Managers' Lives', *International Journal of Human Resource Management*, 5(4): 893–909.

Whipp, R. and Smith, C. (1984) 'Managerial Strategy and Capital–Labour Dynamics: Participation in Context'. University of Aston, Work Organisation Centre, Working Papers no. 4.

Wilkinson, A., Marchington, M., Ackers, P. and Goodman, J. (1992) 'Total Quality Management and Employee Involvement', *Human Resource Management Journal*, 2(4): 1–20.

Williams, K., Haslam, C., Williams J. and Cutler, T. (with Adcroft, A. and Johal, S.) (1992) 'Against Lean Production', *Economy and Society*, 21(3) 321–54.

Willmott, H. (1995) 'The Odd Couple? Reengineering Business Processes, Managing Human Resources', *New Technology, Work and Employment*, 10(2).

Womack, J.P., Jones, D.T. and Roos, D. (1990) *The Machine that Changed the World*. New York: Rawson.

Wright, C. (1994) '*Recycling the Past: Job Redesign and New Production Concepts in Australian Industry*'. Paper presented to 8th Conference of Association for Industrial Relations in Australia and New Zealand (AIRAANZ), Coogee, Sydney, 10–12 February.

10

The Axeman Cometh: the Changing Roles and Knowledges of Middle Managers

Harry Scarbrough and Gibson Burrell

And here comes a chopper to chop off your head. Chop, chop, chop.

'Oranges and Lemons', traditional

Given the current dominance of managerialist thinking in the industrialized world, the view of management that we pursue here is certainly unfashionable and possibly mischievous. Our starting point is to analyse management not as a set of functions, nor even as a range of behavioural competencies, but as a social group with a significant yet finite history. Within this group our particular concern is middle management, those who occupy a specific and distinctive class position as a fraction of what current sociological parlance terms the 'service class'; i.e. a class whose orientations, roles and interests sit precariously between the positions of labour and capital (Child 1969; Lash and Urry 1987).

Separating management as a social group from the performance of managerial tasks is no easy matter. Increasingly, recognition attaches to the inculcation of managerial practices in groups without the formal title or status of managers (e.g. Townley 1993). Yet, much more attention still attaches to 'what managers do' than to their historical evolution. Supporters and critics alike define management in relation to the functions they perform, and not as an important, if diffuse, constituency in society.

The absence of a historical perspective is all the more telling because it inhibits our ability to take due account of the societal implications of current trends in organizational and technological forms. These include the downsizing and delayering of organizations (Dopson and Stewart 1990), the impact of IT (Dopson and Stewart 1993), and the institutionalization of managerial practices through forms of surveillance and discipline (Dandeker 1990). The assumption that these trends simply mean a shrinking of the managerial cadres in each setting is to confuse a quantitative phenomenon with its qualitative effects. We wish to argue that these trends have fundamental significance for the future of middle management.

This is not to say that there is a direct mechanical linkage between the shifting distribution of organizational functions and the class position of organizational members. This was precisely the kind of category error made by proponents of the embourgeoisement thesis in the 1960s: the idea that the then 'new' technology so changed job content that working-class employees would progressively assimilate into the middle class (Goldthorpe et al. 1968; Blauner 1964). One may press the same charge against some writers in the labour process literature who took a contrary position on the basis of perceived deskilling effects produced by technological change (see Attewell's 1987 critique of Braverman). Reading off class position from roles at the point of production (Salaman 1981) is like trying to tell the time by taking an analogue watch and dismantling it to see how the wheels and springs move the hands. As Lockwood (1958) pointed out in a pioneering study of white-collar workers, class position involves a complex interaction of labour market forces, social relations at work, and ascribed social status.

For our purposes, the key point to be drawn from such debates is the recognition that social class position and organizational change loosely couple and demand different kinds of evidence. The immediate configuration of skills at the point of production is an unreliable guide to questions of class position and social identity (Knights and Willmott 1990). However, recognizing the loose coupling between one phenomenon and the other simply requires a more complex or holistic analysis. In this chapter, we aim to outline such an analysis by putting the organizational roles of middle management into a wider socio-economic context. First, this involves acknowledging their contribution to the whole circuit of capital (i.e. not simply roles at the point of production). Second, it means viewing changes within that circuit in terms of their implications for middle managers' share of the *totality* of knowledge involved (Armstrong 1988). Relative shifts in skill and knowledge, be they up- or down-skilling, actually tell us little about the *societal* connotations of change.

Development of Management

Our argument begins with a history that is in danger of being buried under the myth-making capacity of the management literature. Historical research suggests that the social origins of management are humble – extremely humble, indeed. Mant (1983) suggests that the term 'management' derives from *maneggiare* in Italian and *ménager* in French. The former implies horse-handling, but clearly referring to the role of the ostler and not the horseman. The French word, meanwhile, denotes the direction and control of domestic services. Again, it is a service position to which the butler or housekeeper is a key approximation. In *Jane Eyre*, for instance, Mrs Fairfax claims to be a 'mere manager' when Jane wrongly assumes she is the owner of the house. As a putative occupational group management signified an association with horse-droppings or chimney soot that besmirched it at the outset. It was 'dirty work' (Ackroyd and Crowdy 1991).

The definitive Victorian view of the manager comes, like so many other archetypes, from Charles Dickens. This is the obsequious figure of Uriah Heep in *David Copperfield*. The implication within the novel, and not lost upon the readership, was that the latent function of managers was to rob the bourgeois of their rightful possessions, including their loved ones and their business. They were oleaginous, untrustworthy creatures, whose services polite society shunned or at best treated with disdain. In the face of this genteel hostility, it is little wonder that management in this period appeared in the eyes of many to be a highly fragmented, low-status group (Pollard 1965; Reed and Anthony 1992).

In Britain at least, management took a long time to overcome the stigma of its social origins. Urry suggests that the legitimacy and status of this group was not completely secure even up to the Second World War:

> Management did not develop in Britain as a relatively autonomous set of interrelated professions, able to force through further widespread educational, technical and organizational reforms . . . the service class in Britain before the Second World War did not possess sufficient organizational and cultural resources to produce a substantial restructuring of British society. (1984: 43)

Clearly, the view of management changed as the service class grew, but the real transformation in the fortunes of management was not the growth of scientific management (important though this was) but the development of nationalized industries and the welfare state under the post-war Labour Government. The process of sanitizing the besmirched image of management then gathered pace in the technocratic 1960s. Probably, it was the 1980s that proved to be the apotheosis of the managerialist ethic: Reaganomics, Thatcherism and the enterprise culture allowed certain kinds of managers to cut a heroic dash by posing as the ultimate wealth creators in societies obsessed with wealth. The yuppie triumphalism of this period provides a striking contrast with even the feigned humility of a Uriah Heep. As Hansen (this volume) notes, it would have been unthinkable for nineteenth century business people to produce the kind of self-aggrandizing autobiographies that now litter airport bookstalls. The Bible says the rich man's chances of a heavenly afterlife are about as likely as a camel passing through the eye of a needle. But nowadays, as Hansen says, 'The eye of the needle has become the arch of triumph.' In contemporary times, marching through this arch came not only the great leaders and entrepreneurs of the 1980s but their massed battalions of middle managers too.

Even with the chastening effects of the 1990s recession, the ideological and political dominance which management achieved in the previous decade seems to linger on – not so much invulnerable as simply unchallenged. However, what our genealogical detour has helped establish is the historical specificity of the managerial classes. We can at least consider the possibility that the 1980s were indeed the high-water mark for whatever coherent class position they have achieved.

Various kinds of evidence provide the ammunition for this argument.

First, there is the failure of management, especially in Britain, to develop a coherent project for professionalizing themselves and thereby cementing their societal position. As Reed (1989) shows, for all the credentialist trimmings of the 1980s upsurge in management education, British management continues to exhibit a socially fragmented, economically polarized and culturally stratified occupational structure.

Then there are the ideological ambiguities surrounding management's role. As we have seen, even in the home of the industrial revolution, management's social position has frequently been insecure and uncertain. Tracing the ideological debates around management shows that a major source of this insecurity has been a periodized series of assaults upon management's *raison d'être*. Where the 1980s exalted managers as entrepreneurs, previous generations have reviled them as *apparatchiks* of various forms of bureaucracy.

We only need to note, for instance, the antecedents of the word 'bureaucracy', coined around the year 1764 by a French nobleman (Warwick 1974) as a term of abuse for the encroachment of paid officials into jobs previously held by noblemen. One telling aristocratic phrase described it as 'the giant power wielded by pygmies'. The developments to and within the French absolutist state and the major infrastructural work such as road-building, carried out under the reign of Louis XIV, all contributed to the threat to the aristocracy. Even at this stage there was a clear recognition that bureaucratic structures with their pyramidal form are a perfect 'breeding ground' for middle managers – pygmies to be derided, abhorred, certainly subject to tight control and dispensed with whenever possible.

Ever since these aristocratic antecedents, periodic assaults upon middle management grew, under the guise of a loathing for bureaucratic power and even the very existence of bureaucrats, questioning the social aspirations of managers (Berle and Means 1932; Burnham 1941). In the more recent period, as Dopson and Stewart (1993) show, commentators have fixed upon technology as the destroyer of middle management jobs and functions. Leavitt and Whistler (1958), Hicks (1964) and Neumann (1978) all argued that new information and production technologies threatened middle management. There were also critiques of the sheer inefficiency produced by large bureaucracies. These ranged from the implicit message of the Aston Studies (Pugh and Hickson 1976) to Schumacher's (1973) assertion that *Small is Beautiful* and Illich's (1971) wider-ranging social critique in *De-Schooling Society*.

Somehow or other middle management survived the technological and bureaucratic onslaught of the 1950s and 1960s. It took someone broadly sympathetic to their circumstances to produce an account that still resonates today. Fletcher (1973) pointed out that the great cause of insecurity to middle management was not new technology *per se* but the danger of being progressively managed out of existence. Their position, he noted, was inherently unsafe:

Unsafe from what? Well, in addition to attrition by cabals there is the constant possibility of being planned out of the present job. The management hierarchy is regularly reorganized. A pendulum swings from central control to regional autonomy. New advisers; liaisons with accounts or finance; development teams; executive development programs are all on the drawing board. Management is always susceptible to rationalization and middle management positions especially . . . A new norm may be decided upon 'on consultants' advice . . . it involves a bit of a shake up, a complete face lift' or 'an organization set for the seventies'. (1973: 138)

Unfulfilled prophecies about middle management redundancy should, of course, make us wary of linear extrapolations based on any single factor. However, recent trends provide powerful evidence that the middle-ranking layers of organizations are being managed out of existence in ways perceptively, if prematurely, indicated by Fletcher. As Deetz (1991: 228) says, some middle managers may have managed themselves out of existence by rationalizing and codifying their own activity: 'They success-fully managed themselves, but as in the original manège, the trained horse needs no trainer.'

Within the Western industrialized world, the last five years has seen a wave of organizational downsizing and delayering. The former refers, of course, to cuts in the number of employees utilized by the organization in carrying out its tasks; the latter to a form of corporate 'liposuction' in which reduction in staff is achieved through the removal of the middle layers of the organizational pyramid. The elision between the two terms has come about obviously because much of the recent wave of downsizing has been in the form of delayering.

Empirical evidence on these trends is never likely to be unequivocal. The discrepant economic cycles of particular business sectors effectively preclude much homogeneity in organizational change. However, data from the USA and Britain give little room to doubt that significant changes are taking place in the composition and character of the middle management group. Some of this is recession related (though unless we believe that growth is the natural state for capitalist economies, one should hardly discount this). Yet, even post-recessionary data confirm the trend. Thus, in the USA, *Business Week* (14 June 1993) claims that despite US economic growth of 2.6 per cent, more than 500,000 clerical and technical staff positions disappeared in the preceding year. This compares with 1 million professional jobs disappearing between 1979 and 1990 (Heenan 1989).

In Britain, where the recession is a more recent memory, one must, from force of circumstances, rely on more impressionistic assessments of current trends. For example, the most recent Institute of Personnel Managers' conference heard claims that nine out of ten large organizations had removed at least one level of management within the last five years. Indeed, the chastened chief executive of IBM in Britain issued a gloomy warning to all aspiring managers, saying that 'secure jobs are a thing of the past.'

The published reasons given by corporate headquarters for these significant reductions in managerial staff are many and various (Cascio 1993), but CEOs in confidence will firmly put the blame on middle managers themselves. No longer are middle management seen as the solution to organizational problems. Instead, the perception of them as the problem grows. They are costly, resistant to change, a block to communication both upwards and downwards. They consistently underperform; they spend their time openly politicking rather than in constructive problem solving. They are reactionary, undertrained and regularly fail to act as entrepreneurs.

Knowledge and Management

Having noted the evidence on trends and senior management perceptions, however, we want to move beyond it. We are aiming not to build a detailed empirical case here for the qualitative changes we describe, so much as to map out a predictive line of enquiry. Nor do we think that job numbers and organizational roles translate directly and mechanically into class positions, for the reasons noted earlier. We certainly do not accept senior management's demonization of this group unquestioningly. Our preferred strategy is to analyse the relationship between organizational roles and class positions in two steps: first, by examining the changing distribution of knowledge in organizations; and second, by mapping the effects of such change onto the social position of middle managers through the Marxian categories of alienation, immiseration, homogenization and polarization (Marx 1957; 1963; 1970).

The first of these steps, though, has to be a cautious one. Knowledge is a slippery and elusive concept, and every discipline has its own secret realization of it. Problems of interpretation haunt every attempt to use the concept effectively, such that even basic typologies that talk about, say, formal versus tacit knowledge (Polanyi 1967) actually can be quite meaningless in certain contexts.

Studies of knowledge in management demonstrate these problems to the full, with heterogeneity and incommensurability being probably the only things they have in common. However, for our specific purposes here, we make a rough and ready distinction between two basic epistemological positions. In one camp, which we term 'content theories' of knowledge, are writers who assert that knowledge has some technical substance, and can be developed, possessed and traded by groups and individuals. Many subscribers to this view reify or objectify knowledge. They define it, for instance, as hierarchically nested (Lyles and Schwenk 1992; Kogut and Zander 1992), and possessing qualities such as fluidity, adhesion and porosity (Badaracco 1991; Cohen and Levinthal 1990).

Against 'content theory', we see arrayed a whole series of studies whose terms, broadly, suggest a 'relational theory' of knowledge. In other words, knowledge needs understanding not as a free-floating entity, and certainly not as an approximation to scientific truth, but primarily in terms of social relations. Thus, we note that knowledge selectively is available to particular groups on the basis of class, gender, etc., implicated in the production and reproduction of social relations, and in the unequal distribution of power. Asking not what *is* knowledge, but what *counts* as knowledge, relational theorists may deny it any substantive content whatsoever: it is all to do with the manipulation of social relations. Thus, Alvesson (1992) claims that organizations lay claim to knowledge rather than possess knowledge itself, and other writers (e.g. Latour 1987) emphasize the rhetorical nature of such knowledge claims. The perceived advantages of 'impression management' over 'merit' (Goffman 1971), and the importance of 'networking' (Kotter 1982) in the micro-politics of managerial roles, give added credence to this view. As Whitley (1988) notes, the fragmented and discursive form of management practice is not amenable to a purely technicist account of its knowledge base.

The problem with these theories is that each denies the other the capacity to provide a completely adequate account of changes in the distribution of knowledge. If we look at studies of technological change, for instance, it is difficult to explain their social implications except in terms of technology-related changes in the kinds of knowledge which different groups possess. The need to acknowledge the relational bases of technology design and the way its effects are mediated immediately qualifies the relevance of content theories of knowledge. Thus, Pettigrew's (1973) analysis of the role of 'technological gatekeeper' shows that the possession of knowledge has important social effects, but only when channelled through a strategic position in the organization.

Rather than privileging one view over another, we propose a binocular view of managerial knowledge – i.e. acknowledging both content and relational dimensions. This makes us sceptical about the many accounts of middle management roles that take a one-sided view. The late 1950s predictions of the eventual but inevitable demise of middle management provides a good example. These accounts, typified by Leavitt and Whistler (1958), focused simply on the effects of computers on the content of managerial knowledge: improved information flows would simply eliminate the need for the 'go-between' role of middle managers. However, in treating information as a neutral commodity, such studies neglected the persistent relational aspects of the middle management job. Organizations continued to need someone 'in the middle' to mediate social relations and to exercise delegated authority, and this greatly conditioned the design and use of computing systems.

Scepticism about late 1950s predictions should not blind one to the radical changes evidenced by 1980s trends in organizational and technological forms. Indeed, these trends imply that middle managers suffered a historic reversal in their fortunes in the last decade. Compare the pattern of events in say the last five years, with the long term secular trends that helped to boost middle managers to their peak position in the 1980s. From the early years of this century, this group engaged in progressively absorbing and objectifying an ever greater share of the practical and technical knowledge of the organization. While Taylorism and Fordism focused on the appropriation of the workforce's practical knowledge, specialisms within management itself were colonizing new areas of expertise with consequent implications for growth and differentiation in the ranks of middle management. Thus, the expansion of the knowledge base controlled by management went hand in hand with expansion in their organizational role and status.

However, current trends in the organizational and technological context for management – confused and inconclusive as they may be (Dopson and Stewart 1990) – suggest that this historic marriage between the needs of capital and the expansion of the service class may be heading for a divorce. No single factor is responsible for this, for the complex formation and distribution of managerial knowledge clearly reflect the interplay of a variety of factors. However, the concerted implications of technological and market change certainly suggest the incipient redefinition of managerial roles.

Taking technology as a case in point, the advent of information technology (IT) has enormous repercussions not only for jobs but also for the distribution of working knowledge in the organization. The spread of information systems produces greater *transparency* in operations, as managers and employees alike experience information as a shared resource rather than the bureaucratic property of a particular group or function. The most obvious effect of this is to produce surveillance effects that stimulate particular kinds of managerial performance (Buchanan and McCalman 1988). However, such systems can also help cause a redefinition of the role itself. Transparency acts to decompose concentrations of knowledge from flows of information. Managers whose roles are primarily information handling are clearly vulnerable. Thus a recent survey of accountancy practices in the UK (Ezzamel et al. 1993) shows how IT is bringing a potentially enormous degree of job loss and restructuring in its wake. A dramatic, but not untypical, illustration comes from a finance department that reduced its staff numbers from one hundred to fewer than twenty by substituting electronic payment methods for the traditional paper invoices and receipts. As Ezzamel et al. (1993: 13) note, 'even accountants appear to be no longer immune to the vagaries of economic recession, structural reorganization and technical innovations'.

At the same time, information systems may encourage organizational restructuring around those groups whose formal or tacit knowledge is least susceptible to routinization or automation. This poses a twofold challenge to the hierarchical principle of control: firstly, through the need to enlist the knowledge of certain rank and file work groups; and secondly, by the generalization and internalization of management through forms of surveillance (Bloomfield 1991; Poster 1990). In both instances, the need for formal managerial control greatly diminishes.

When the effects of IT combine with market-induced organizational change these tendencies seem most extreme. A few examples suffice to make the point. Total quality management is a cluster of techniques that seeks to shift power from the producer to the customer. It involves changes in work organization, and the extensive application of techniques to measure output. Although dismissed in some quarters as simply a means of legitimating increased surveillance of the workforce (Sewell and Wilkinson 1992), this is to neglect its powerful effects on both the kinds of knowledge held by management and on managers' relations with other groups of employees. Significantly, TQM displaces the 'heroic manager' in favour of surveillance systems, workforce empowerment, and the rhetoric (and pressures) of continuous improvement.

A related set of innovations in work organizations comes from the advent of 'lean production' in the auto industry (Womack et al. 1990). Here, the explicit agenda is to do with getting middle management to disgorge production knowledge to better enlist workforce knowledge in the pursuit of 'continuous improvement'. This recruitment of worker know-ledge connects, certainly, with a strategy of cooptation: a union report on the application of lean production techniques in a Canadian plant even suggested that 'the plant designers deliberately established less than optimum operations so that the workers would get involved in the suggestion program' (CAMI 1993).

However, the cooptation of the workforce is part of a production regime that economizes on the deployment of middle managers, and places those who remain under tremendous strain. In a case study of lean production in the Australian car industry, Shadur and Bamber found that

> only a minority of the workforce agreed there was too much pressure or stress in their work, and supervisors were more likely than operators to report excessive pressure in their work. . . . Lean production systems place greater demands on supervisory staff and managers than under mass production since they are responsible for managing a broader range of issues in their unit. . . . There are also more demands on them to maintain the extensive information system for each unit and optimize performance on each item they measure. (1993: 22)

In some contexts, such systems inflict tremendous stresses on a dwindling band of middle managers. Indeed, Calás and Smircich (1993) argue that sometimes the psychic wounds are so great that certain managerial skills are being progressively feminized as a kind of coping strategy. This may be creating increasing opportunities for women in nationally based manager-ial structures, but there is a sting in the tail. Calás and Smircich note that the feminization of these management structures happens to coincide with a parallel globalization of business functions involving the transfer of power away from the national to the global level. It follows that this process of feminization represents not so much the enhancement of women's societal position but a derogation of the middle manager's. Kanter (1977), of course, pointed out that the feminization of an occupa-tion (such as the role of secretary) generally implied its downgrading in the occupational structure.

Our final example of this displacement of middle manager knowledge and roles is the process known as 'business re-engineering'. This explicitly targets middle management in that it aims to sweep away the vertically differentiated, functional structures that are their natural habitats. In their stead, it proposes a series of low-level horizontal work processes that do the same tasks but with significantly fewer layers of management.

Achieving this goal, according to Hammer and Champy (1993), involves the application of ten key principles:

1   a switch from functional departments to process teams
2   a move from simple tasks to multidimensional work
3   a reversal of the power relationship from superordinate to subordinate empowerment
4   a shift from training to education
5   the development of reward systems that drop payment for attendance in favour of payment for value added
6   a bifurcation of the link between reward for current performance and advancement through assessment of ability
7   the overturning of employee focus from concern for the boss to concern for the customer
8   changes in management behaviour from supervisors to coaches
9   the flattening of hierarchies
10 changes to executive behaviour from 'scorekeepers' to leaders.

The aim of these design principles is to polarize the distribution of knowledge and functions between an 'educated' and 'empowered' work-force and a much smaller group of corporate leaders, in whom concentrates managerial power and discretion. Middle managers are no longer the beneficiaries of organizational change, as they were under Fordism (though not necessarily under Henry Ford himself: Sward 1948: 185). Rather, they are its primary victims.

As this and other examples indicate, the restructuring of organizations is more than a question of 'streamlining' or a simple numerical reduction in the ranks of middle management. The 're-engineering' of business processes involves institutionalizing cardinal elements of management activity within a regime of informational controls and quasi-market relationships. In the process, not only do managerial jobs alter but there are irreversible changes in managerial careers. The rigid climbing-frame of bureaucracy and internal labour markets (Edwards 1979) gives way to more 'flexible' forms of organization. In every major boardroom, the sacred cow of the managerial career is being slaughtered (Kanter 1989):

> Nearly a million US managers earning more than $40,000 a year lost their jobs in 1991 and, in fact, each year for the past three years, between 1 and 2 million middle managers were laid off. (Cascio 1993)

The manufacture of fine-sounding euphemisms covers senior management's shame-faced participation in this blood-letting – 'we're giving you ownership of your career', or 'we're freeing up your future' – but neither the empty phrases nor the tell-tale outpouring of self-help 'career management' texts can disguise a nascent change in the stature and knowledge base of the managerial class. The politics of expansion are giving way to a politics of decline.

Implications for Middle Management

The key point about the above examples is that they share a common dedication to the elimination of middle management – not of the shop-floor workforce as would have been the case a couple of decades ago. Moreover, their effect is to change not only knowledge content – bringing workforce knowledge into the loop – but also the social relations that channel the application of that knowledge.

We can conceptualize the motives behind these changes in a number of ways. Technological and market forces are clearly an important part of the equation, but so too is capital's quest to economize on the costly business of fostering trust and commitment within large-scale distended bureaucracies (Armstrong 1991). Suddenly, it seems much easier (and cheaper) to 'flatten' middle management and develop trust-based relations with a small cadre of corporate managers. Meanwhile, a debased version of self-management, based on worker empowerment, technological surveillance and the unforgiving pressures of the market, controls the productive part of the organization.

All of this makes Fletcher's (1973: 147) analysis of 'lumpen-managers' an increasingly persuasive formulation. Following his lead, we will consider the implications of these changes in terms of the proletarianizing tendencies associated with the immiseration, homogenization, polarization and alienation of middle management. This is not to equate middle managers with the proletariat *per se*, but to suggest that our account so far – plus other evidence from the British context – suggests that they may indeed be subject to the *process* of proletarianization.

The analysis of that process comes in Volume 2 of *Capital*, where Marx describes the social trends that eventually reveal the common class position of the proletariat, thereby engendering revolutionary consciousness. One important factor here is the in-built tendency of capitalist societies to condemn large segments of the working class to immiseration or pauperization. The specific question that faces us in applying this concept to middle managers is whether immiseration is a relative term, i.e. comparing worker income to that of the capitalist class. If we view it in this relative way, then there is a real sense in which middle managers are increasingly experiencing immiseration.

The evidence for this is less to do with the salaries paid to middle managers (though more on that later) than with job insecurity and the foreshortening of managerial careers. Rosabeth Kanter's revised edition of *Men and Woman of the Corporation* (1993) presents the breakdown of career structures as the biggest change in corporate life over the last fifteen years. Perhaps characteristically, she argues that individuals need to adapt to these new circumstances by pursuing an ethic of personal employability. Phrasing this in the euphemistic vein we noted earlier, they take 'ownership of their own careers'.

In Volume 3 of *Capital*, Marx continues the analysis in terms of homogenization: that is, the set of processes that come to engender a sense of shared objective conditions amongst the proletariat. Their relative poverty, the physical misery of the reserve army of unemployed, the very significant diminution in wages and the huge rise in unemployment provide a source for a community of interest. The factory system itself further exacerbates this process by providing a single locale for the development of a recognition of mutual interests. Self-consciousness becomes possible, and class consciousness then develops at a pace.

Without making a simplistic equation between the technological changes embodied in the factory system, and the pervasive but diffuse effects of IT, there is certainly plenty of evidence for a trend towards homogenization amongst the salariat. Thus even John Monks, the head of Britain's Trades Union Congress (TUC), is able to see the traditionally ultra-conservative ranks of middle managers as a potential source of membership for British trade unions. He believes that the labour movement 'can connect' with frightened professionals: the argument resonates because 'the ordinary guy [*sic*] with a full-time stable job is now an endangered species' (in Cohen 1993: 17).

As for polarization, this refers to the processes whereby the concentration and identification of shared interest in the proletariat symmetrically oppose centralization and concentration of capital. In general terms, Marx claims that capitalism bases itself upon a structurally rooted antagonism between capital and labour experienced day to day. Polarization is important because it creates political expressions of this antagonism.

When we look at one of the most extensive recent sociological studies of British management, we find a dramatic account of polarization in both interests and consciousness. Scase and Goffee claim that a polarization of management is indeed taking place, with a 'growing divide, between on one hand senior executives, and on the other, middle and junior executives' (1989: 186). Even the *Financial Times* (15 May 1993: 12) feels moved to record the 'frustration' of middle managers over the growing gap between their salaries and the soaring pay increases awarded to top management. It quotes an expert from Hay Management Consultants as saying that: 'His [i.e. the middle manager's] differential over the people below him hasn't increased as fast as the director's differential over him. The gap has widened quite significantly over the past decade.'

This split between middle and senior management levels becomes quite central to current debates: it is here that a polarization effect is most visible. One section of management is facing a process of proletarianization, clearly signalled by the spread of 'harmonized conditions' agreements (*Industrial Relations Review and Report* 1992). The latter bring managers and workers alike under the same regime for pay, timekeeping, and holidays, and give symbolic expression to the new corporate team through the wearing of standard uniforms and the operation of single-status canteens (Wibberley 1993). Significantly, senior managers form a typical absence from these agreements (Yeandle and Clark 1989). Through the development of highly lucrative personal contracts they become locked in ever closer embrace with the capital that employs them.

We would expect these changes in the objective circumstances of middle management – greater insecurity, stress, decline in pay relative to top management – to produce a high level of alienation. This concept, of course, even more than the other Marxian 'process' concepts, has been subject to much debate and criticism. In brief, it is possible to say that under capitalism, human beings become less valued, in direct proportion to the increasing value attached to the world of 'things'. This objectification leads to 'a loss and servitude to the object' (Marx, *Early Writings*, in Bottomore 1964: 121). Alienation, produced by individuals experiencing a loss of control, feeling that their lives are in the grip of some unnamed external power, manifests itself. They become alienated from the product of their labour, from the tasks they perform, and even from themselves and species being.

Again, the empirical world yields some important signs of middle management alienation. For example, John Hunt (1986) argued that the rise of managerial alienation was taking on epidemic proportions. By 1989, Scase and Goffee in *Reluctant Managers* were able to contend that many British managers were:

> less than fully committed to their jobs and . . . have great reservations about giving priority to their work, their careers and indeed their employing organizations. They are more careful, perhaps, than in the past about becoming psychologically immersed in their occupations and seek instead to obtain a balance between their work and private lives. They are reluctant to strive for career success if this can be gained only at the expense of personal and family relations. Consequently, they are less prepared to subordinate their personalities to the requirements of their work and their careers. (1989: 179)

However, there are also counter-tendencies to the emergence of managerial alienation. One of them is simply the in-built expectations of personal improvement produced by the traditional career structure. Galbraith, for example, has said recently that

> people who are shed, if I may use the subtle modern term, expect one day to be shedders again, even if they experience how the great majority of insecure people live . . . If you have been a middle manager in a corporation, I think you will always stick with the ideas, or lack of them, which corporate life cultivates. (quoted in Cohen 1993: 17)

Also, the unpredictable psychological response to insecurity might preclude outright alienation. The so-called 'Stockholm syndrome' – that is, the hostage's identification with his/her captor – suggests that threats of insecurity and restructuring may even increase the middle manager's commitment to senior management. In short, this 'delicious uncertainty' may provide the basis for love as much as hate.

Conclusions

We know that the processes are unclear and we know that politicization of the middle management ranks is unlikely. Although it is a commonplace observation that *déclassé* groups spark revolutions, this is the merest fantasy when applied to middle management. Even a Durkheimian kind of managerial solidarity seems an unlikely response given this group's intense attachment to a personal ethic of possessive individualism.

Yet, even our brief and eclectic sketch of middle management roles suggests that events are conspiring against this group. Their attachment to individualism may prevent an overtly political or class-conscious response to these events, but the foundation of such individualism – the normatively competitive career – is certainly under threat. Changes in organizational form are gradually taking both the content and the relational components of organizational knowledge out of the control of middle management groups. The resultant effects on class structure will get worked out through the apolitical, individualized responses of the newly dispossessed middle management cadres. This means they are unlikely to take the conventional forms we associate with class struggle, and certainly not the revolutionary form which Marx associated with proletarianization.

Such considerations prompt us to look to unlikely and even outlandish possibilities as elements in the future of middle management. Simply as an illustration, we offer the possibility of an emergent 'kleptocracy' – rule by thieves – as an outlet for the displaced economic drive of this group. This might emerge, for instance, through a division between a socially legitimate group enjoying reasonable job security and an insecure, marginalized mass who make the short term and illicit gains of white-collar crime substitute for the rewards of a long term career. From the US robber barons in the late nineteenth century to some of the most senior executives in Italy and Japan, to the nascent 'entrepreneurs' of Eastern Europe, history shows how far economic activity may be lubricated and even controlled by corruption and criminality.

Conjecture of this kind may currently seem implausible for most Western nations. But with the impending threat of radical changes in their jobs and prospects, the middle managers of the future, lumpen and otherwise, will certainly constitute a radically different fraction of the service class from the 1980s grouping. Supposedly, the 1980s pointed Western managers to the warm embrace of an enterprise culture. Perhaps: but many will find that capital's ultimate embrace wrings them, warmly, by the neck.

References

Ackroyd, S. and Crowdy, P. (1991) 'Dirty Work: the Case of the English Slaughtermen', *Personnel Review*.

Alvesson, M. (1992) 'Organizations as Rhetoric: Knowledge-Intensive Firms and the Struggle with Ambiguity', Paper presented at the Conference on Knowledge Workers in Contemporary Society, Lancaster, September.

Armstrong, P. (1988) 'Labour and Monopoly Capital', in R. Hyman and W. Streeck (eds), *New Technology and Industrial Relations*. Oxford: Basil Blackwell.

Armstrong, P. (1991) 'Contradiction and Social Dynamics in the Capitalist Agency Relationship', *Accounting, Organizations and Society*, 16(1): 1–25.

Attewell, P. (1987) 'The Deskilling Controversy', *Work and Occupations*, 14: 323–46.

Badaracco, J. (1991) *The Knowledge Link: How Firms Compete through Strategic Alliances*. Boston: Harvard Business School Press.

Berle, A. and Means, G. (1932) *The Modern Corporation and Private Property*. New York: Macmillan.

Blauner, R. (1964) *Alienation and Freedom*. Chicago: University of Chicago Press.

Bloomfield, B. (1991) 'The Role of Information Systems in the UK National Health Service: Action at a Distance and the Fetish of Calculation', *Social Studies of Science*, 21(4).

Bottomore, T. (1964) *Karl Marx: Early Writings*. New York: Macmillan.

Buchanan, D.A. and McCalman, J. (1988) 'Confidence, Visibility and Pressure: the Effects of Shared Information in Computer Aided Hotel Management', *New Technology, Work and Employment*, 3(1): 38–46.

Burnham, J. (1941) *The Managerial Revolution*. New York: Day.

Calás, M. and Smircich, L. (1993) 'Dangerous Liaison: the Feminine in Management Meets Globalization', *Business Horizons*, April: 73–83.

CAMI (1993) *The CAMI Report: Lean Production in a Unionized Auto Plant*. Ontario: CAW-Canada Research Department.

Cascio, W. (1993) 'Downsizing: What Do We Know? What Have We Learnt?, *The Executive*, VII(1): 95–104.

Child, J. (1969) *British Management Thought*. London: Allen and Unwin.

Cohen, N. (1993) 'Nobody is Safe', *Independent on Sunday*, 24 October: 17.

Cohen, W.M. and Levinthal, D.A. (1990) 'Absorptive Capacity: a New Perspective on Learning and Innovation', *Administrative Science Quarterly*, 35: 128–52.

Dandeker, C. (1990) *Surveillance, Power and Modernity*. Cambridge: Polity.

Deetz, S.A. (1991) *Democracy in an Age of Corporate Colonization*. New York: State University of New York Press.

Dopson, S. and Stewart, R. (1990) 'What's Really Happening to Middle Management?', *British Journal of Management*, 1: 3–16.

Dopson, S. and Stewart, R. (1993) 'Information Technology, Organizational Restructuring and the Future of Middle Management', *New Technology, Work and Employment*, 8(1): 11–20.

Edwards, R. (1979) *Contested Terrain*. London: Heinemann.

Ezzamel, M., Lilley, S. and Willmott, H. (1993) 'Accounting for Management and Managing Accounting: Reflections on Recent Changes in the UK'. Paper presented at Staff Seminar, Warwick Business School, 17 November.

Fletcher, C. (1973) 'The End of Management', in J. Child (ed.), *Man and Organization*. London: Allen and Unwin.

Goffman, E. (1971) *The Presentation of Self in Everyday Life*. Harmondsworth: Pelican.

Goldthorpe, J., Lockwood, D., Bechhofer, F. and Platt, J. (1968) *The Affluent Worker in the Class Structure*. Cambridge: Cambridge University Press.

Hammer, M.E. and Champy, J. (1993) *Re-Engineering the Corporation*. London; Nicholas Brealey.

Heenan, D.A. (1989) 'The Downside of Downsizing', *Journal of Business Strategy*, 18–23.

Hicks, R.L. (1964) 'Developing the Top Management Group in a Total Systems Organization', *Personnel Journal*, 50: 675–82.

Hunt, J. (1986) *Managing People at Work* (2nd edn). London: McGraw-Hill.

Illich, I. (1971) *De-Schooling Society*. Harmondsworth: Penguin.

Industrial Relations Review and Report (1992) 'Report on Thames Water', 520.

Kanter, R.M. (1977) *Men and Women of the Corporation*. New York: Basic Books.

Kanter, R.M. (1989) *When Giants Learn to Dance: Mastering the Challenge of Strategy, Management and Careers in the 1990's*. New York: Simon and Schuster.

Kanter, R.M. (1993) *Men and Women of the Corporation*. (2nd edn). London: Harper Collins.

Knights, D. and Willmott, H. (eds) (1990) *Labour Process Theory*. Basingstoke: Macmillan.

Kogut, B. and Zander, U. (1992) 'Knowledge of the Firm, Combinative Capabilities and the Replication of Technology', *Organization Science*, (3)3: 383–97.

Kotter, J. (1982) *The General Manager*. New York: Free Press.

Lash, S. and Urry, J. (1987) *The End of Organised Capitalism*. Cambridge: Polity Press.

Latour, B. (1987) *Science in Action*. Milton Keynes: Open University Press.

Leavitt, H. and Whistler, L. (1958) 'Management in the 1980's', in H. Leavitt and L.R. Pondy (eds), *Readings in Managerial Psychology 1964*. Chicago: University of Chicago Press. pp. 578–92.

Lockwood, D. (1958) *The Blackcoated Worker*. London: Allen and Unwin.

Lyles, M.A. and Schwenk, C.R. (1992) 'Top Management, Strategy and Organizational Knowledge Structures', *Journal of Management Studies*, 29(2): 155–74.

Mant, A.D. (1983) *Leaders We Deserve*. Oxford: Martin Robertson.

Marx, K. (1957) *Capital*, vol. 2. Moscow.

Marx, K. (1963) *Capital*, vol. 3. Moscow.

Marx, K. (1970) *Capital*, vol. 1. London.

Meyer, J.W. and Rowan, B. (1977) 'Institutionalized Organizations: Formal Structure as Myth and Ceremony', *American Journal of Sociology*, 83: 34–63.

Neumann, P. (1978) 'What Speed of Communication is doing to Span of Control', *Administrative Management*, 39: 30–1.

Pettigrew, A.M. (1973) *The Politics of Organisational Decision Making*. London: Tavistock.

Polanyi, M. (1967) *The Tacit Dimension*. New York: Doubleday Anchor.

Pollard, S. (1965) *The Genesis of Modern Management*. Harmondsworth: Penguin.

Poster, M. (1990) *The Mode of Information: Post-Structuralism and Social Context*. Cambridge: Polity Press.

Pugh, D. and Hickson, D. (1976) *Organizational Structure in its Context: the Aston Programme I*. London: Saxon House.

Reed, M. (1989) *The Sociology of Management*. London: Harvester.

Reed, M. and Anthony P. (1992) 'Professionalizing Management and Managing Professionalization: British Management in the 1980's', *Journal of Management Studies*, 29(5): 591–613.

Salaman, G. (1981) *Class and the Corporation*. London: Fontana.

Scase, R. and Goffee, R. (1989) *Reluctant Managers*. London: Unwin Hyman.

Schumacher, E.F. (1973) *Small is Beautiful*. London: Blond and Briggs.

Sewell, G. and Wilkinson, B. (1992) 'Empowerment or Emasculation: Shopfloor Surveillance in a Total Quality Organization', in P. Blyton and P. Turnbull (eds), *Reassessing Human Resource Management*. London: Sage pp. 97–115.

Shadur, M.A. and Bamber, G. (1993) 'Towards Lean Production? The Transferability of Japanese Management Strategies to Australia'. Paper presented at the 11th EGOS Colloquium, Paris.

Sward, K. (1948) *The Legend of Henry Ford*. New York: Russell and Russell·.

Townley, B. (1993) 'Performance Appraisal and the Emergence of Management'. *Journal of Management Studies*, 39(2): 221–38.

Urry, J. (1984) 'Scientific Management and the Service Class'. Lancaster Regionalism Group, Working Paper no. 12, Lancaster University.

Warwick, D. (1974) *Bureaucracy*. London: Longman.

Whitley, R. (1988) 'Social Science and Social Engineering'. Working Paper no. 171, Manchester Business School.

Wibberley, M. (1993) 'Does Lean Necessarily Equal Mean?', *Personnel Management*, July: 32–5.

Womack, J., Jones, D.T. and Roos, D. (1990) *The Machine that Changed the World*. Oxford: Maxwell Macmillan.

Yeandle, D. and Clark, J. (1989) 'Personnel Strategy for an Automated Plant', *Personnel Management*, June: 51–5.

11

Management Knowledge for the Future: Innovation, Embryos and New Paradigms

Stewart R. Clegg, Mary Barrett, Thomas Clarke, Larry Dwyer, John Gray, Sharon Kemp and Jane Marceau

Management knowledge is irredeemably political. It is becoming more so as contemporary industry trends require employees to be more reflexive as producers (and, one might add, as consumers). Shorter product runs and micro-markets mean that in emergent and postmodern[1] industries

> employees must make decisions more often on the best processes suited for new products. Reflexive in the sense that much work must go into the design of new products; these are typically long-cycle job-tasks entailing a whole series of judgements and decisions between alternatives in regard to product quality and process optimality. It is reflexive in regard to individualization. Employees must take more individual responsibility with the 'slimming' of the firm's management structures. (Lash and Urry 1994: 122)

It is not only these industry trends in the heartlands of 'Western' firms that indicate increased pressure and political need for change. There is also the realization that the business recipes of successful firms in some of the East Asian 'newly industrialized countries' differ, politically, from predominant Western models (Clegg 1990; Clegg et al. 1986). Moreover, global changes have an impact not only on established industries but also on those 'embryonic industries' presently emergent and yet to be established (see Appendix).

The novelty of embryonic industry lies in the application of distinctive practices to production, service or problem resolution in ways that are discontinuous with existing technologies, values and knowledge. The root metaphor is that of an 'embryo'. If there is not something that is new and discontinuous then there would be no new conception, nothing in embryo. Thus, embryonic industry is new and emerging. Without it a country will have diminished 'national' tomorrows of economic consequence, no bright new dawns, no expanded opportunities for employment and wealth generation. Increasingly, management theorists argue that the creation of tomorrow's industries means renouncing yesterday's management by imperative in favour of more reflexive management, thus emphasizing discontinuities already evident.

At the core is innovation in products and processes. Moreover, innovation is also organizational and managerial. Not only this: culture can play a central role in innovation that derives not only from technological discontinuity but also from cultural roots. Effective innovation harnesses innovation in products and processes to social systems that can manage, organize and deliver them to markets effectively (Eriksson 1990). Embryonic industry is important because it contributes to employment, provides spillover benefits to industries, opens new markets, is a major source of 'emerging exporters' and, in general, creates wealth.

Embryonic Industry and Innovation

The case of AMRAD is an exemplar of the wealth creation and export opportunities that successful management of an embryonic industry can provide. In Australia, Melbourne-based AMRAD is an unusual company in that, as well as running a successful drug distribution business that turns over Aus$45 million a year, it acts as a commercialization agency for ten medical research institutes spread around Australia. External agencies conduct the research. AMRAD emerged out of public policy initiatives in Victoria in the late 1980s. AMRAD pays participating institutes to research new drugs to the commercialization stage. Once it has a finished product on the market it also pays a royalty stream to the creator. Its product lines include an agent to speed up the production of blood clotting cells, a vaccine against the rotavirus that causes life-threatening diarrhoea in babies, a new treatment for glaucoma and a drug to assist the treatment of bladder cancer.

Until the late 1980s Australia had a fairly insubstantial pharmaceutical industry except in over-the-counter drugs, owing to the tremendous investment requirement in capital and equipment and because so much of the entrepreneurial and business skills needed for success in the world pharmaceutical market remained overseas. AMRAD, as a commercialization agency, accelerated the national 'catch-up' process. The wealth creation opportunities are considerable. In 1995 AMRAD was involved in an Aus$200 million listing on the market. Several of the nation's largest financial organizations as well as overseas institutional investors and a major Japanese drug company, Chugai Pharmaceuticals, register in the shareholdings.

AMRAD demonstrates a number of key points that are widely applicable in the development of national embryonic industries. First, there is the important role that public policies played in its development. Second, there is the spectacular growth potential realized in a successful embryonic industry. Third, there is the example of a national embryonic industry being created where previously the niche had been colonized principally by overseas firms. Fourth, the relationship between market intelligence and innovation is central to the emergence of a successful embryonic industry. Markets are as important as innovation and innovation is not just technological. New markets open not only because of novel technologies;

shifts in values and culture also are potent sources of innovation. It is not only technological innovation that creates markets for embryonic industry. Cultural innovation is important as well. Another case study, this time drawn from Brazil, can demonstrate how and why cultural innovation, and renovation, may be vital for local economic development.

The Rhythm of the Saints: the Importance of Cultural Diversity for Embryonic Industry[2]

The Rhythm of the Saints was the title of a best-selling record released by Paul Simon in 1990. The opening track introduced something new to many ears: the sounds of Olodum, recorded in Pelhourino Square, Salvador, Bahia, in Brazil. A martial, insistent, hypnotically rhythmic beat, the sound of a troupe of drums, percussive and shuffling, behind a typical Paul Simon lyric, 'The Obvious Child'. The name of the troupe of drummers was Grupo Olodum.

Olodum has become inseparable from Pelhourino since its founding on 25 April 1979. Olodum means 'the God of Gods' or 'the Supreme God' in Yorubá, the West African language. Although music fans may know Olodum as a band, the band's members are much more than that. They are a social and a cultural movement. Inspired by the profound impact of Bob Marley on black consciousness they began as a movement of cultural resistance, a movement of the outcast, the dispossessed and the despised, drawn from the ranks of the *droguistas* and *prostitutas* who congregated in Pelhourino, the then decaying heart of Salvador, Bahia. While the voice was inspired in part by the reggae music of Marley, and the Bahiano traditions of *tropicalismo*, to be found in Caetano Veloso, Gilberto Gil, Gal Costa and Maria Bethânia, to name only the most famous Bahian artists, it also drew nourishment from the surrounding culture of syncretic religion, the blend of African animism and Catholic rite that is institutionalized as the church in Bahia.

Samba is the music of the people of Brazil, brought from Africa as slaves to work the sugar plantations and the latifundia economy of imperial Portugal in the New World. Forced to adopt the religion of their oppressors, the people infused it with a parallel system of beliefs, deities, and saints, in the Macumba, which preserved and recreated the animism of traditional belief systems in Africa. Olodum built on this heritage, taking it further to create an imagined community (Anderson 1983) through its imagery of Africa, especially in the re-creation of the Ashanti rhythms of Ghanaian music. Moreover, it had a particular liminal space in which to develop – the traditions of Bahiano *carnaval*.

Carnival has common characteristics wherever we encounter it: theatricality; being, however briefly, what ordinarily you are not; a zone and a space in which one can try out various masks, sometimes literally, sometimes more metaphorically as identities which define sensibility. Traditionally, carnival reversed social orders and sanctioned transgression, a space of release prior to Lent, a space of pleasure prior to a period of denial.

In Bahia, since about 1950, carnival has been synonymous with the *trios elétricos*, which are now a spectacular procession of articulated trucks, each with musicians and dancers on top of a revolving platform, itself built over a massive bank of speakers flanking each side of the truck. The amplification is loud, the music pulsating, the costumes colourful and the dancing marvellous. This display has evolved from a simple old 1929 Mustang, with a loudspeaker transmitting the music of Dodô and Osmar, musicians from Recife, and today the *trios* are predominantly the voice of the *afro-blocos*, the black Bahiano version of the *escolas de samba*. The *blocos* are the more or less formally organized music, dance and supporter troupes that parade in carnival. Historically the *afro-blocos* started with the Filhos de Ghandy, an organization of black dockworkers and fishermen that first imagined, and thus created, a space in the Latin carnival in which black people could parade with dignity and without fear. There are exceptions – some *trios* are more commercial and often somewhat paler in complexion – but in the music of the *trios*, and especially in Olodum, is to be found the heart of Bahiano *carnaval*.

Through the cultural innovations associated with *carnaval*, Salvador became revalorized from a space that was declining and dangerous to one that was considerably entrepreneurial. Salvador provides an object lesson in how cultural innovation can seed and produce embryonic industry, even in the least likely circumstances. Moreover, it stands as a case of an authentic and glamorous postmodernism emerging from a space previously bleak and borderline, a place of darkness and dangerous desires.

Salvador was founded in 1549 by Tomé de Souza, first Governor-General of Brazil, on a hill overlooking the Bay of Bahia, in a strong defensive position. At the centre of the settlement was a plaza, known since 1807 as Pelhourino, named thus when the authorities established there the pillory at which slaves were whipped. The old historical district of Salvador takes its name, Pelhourino, from that instrument of torture once located in its heart. In times past, at the dawn of the eighteenth century, Pelhourino housed the elite and the aristocracy of Brazilian society. They lived in large mansions and town houses, built from fortunes amassed from the profits of the *Recôncavo* sugar plantations, the expropriation of slave labour. In and amongst their homes were many beautiful churches, ornate in the Portuguese way, testament to the economic surplus extractable from slaves, sugar and surveillance reinforced by the whip.

By the nineteenth century sugar was not the staple element of the Brazilian economy that it had been. New colonists elsewhere in the Caribbean had realized the profitable combination of black bodies, green fields and white expropriation, and the profits accruing to the prime movers lessened greatly. By the end of the nineteenth century the old elite were down at heel. New bourgeoisie took their place: businessmen and bankers – capitalists – who, influenced by the prevailing positive philosophies of progress, sought a space outside the unhealthy, crowded and unsewered historic city. Slowly Pelhourino changed. No longer the social magnet of this city, its population shifted as the wealthy set up homes elsewhere. Not all abandoned Pelhourino but seepage produced a net outflow.

The 1930s saw the complexion of the district rapidly change. Many Syrian, Lebanese and Italian migrants moved there. In 1932 the police moved the prostitution district into Maciel, in Pelhourino. The area declined rapidly into a largely ungovernable space of drug addicts and prostitutes in which few 'respectable' people ventured easily at night, in which many people lived illicit lives, the old town houses being subject to multiple occupancy, often by squatters, who practised lifestyles far removed from those of the rich and famous who had once lived there. Fires, started by unsafe and illegal tapping into the electricity supply, decay, and dereliction, threatened to wipe out the legacy that imperial settlement had bequeathed to the world in Salvador – the finest collection of Portuguese baroque colonial architecture in the Americas. By 1991, the area was completely derelict, with over thirty buildings a year collapsing, despite it having been placed on the World Heritage Registry of UNESCO in 1984, after an initial report on the district in the 1960s.

By 1994 the picture had been reversed totally. Today the whole district has been sewered, repaired, refurbished, and repainted in the vibrant pinks, blues and yellows of the colonial stucco that fronted the buildings. The initiative was taken by the state government in 1991 to commit the funds necessary to save Pelhourino before it was too late. Why, in 1991, after the need had been evident for many years, did the project start? Many explanations have been advanced: that the State Governor, newly embarked on a third term, had intimations of mortality and wanted to have done one really big good thing while he still had opportunity to do so, is a popular explanation in governmental periodicals. One contributory factor, however, as Caetano Veloso (1994: 83) acknowledges, was undoubtedly the organizational basis provided by the cultural resistance that Olodum, and other *blocos* like them, generated.

Pelhourino, as its social mobility went inexorably downward, had become the authentic heart of darkness in Bahia. From an eighteenth century slave market, through a nineteenth century pillory, to the twentieth century revival, it had always had an Afro-Brazilian connection. In Bahia it is impossible not to have this. But the recent revival would have been almost unimaginable without the efforts of the cultural movements like Olodum to positively valorize the cultures of colour in Bahia through (re)imagining Africa in Brazil.

The headquarters of Olodum, Casa de Olodum, was formed there in 1985, and the social movement that they represent, as well as the thousands who form their *bloco* at *carnaval*, are what made revitalization possible. Because of the resistance orchestrated by the *blocos*, the Filhos de Ghandy, Olodum and all the others, there was a cultural capital waiting to revalorize the space. They provided a hermeneutic reflexivity, one that inscribed cultural innovation, meaning-making and resistance through the creativity of *carnaval*, that gave Pelhourino its 'postmodern' form, as a visual form of 'de-differentiation':

> Postmodernity involves de-differentiation. There is a breakdown of the distinctiveness of each sphere and of the criteria which legislate within each vertical dimension. There is implosion as a result of the pervasive effects of the media and the aestheticization of everyday life. Cultural spheres are much less auratic. There is a shift from contemplation to consumption, from 'high culture' to 'high street'. Some of the differences between the cultural object and the audience dissolve as legislation is replaced by interpretation. And finally postmodernity problematizes the relationship between representations and reality. Since what we increasingly consume are signs or images, so that is no simple 'reality' separate from such modes of representation. What is consumed in tourism are visual signs and sometimes simulacra; and this is what is consumed when we are supposedly not acting as tourists at all. (Lash and Urry 1994: 272)

We might say that postmodernity represents the carnivalization of everyday life. In Pelhourino, *carnaval* has escaped its liminal space, seeped out into the streets of everyday life, and transformed a baroque masterpiece into a postmodern arena. The buildings may be the re-creation of premodernity but the cultural activities and spaces that they house are the context that valorizes Pelhourino. The physical context is also a symbolic and semiotic context. The place that is Pelhourino is marketing less the image of a dead colonial past and more a lively Afro-Brazilian present and presence. Its creation as such can be said to begin from the 1930s, with the picaresque novels of Jorge Armado. However, it is through the popular music of the more recent past that the contemporary inhabitants of Pelhourino found their identity.

It should be understood that this identity, one here labelled postmodern, was never consciously contrived as such from the outset. Instead, it was a form of resistance to the rationalizing disciplines of modernity, that marginalized certain spaces and the people who occupied them as premodern, as almost anti-modern. In the case of Bahia as a whole, its blackness, its Africanness, marked it out as different from the southern industrial cities, notably São Paulo. Pelhourino, special home of those excluded or expelled from civil society, was clearly the most marginal and least colonized zone, a wild space where the rhythms that disciplined every day of modernity barely registered. Pelhourino's rhythms were resistant. While they were resistant to the labels attached to the marginalized space occupied, their resistance was orchestrated not just against discipline but through discipline – the discipline of the drum school.

The identity of Pelhourino is, above all, symptomatic of racial resistance creating a centre of consumption grown from black consciousness. Olodum's project began in April 1979, to restore dignity to those outcasts who, from the 1930s, had moved into Pelhourino; dignity built through collectivist organization (Fischer et al. 1992). Here, collectively orchestrated, the experience of participation provided a crucible for cultural revivification through an imaginary of Africa, signified in part through colour. In Pelhourino, Olodum's imaginative use of symbols expresses its individuality most strongly in the colours of green, red, yellow, black and white. Each colour has a symbolic significance: green represents the rainforests of Africa; the deep red is symbolic of the blood of the people, shed in so many centuries of suffering from the slavery days; golden yellow represents prosperity; black is for the colour and the pride of the people; while white is symbolic of world peace. Together, these colours are symbolic of the African diaspora, 'the movement of Jah people', as Bob Marley (1977) once put it. The vision that Olodum developed latched on to the dereliction of what had been the architectural heritage of the Americas. The *blocos'* aesthetic interest in projecting a positive image of Africa, and of negritude, for and to the dispossessed, created a counter-hegemonic project that not only became hegemonic in its own space, but also became so as a space for a cultural entrepreneurship that *The Rhythm of the Saints* broadcast globally.

The local project of cultural hegemony, plus the resources that the state government brought to the restoration of Pelhourino, produced a conjuncture that mirrors almost exactly that which Lash and Urry (1994: 216–17) propose as the scenario of a successful postmodern, consumption and tourist-based place-image. Born from resistance, matured through a type of collectivist organization, and articulated in accord with other, more official, projects, the relation of Olodum and Pelhourino is a perfect example of an embryonic industry forged from cultural innovation. Today, Salvador, the city in which Pelhourino exists, is the second most visited tourist spot in Brazil (Lamb 1994: 42). Just four years previously it was only the eighth most visited. Today, many bars, restaurants, museums, arts and crafts shops, workshops, cultural troupes and schools occupy space that previously was virtually ungovernable, non-taxable and unliveable. Few spaces can combine the elements for marketing place-image as successfully as Pelhourino, but, it is worth recalling, just four years previously it existed as such a place-image hardly at all. It appeared, to all intents and purposes, an ungovernable space, peopled by an underclass.

Readers may accede that culture can seed embryonic industry in what may seem an exotic Afro-Brazilian example. Yet, crucial to the example is not the exoticness of the culture signified – after all, it is hardly exotic to the people concerned – but the sense of identity that cultural symbols provide. In Brazil, the salience of Africa for the people of Bahia is unquestionable. Forced migration, expropriation, and exploitation through slavery made it so, even many generations after the end of slavery.

Building Cultural Competences

A focus on innovation for embryonic industry can be cultural just as much as technological. Cultural competences can generate innovation. Cultural competency refers to the ability to be able to harness and use culturally diverse myths, symbols, rituals, norms and ideational systems creatively to add value to an organization's activities. Culture always derives from lived experience; the more diverse that experience, the more diverse the cultures. Hence, we hypothesize that in postmodern societies it is not simply the pecularities of a cultural project coalescing with a place-image that can reap embryonic industry, as in Bahia. Diversity, in itself, can drive innovation. A shift in focus back to Australia helps to make this clear.

Brazil had African slavery as well as European migration contributing to its demographic mix. Australia never shipped slaves from Africa, but began by shipping convicts from Britain, and then surplus population from the British Isles and Eire, who, by the end of the nineteenth century, were free to participate in what, because of wealth generated from sheep, gold and wheat, had become the best-paid labour market on earth (Connell and Irving 1979).

High wages had their price. In Australia the cost included exclusionary policies on the part of labour designed to keep the supply of workers short and their price high in a country largely peopled by migrants and early generation settlers. For many years a so-called 'white Australia' policy effectively excluded Asian migration, and it was only after the Second World War that migration began to be welcomed from a wider array of countries than Britain and those in Northern Europe. Australia is now the most multicultural and least officially hegemonic culture on earth, partly as a result of the development of 'multiculturalism' as an ideology that articulates the lived experience of the many ethnic groups that comprise the country today.[3]

Some would argue that cultural memories from that time underly the Australian psyche (see Bronowski 1992) and that, whilst Australia has now earned a reputation of good neighbour and trader in the Asia Pacific region, continuous attention to this background is necessary. Bronowski (1992) interestingly traces the symbols which Australians historically have used to portray Asia and convincingly argues that Australia's trade myopia (when it came to Asia) was a consequence of its cultural myopia, one born originally from a tradition of defensive 'labourism' concerned, above all, to minimize competition in a labour market that shortages made more favourable to suppliers, rather than buyers, of labour. The very serious efforts that Australia's contemporary multicultural policy makes to promote cultural diversity, and the debate it creates, are signs of Australia's current bona fides and the corrective spectacles which it now wears to remedy the historical condition. In a country like Australia today, one where diversity flourishes, this diversity of cultures offers major sources of value for enterprises.

First, we can say that it does so by virtue of the introduction of cultural novelty. Socially, innovation comes from cultural diversity just as it comes from a diverse gene pool biologically. The food industry complex is the most evident case in point. The emergence of a 'Mediterrasian' cuisine that is distinctively Australian as a source of culinary excellence has only been possible because of the culturally diverse ethnic traditions represented in the country. Innovative chefs can draw on the diverse traditions that their skills and their biographies have exposed them to. From the cultural overlays come innovations. Shifts in values that derive from culture create new market opportunities. It is market intelligence that identifies these as opportunities. Innovators respond to these opportunities and, if successful, seed an embryonic industry. They transfer their knowledge and practice into other markets (Micronesia and Thailand are two that spring to mind in this area of endeavour).

A second major source of value for industry comes from the diversity of the personnel who comprise it. In selling overseas, whatever the product, whether traditional or innovative, national enterprises in a country such as Australia have a remarkable opportunity to do good business through the serendipity of multiculturalism. Australians who are also competent speakers of a customer's language, because they already know the language as their community language, have a head start in doing good business in that culture. This is because they already have much of the tacit knowledge and implicit learning that those who are alien can acquire only slowly and painfully. In general, a great deal of learning occurs through making mistakes. In business this can be costly. Multiculturalism presents the possibility of much lower-cost learning. However, diversity requires good management if it is to generate innovation.

There is a third important attribute of culture in relation to embryonic industries. Recent studies assess and compare cultural attitudes towards technology. Such attitudes mediate the effective use to which technological innovation may be put (Gattiker and Willoughby 1993; Gattiker and Nelligan 1988; Early and Stubblebine 1989). Evidence suggests that countries with a positive governmental and public policy culture with regard to education for technology, such as Germany (Littek and Heisig 1991), have better prospects for the development of embryonic industry.

The role for public policy is not reserved merely for technological innovation: the case study of Pelhourino makes this clear. Within Australia there is another example. The recent policy of the Australian Government in launching the 'Creative Nation' initiative is an indication of public policy spending on culture that couples public support of cultural activities with investment in state-of-the-art CD-ROM technologies for the production and dissemination of cultural production. Increasingly it seems that the division between 'culture' and 'technology' as sources of innovation will blur: it is likely they will blur furthest and fastest in those democracies whose public policies support open communication rather than distort it in the name of the ruling party, ideology, families, ethnicity or whatever. Here, Australia has a considerable regional advantage, compared to other of our northern neighbours.

That Australia is now a country of great cultural diversity is axiomatic. Goldstone (1987) has suggested that situations characterized by cultural diversity and ferment are those that most readily foster innovation.

Enforcement of a state of orthodoxy, the preservation of tradition as the yardstick of action, the veneration and conservation of the past, these promote nothing so much as intolerance, hostility and resistance to innovation. Pluralism encourages innovation organizationally to the extent that its diversity is competitive (Perry and Sandholtz 1988).

In the appropriate conditions, Gattiker and Willoughby observe,

> If a firm or region can develop technological competence and manage the multicultural workforce successfully, and thereby improve its competitive advantage in global markets, it will ultimately succeed in securing more resources and wealth. (1993: 474)

While this view is correct, it underestimates the role that culture can play. While good management of the multicultural workforce is vital, there is more to culture than merely its proliferation across the diversity of employees. There is also the question of cultural identity of customers and consumers in the marketplace. In all 'postmodern' societies, by definition, these identities will be fragmented, disparate and heterodox.

Considering identity and 'culture' leads us to break ranks with the predominant wisdom. Since at least Peters and Waterman (1982), when management theorists and practitioners began to emphasize the importance of 'culture', they have done so in terms that euologize the importance of a 'strong culture'. It has become almost axiomatic to discuss the necessity of having a unitary culture for organizations that are to achieve excellence. Rather than contribute further to a discussion of culture that mistakes strong symbols and rituals for signs of unitary culture, rather than recognizing them as mechanisms designed to try and create one where it is usually absent, we believe cultural diversity should be seen as a strength rather than a weakness.

Multiculturalism, the widespread use of community languages and the vitality offered by ethnic communities that are not being forced into a melting pot are all major advantages. Australian management education can build upon these to gain competitive advantage in the markets that our community languages and cultures represent. There needs to be a conscious realization and development of ethnic diversity as a strategic resource for the management of embryonic industries that seek to build an export base. It may also be recommended that the teaching of management and the teaching of what are usually considered to be 'arts' subjects in tertiary institutions need to be brought into a more systematic and symbiotic relationship.[4] It is not only the integration of cultural and language elements with the curriculum of management that is important. One of the fastest-growing areas in the United States Academy of Management's portfolio is 'the management of diversity'. A great deal of management is culturally implicit behaviour, as feminist critiques of the masculinist bias of management have identified. Yet it is not only gender cultures that are at work in organizations. There are also cultures of ethnicity that require surfacing and managing. The development of the management of diversity is a necessity for the management curriculum, particularly for embryonic industry. This is because there is a central role for cultural entrepreneurialism to play in developing innovation. Yet, if it is to be not only in the area of ethnic businesses that these innovations occur, then other organizations have to develop capabilities that allow them to add the value that cultural diversity makes implicitly available, rather than to resist it in the name of a strong and hegemonic culture. Of course, not all competences are cultural.

Technological Competences

For any organization to survive it must have some distinctive competence (Selznick 1957), those things that it does especially well when compared with its competitors in a similar environment. The emphasis on cultural innovation is not usual. Typically, the literature of innovation concentrates on questions of technological innovation and emphasizes radical transformations of product technology. Technological competence may be defined, following Gattiker and Willoughby (1993: 463), as the ability to receive and use information for solving both technology and economically related problems and creating opportunities in which appropriate decisions may be made. Three aspects define this technological competence. The first aspect is the cluster of 'learning-related' aspects. The second aspect also concerns a cultural dimension, the cultural embeddedness of competence in organizations and countries by individuals and groups. The third aspect refers to the degree of scarcity of the allocation of the competence in a particular locale (Willoughby 1990; 1992; Gattiker and Willoughby 1993).

The concern with innovation does not necessarily relate to the management of embryonic industry, although the Pelhourino case raises management issues. Olodum, in common with the other *afro-blocos*, is very largely self-managed, a collectivist organization.[5] Do the characteristics of what Rothschild-Whitt (1979) named 'collectivist organizations' foreshadow the management of embryonic industries more generally? The contemporary discussion of collectivist organizations, like the ancient god Janus, is two-faced. One face looks back while the other looks forward. Half looking back to an older tradition of socialism, with a stress on workers' control, on cooperatives, on industrial and economic democracy, and half looking forward to a world of lean organization, *kanban*, *kaizen*, empowerment and flat organizations, elements of the collectivist tradition seem as much at home in the visions of a Tom Peters (1992) as in the values of the 1960s hippies that Joyce Rothschild and Alan Whitt (1986) researched, in 'alternative' organizations. This Janus-like quality is reflected in an emergent 'new paradigm' of management which suggests that while the 1960s expression of the idealism of 'collectivist culture' may be dead the ideas that were generated then have a continuing, and a commercial, relevance today. However, their complexion is considerably different.

New Paradigms of Management

In many institutions of higher education, it has become customary for management courses to include a lecture or two on 'management issues of the future'. Usually late in the course, discussion will sometimes centre on organization-specific developments such as continuing technological change or flatter organizational structures. Often it will include discussion of the increasingly 'global' nature of business enterprises. Other times it centres on the 'greening' of business, or the impact of social trends on management and organizations, such as the increasing education levels of the workforce and employees' consequent awareness of their rights at work, or other demographic trends in workforce gender and age composition. Usually, students are urged to notice the increasing need for rapid adaptability to change that these social trends impose.

In this regard may be explored the increasing impact upon business and its management of the two most significant 'post-materialist' trends of the late twentieth century: the growth of feminist and ecological consciousness. We shall consider the latter first. Ideologies of environmentalism are potent postmodern rallying points for contemporary cultural formation, much as the ideologies of progress were for modernity. And, just as progress as an ideology was able to turn a business trick or two, so it is the case with environmentalism. The green movement may be seen as many things. To some elements in the community it is a source of mischief, an irritation, an unnecessary constraint on economic and community activities. For others it is almost a sacred cause. For embryonic industry it can be an important source of competitive advantage. The values of green culture can be a major push for the adoption of processes that add value, as industries adapt to their demands. An unspoilt environment and ecologically sound produce have a competitive edge in polluted markets.

The Sydney Olympics present a case study of 'green' business, of what it means in practical terms. Greenpeace were consultants to the successful Sydney Olympic 2000 bid, developing guidelines as the basis for a 'green' chain of 'organization learning'. The guidelines are simple but exhaustive. The Olympic village will:

- maximize the use of recyclable and recycled materials such as glass, paper and metals
- use only recycled plastics
- use CFC-, HFC- and HCFC-free refrigerants and processes
- use renewable sources of energy, including solar power
- use building materials from sustainable sources
- prepare pre-site audit of habitat and species
- develop passive solar design of houses
- maximize use of public transport and elimination of leaded fuels
- utilize water conservation and recycling practices including dual-flush toilet systems, roof-fed water tanks and water-saving shower roses

- recycle treated storm water and sewage effluent.

Companies that tender for contracts for the site, according to the initial contract, will have to show how they are going to follow these guidelines. Components will be subjected to 'life-style costings', an audit that takes into account the environmental impact of their manufacture, use and future disposal. All merchandizing contractors will be scrutinized as well. As a result of following these policies Greenpeace and the ecology group Ark will develop a data base on international best practice and products to cover every construction requirement. In addition, best practice definitions will be specified for recycling processes, waste management, energy conservation, water reuse and recycling, toxic use reduction and renewable energy resources (*Greenpeace Business* 1993). Green charters, we believe, will be of increasing business relevance in sophisticated post-materialist business cultures.

Other aspects of the post-materialist business environment that relate to broader ideological changes include the impact of feminist thinking on management paradigms. Under the impact of this some commentators see the ethos of management changing fundamentally, away from a hierarchical and authoritarian mode towards more collectivist concerns, under pressure from feminist agendas. Optimism is a frequent hallmark of social movement members' belief that ideas can change the world: feminism's optimism contributes a different perspective to management debate. What some might call a 'female ethos' or a 'feminization of management' is increasingly prominent as a contemporary expression of some older collectivist ideals. This 'feminization' does not mean that the ranks of management are becoming staffed with more women than in the past. The reference is, instead, to the substantive content of management activity, where 'masculinism' characterizes older, military-derived models. To make the point clear, the adoption of such masculinist models could be the hallmark of 'feminine' occupations as much as 'masculine' ones. Nursing, historically, was a case in point (Chua and Clegg 1990). Here the employees were principally women but because of the history of hospitals the organizational model derived from the male world of the military, with its bureaucratized ranks, uniforms, distinctions and command structure. Certainly, the new 'ethos' is very different from older models of management derived from the military, through public sector bureaucracies (Weber 1978) and engineering practice (Taylor 1911), in the earlier years of this century. Not all practitioners who in the past have been habituated to masculinist and military models will find more feminized practice easy.

The increasing interest in a different, 'female' way of doing things arises from developments in a variety of disciplines. An often quoted example from psychology is Gilligan's (1982) exploration of women's moral development, in which she argued that women see the world as networks of relationships, in contrast to men's vision of hierarchical power and rights-based systems of justice. As a consequence, women value 'integrative', caring systems of morality above abstract analyses of rights. As Rogers (1988) points out, the notion of interconnectedness and its importance in women's reasoning structures has been reinforced in several additional studies, including Belenky et al. (1986) and Benack (1982).

At one level the qualitative 'feminization' of management is not surprising. Managers, particularly in the newer information industries, point out that the complexity and short span of their product life-cycles mean that 'windows of opportunity' require rapid and widespread sharing of knowledge rather than its concealment from competitors. Yet in older industries too, the technological and demographic changes mentioned above mean that the reliance on formal planning for predictable outcomes has become less effective.

While the 'female' ethos may be gaining impetus in the workplace, it has been less successful within management education. The reason for this stems from the diverse disciplinary origins of management as a field of study. At the very least, it is possible to discern tributaries of management thinking in economics, history, science, engineering, political theory, psychology and sociology. Each of these different disciplinary perspectives has brought a different emphasis to the discipline of management – often via the offer of 'salvation' in response to a succession of management crises. An example is 'scientific management', the application of the principles of science (conceived as empiricism) to the problems of efficiency, coordination and elimination of waste found in large corporations. The problems that scientific management created in terms of the dehumanization of work through the over-emphasis on specialization of tasks were, in turn, addressed by the theorists of the human relations school.

However, one blind-spot remains: the traditional tributaries of management thinking have not suggested ways to account for the perceptible shift towards a feminization of management. This is because, as pointed out by feminist scholars and critics such as Gilligan (1982) in the case of psychology, Hurley (1991) in the case of sociology, and Evans (1986) in the case of political theory, these disciplines have largely addressed themselves to the male world. The paradigms they rely on have largely left out – and hence devalued – women's experience. An example of such a paradigm is the Aristotelian division of the world into the private and public spheres. Many feminist scholars (and, paradoxically, in the light of the relative absence of feminist thinking in management education to date, the economic philosopher J.S. Mill) have demonstrated how the public/private dichotomy has been used to confine women to passive ('being') states in the private sphere and men to active ('doing') states in the public sphere. The result within feminist scholarship has been to examine the myriad ways in which 'the personal is political'. Perhaps because of the lack of legitimacy of women's studies in some academic circles – a situation which has been echoed in the management discipline – feminist concerns have remained peripheral, at best, in the streams of thought which have traditionally provided the impetus for change in management thinking. This can be seen in the specific case of research into women's entrepreneurship. As is increasingly being argued, even in the mainstream journals of entrepreneurship, the study of women's contributions to economic development and also to the theoretical development of the field of entrepreneurship has been held back by the fact that their businesses are more likely to be run from home (the private sphere) and hence overlooked, despite their significant and growing contribution to the economy. The preceding discussion should not be taken as indicating that women have won the struggle for a place in senior corporate ranks. Considerable contextual empirical variability has to be taken into account. Further, the idea that only women and not men are able to operate according to the new management paradigm is not necessarily supported by even the most fervent adherents of the new approach. In the past, while formal structures of imperative command crystallized as bureaucracy could aspire to control all that was within the reach of the organization, that control could never be total. The many 'vicious circles' of management attempts at control to repair a perceived power deficit, leading to increased employee resistance, are well recorded from Gouldner (1954) onwards (see Clegg and Dunkerley 1980). It should be self-evident that control will be far less and attempts to achieve it far more inappropriate when the most important relations that the organization enters into are not within its grasp as a legally fictive individual. As networks expand and as markets intrude into organizations, intra-organizational hierarchies, and control premised on them, recede in importance. As organizations seek value through the strength of their ties to and networks with other organizations, attempts at imperative managerial control become more intrusive and inappropriate.

The old paradigm of management tradition and practice is increasingly obsolete for the managers of embryonic industries. If the older paradigm was the hallmark of 'modern organizations' then the emergent or new paradigm may be seen, as Clegg (1990) has suggested, as the sign of 'postmodern organizations'. While there is no one actual model of 'postmodern organizations' (just as there were variations in practice in 'modern organizations') we can identify some of the 'new paradigm' elements that contemporary research suggests will be important in its constitution. In respect of the issues that the new management paradigm addresses there is considerable overlap with earlier accounts of 'postmodern organizations', although the specificity is different (Clegg 1990). If postmodern organization can be identified in the emergent management practices of embryonic industry then the concept achieves more robust and empirically specifiable expression. More especially, six years after the original expression of 'postmodern organizations' (Clegg 1990), we are in a position to identify the management dimensions more explicitly than in the earlier, itself embryonic, expression (Table 11.1).

More generally, proponents of the new paradigm distinguish themselves not only by incipient feminization but also by new approaches to learning,

Table 11.1 *'Old' and 'new' paradigms of management*

New paradigm	Old paradigm
Organization learning	Organization discipline
Virtuous circles	Vicious circles
Flexible organizations	Inflexible organizations
Management leaders	Management administrators
Open communication	Distorted communication
Markets	Hierarchies
Core competencies drive product development	Strategic business units drive product development
Strategic learning capacities are widespread	Strategic learning occurs at the apex of the organization
Assumption that most organization members are trustworthy	Assumption that most organization members are untrustworthy
Most organization members are empowered	Most organization members are disempowered
Tacit and local knowledge of all members of the organization is the most important factor in success, and creativity creates its own prerogative	Tacit and local knowledge of most members of the organization must be disciplined by managerial prerogative

to structure, to leadership, to communications, to life-cycles, to competences, to people, and to knowledge.

New Paradigm: Organization Learning

Dodgson (1993a: 375) notes that organizations today need to learn quickly and continuously. Influential consultants urge that competitive edge attaches to those organizations that succeed in doing so (Peters and Waterman 1982; Kanter 1989; Senge 1990; Garrat 1987). Research suggests that it is the differential ability of smaller firms to learn quickly, particularly about technological opportunities, that has been responsible for a changing pattern of competitive relationships between large and small firms in favour of the latter (Rothwell 1992). For larger organizations, the rapidly accelerating pace of technological change demands learning because of the complexity of new product development processes (Rothwell 1992). Product life-cycles shorten and 'lean production' emerges (Womack et al. 1990), based on alternative East Asian, particularly Japanese, forms of organization using JIT, TQM, etc. (Clegg 1990; Clegg et al. 1990; Marceau 1992).

Learning may be 'single-loop' or 'double-loop' (Argyris and Schon 1978). Single-loop learning feeds back on to present competences and routines of knowledge and their application in order to remove obstacles to their functioning; double-loop learning, by contrast, is learning that transforms the existing stock of organizational know-how contained in these routines and competences. Organizations need both, although the evidence suggests that learning which is double-loop is far more difficult to achieve (Argyris and Schon 1978).

Learning implies both outcomes and processes. The notion of virtuous learning circles suggests comparative improvement in efficiency, however one chooses to measure it, in whatever stakeholder terms: profits; quality of working; supply of jobs; consumer satisfaction; environmental impact; or macroeconomic outcomes. Vicious learning circles, by contrast, imply diminished efficiency. Learning processes concern the achievement of these outcomes, the how and the why rather than the what questions. Organization learning occurs through:

- Learning with clients, asking how, beyond market research, does the organization achieve a constant symbiosis and exchange with clients? (Employees can be encouraged to attend meetings with customers and suppliers as part of the local organizational culture.)
- Learning from outsiders, asking how does the organization tap the knowledge of consultants, academics, subcontractors, the community? (Interpersonal networks of friendship seem most important.)
- Learning from each other, asking how is knowledge passed on within the group, from group to group, from division to division, or even from sector to sector?
- Learning from schemes for systematic knowledge capture and dissemination. Is there a systematic scheme for capturing and disseminating knowledge at a strategic level (Peters 1992)?

According to McKinsey (1993: 57) managers in innovative firms have learned that:

- An appropriate top-manager's role is proactive, committed, hands off the detail, goal-setting and motivating.
- Dream-driven goals should be the company aspirations.
- An ability is needed to 'zoom in' on customer needs, company strengths and the innovations required to ensure their match.
- Project management must stress cross-functional teams, senior management sponsorship of projects and championing separate from the day-to-day organization politics.
- Integrated innovation must deepen existing products and processes, as well as aiming to supersede them, where changes are pursued in close dialogue with the customers by all managers, including senior management.

Organizations and their managers not only need to learn. Goldman and Nagel (1993) argue that they must also unlearn:

- that cooperation is less desirable than competition
- that labour–management relations need be adversarial
- that information is power and can be shared only to one's detriment
- that trusting others makes one vulnerable
- that complex problems admit of single technological solutions
- that breakthroughs are the only targets to aim for
- that markets will create themselves once better mousetraps are invented

- that infrastructure requirements will take care of themselves once pioneers have thrown up superstructures
- that standards are constraining and their formulation dull work
- that only parts can be invented not whole systems.

Comparing companies that are winning with those that are losing market position, Hayes et al. (1988) conclude that the key difference is that winners 'constantly strive to be better, placing great emphasis on experimentation, integration, training, and the building of critical organizational capabilities'. Conceptually, the notion of learning must be central. If management cannot learn then little justification exists for the practice of management development. Firms that are not 'agile', that cannot develop new products or services, that do not attend to their customers' needs will not survive long where they are in increasingly competitive business environments, unsheltered and unprotected. Since the object of innovation is to commercialize products valued by customers, acceleration of the process should not jeopardize the *quality* of the firm's offerings. It requires continuous, open and timely communication sensitive to the need to nurture effective teamwork among all members of a firm and its alliance partners to achieve this acceleration.

Successful new product performance suggests that product innovation is an activity that can be learnt (Cooper and Kleinschmidt 1986; Dwyer and Mellor 1991). The learning cited by the above authors applies predominantly to production issues. Whether it works equally for product innovation is unclear. Incremental product innovation involves modification of existing products in the context of given levels of technology. Discontinuous innovation often transforms these, as it radically alters technologies, occupational definitions and the authority relations that existing knowledge relations constitute.

Top management has an important role to play in the acquisition of the learning skills that institutionalize innovation. This role includes linking the organization to key outside contacts that serve as 'learning agents'; cultivation of particular technical skills within the organization; encouraging an innovative mindset among personnel; locating, defining and linking skills within the organization; matching skills with the organization's strategic plan; and rewarding people for their contributions to innovation. Top management is best able to establish innovation, and its communication, as a central value (McKee 1992).

Highly responsive and agile enterprises can sometimes broker roles as 'virtual companies' that exploit transient or niche markets as they emerge, where management achieves a speed and flexibility that matches that of the technologies involved (Goldman and Nagel 1993). Such agile management, characterized by strategic focus on long term financial performance, seeks opportunities for growth and profit in constant change that flexible management can exploit. Authority diffuses in the agile enterprise rather than being concentrated in a chain of command. Instead of a static corporate structure based on fixed, specialized departments, agile corporations have a dynamic structure, keyed to the evolving needs of cross-functional project teams. They are totally integrated organizations. Work goes on concurrently rather than sequentially and is not necessarily contained within the envelope of the legally distinct corporate entity. Subcontractors, partners, customers and end users interrelate in the concurrent design and production network. Management becomes less functionally oriented and more the management of diverse project teams, creating new alliances with embryonic industry firms. There are implications of this to apply to corporate governance in management education (but see Mathews 1993). Diversity, in all its characteristics, whether premised on diverse knowledge, whether drawing from occupational or other social identities, is today a central issue of heightened salience.

All members of an organization learn but some forms of learning are more strategic than others. Strategic learning is interpretative. Usually this is located at the organization apex, in top management. The leaders and managers of innovative firms in embryonic industries may find it difficult to renounce these traditional ways, particularly where business success seems premised on the special skills and knowledge that they can contribute as technologists to the company. Yet, they will have to do so if the embryo is to grow and develop to maturation. Highly successful new firms in embryonic industries maximize the circulation of learning throughout the 'clever company'.

Daft and Weick's (1982) model of organizational interpretation modes (see Figure 11.1) demonstrates the distinctiveness of organizations in an embryonic industry. It presents four different strategic modes of rational behaviour for innovation. Strategic learning varies in terms of the breadth or narrowness of management search and interpretation mechanisms and the degree of regularity or irregularity with which management actively scans and searches its environment. Narrow search and irregular scanning produce passive receptivity by management of novelty introduced from the organization's environment. Regular, broad and obtrusive scanning through, for example, systematic monitoring of information, participation in training programmes, networks and alliances, produces active creativity. The management of embryonic organizations engaged in innovation in an uncertain environment needs to devote resources to intelligence gathering as an aspect of learning. They need to scan their environments broadly, regularly and actively as 'test-makers' (Daft and Weick 1982). Such management needs to *enact* interpretation, particularly where radical technological innovation creatively destroys or marginalizes existing companies.

Critical axes define the radicalness of innovation: the degree of product innovation; the degree of process variability; and the degree to which the intellectual capital upon which the organization's technical core is premised is changing. It can be shifting in more or less dramatic and strategically different ways, as when an organization moves from one

Organizational
obtrusiveness

	Passive	Active
Unanalysable	**Undirected viewing: reactor strategy** Constrained interpretations Non-routine, informal data Hunch, rumour, chance, opportunities	**Enacting: prospector strategy** Experimentation, testing, coercion, inventing environment Learning by doing
Analysable	**Conditioned viewing: defender strategy** Interpret within traditional boundaries Passive detection Routine, formal data	**Discovering: analyser strategy** Formal search Questioning, surveys, data gathering Active detection

Environmental assumptions (label at left, aligned between Unanalysable and Analysable)

Figure 11.1   *Daft and Weick's model of organizational interpretation modes and strategy*

technological paradigm to another, or it may be more or less deepening, where the changes are far more incremental. Clearly, we are dealing with a continuum.

Where all elements on these axes score low we find a traditional organization. The combination of incremental product innovation with a moderate degree of process variability, allied not so much with dramatic shifts in knowledge but the deepening of existing applications of intellectual capital, defines an organization that is in an embryonic industry. Where product innovation is radical, the degree of process variability is high, and intellectual capital based on shifting paradigms is strategic, we have an organization that is in an ultra-embryonic industry. Figure 11.2 represents these distinctions.

The distinction between an embryonic and an ultra-embryonic industry has important implications, particularly for authority relations in firms. Redefinition of these occurs as the totality of knowledge within which they are organized changes:

> more radical innovations require new organizational forms. It appears that new forms, initially, are better adapted to exploit new techno/market regimes, breaking out from existing regimes within which established corporations for historical, cultural and institutional reasons, might be rather strongly bound. (Rothwell 1992: 234)

Extremely new firms in embryonic industries are distinctive:

> These organizations construct their own environments. They gather information by trying new behaviours and seeing what happens. They experiment, test, and

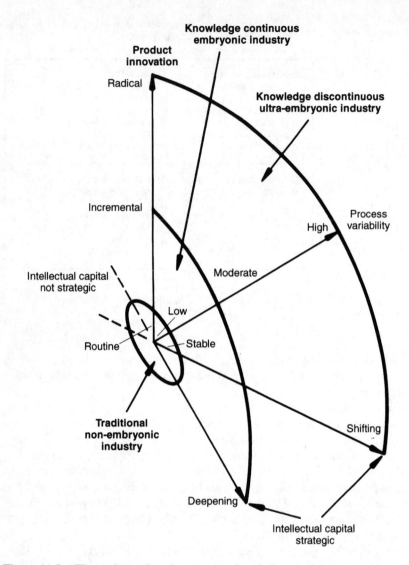

Figure 11.2   *The traditional–embryonic system of organization*

stimulate, and they ignore precedent, rules, and traditional expectations. . . . An organization in this mode tends to construct markets rather than waiting for an assessment of demand to tell it what to produce. (Daft and Weick 1982: 288–9)

The exception would be where they have an inspired founder who operates on undirected viewing. Any firm in an embryonic industry that tries to interpret innovation through conditioned viewing condemns itself to failure. By definition, an organization innovation that creates an ultra-embryonic industry cannot analyse the existing environment: there is none.

Innovations introduce discontinuity into accepted ways of doing things. At their strongest these discontinuities are based on patents. Discontinuities are always challenging but they can be opportunities rather than threats. Virtuous learning makes opportunities while vicious learning confirms threats. It is not the presence or absence of conflict that distinguishes the two types of learning. Conflict will be characteristic of any learning process that challenges deeply ingrained habits with the need to 'unlearn' (Hedberg 1981). Novelty offers variation in industry designs and business recipes for success in that industry, sometimes by chance, sometimes by design. Virtuous learning will be system wide, not just specific to a particular organization's management. Fairtlough (1993) picks up on many of these learning themes in his discussion and description of Celltech as a successful firm in an embryonic industry. Virtuous circles, he insists, build openness, trust, empowerment and commitment. (Also see Dodgson's 1993b account of the central role that both inter- and intra-organizational trust play at Celltech.) Once in motion, virtuous circles have a multiplier effect within the organization. Accordingly, collaborative and open forms of decision-making eliminate the inefficiency of traditional hierarchical styles of secrecy, sycophancy and sabotage. Instead, decisions are based upon expertise, openly elicited and listened to in the organization. Moreover, Fairtlough (1993) argues that innovative firms seek allies to which they can bond for periods of mutual benefit. These may be either mature firms or similar firms in an embryonic industry. Collaborative network arrangements frequently are crucial to the success of embryonic industries.

New Paradigm: Organic Structures

Much management literature recommends organic styles of management. They seem particularly apt for new firms in embryonic industries. There is a freedom from rigid rules; they are participative and informal, horizontal and project based. A mulitiplicity of views characterize the organization. Communication is face-to-face; there is little explicit bureaucracy. Small wins are celebrated and improvement is sought in everything on a continuous daily basis. Recognition and reward of failure should occur if learning is to take place, as consultants such as Peters (1992: 12–13) underscore. Organic structures encourage interdisciplinarity and boundary spanning. Flexibility about changing needs, threats and opportunities goes together with a non-hierarchical structure and a free flow of information up as well as down the organization (Rothwell 1992). Organic structures are also better able to exploit market opportunities as they arise. Markets don't have to be mass or even large. *The Management of Innovation* (Burns and Stalker 1962) suggests strongly that it will be the more organic, rather than the larger and more bureaucratic structures, that are best able to exploit new markets. These new markets are 'microtizing', according to

Peters (1990: 15). '*Successful companies of any size will learn to respect tiny markets, or else*' he warns.

New Paradigm: Leadership

There is a distinction of increasingly dubious worth but it is one used often enough. It is the distinction between 'management' and 'leadership'. All managers may need some leadership skills in flattened organization structures, and vision, rather than being the prerequisite of a charismatic leader, may well be something that is best nurtured by group processes (Bryman 1992; Bennis 1993).

Leadership theory is a specific case of the influence of the broader social trend of feminism on management thinking. In recent years, a number of popular management books such as Loden's (1985) *Feminine Leadership or How to Succeed in Business Without Being One of the Boys* and Helgesen's (1990) *The Female Advantage: Women's Ways of Leadership* have appeared. (Entering the academic reaches of the management discipline via the popular publishing route is almost traditional for management theory, especially leadership theory, as Barrett and Sutcliffe 1993 point out.) The popular trend, as set out in these books, is for leadership to be considered in terms of ideas like 'empowerment', 'vision', and 'culture'. Each of these may be considered in turn.

Specifically, the notion of empowerment means getting things done through sharing power rather than exercising it from above. Indeed, the idea of the placement of people 'above' others is increasingly redundant in this view of leadership, as the traditional organizational hierarchy is replaced by self-directing teams. Leaders provide a vision of the future which is then translated and negotiated in terms of the needs of others in the organization. Through their attention to the culture of the organization, formed through its ceremonies, kinship, underlying feelings and values, leaders find themselves shaped by their followers as much as they shape them. Solutions to problems are reached through negotiated settlements which encompass all members of the team rather than through the traditional exercise of management control. In this way the 'female' approach to management appears as a new development, and not simply a hearkening back to earlier 'participative management' styles in which managers 'took an interest' in employees simply in order to gain their compliance.

The new approach to leadership represents a major shift away from the traditional paradigm embodied in leadership training, which combined a technical emphasis (acquiring skills to solve problems) with political skills (gaining influence and wielding power) and a contingency approach (matching leadership style to the situation). The new approach to leadership is one which women, through their socialization and experience, are well equipped to understand and implement. But as Bennis and Nanus (1985) point out, such an approach runs counter to the traditional and still dominant view of 'tough-minded managers' who are able to take the 'hard decisions'.

Although in management and business, metaphors of military discipline, drill and docility are in decay, and there is realization of management's affinity with activities of listening, learning and launching conversations rather than commanding, controlling and communicating imperatives, legitimacy for the feminine ethos of leadership and management may well still be some way off. Moreover, embryonic firms are not unfocused seminars. Clear leadership, as communicator, integrator and planner (Brown and Karagozoglu 1993), combined with the symbol-laden aspects of the management of meaning and organization *realpolitik* (Clegg 1989; Bolman and Deal 1991), remain vital.

New Paradigm: Communications

Management communications are vital also, as Fairtlough (1994) identifies. They must be frequent, informal as well as formal, and integrative across functional lines rather than down functional hierarchies (Brown and Karagozoglu 1993). Fairtlough's Celltech experience recommends the minimization of hierarchy and the maximization of integrative 'compartments', an analogy that Fairtlough takes from molecular biology. If two kinds of molecule cooperate they can improve their accuracy of replication at least tenfold. If they stay closely associated, they can evolve together and the scientist can aid this joint evolution by putting the two kinds of molecule in a compartment that keeps the compatible variants together and apart from other similar molecules. Once established, compartments start to compete with each other in a Darwinian fashion. Create compartments similarly, within organizations, he recommends. In these compartments all barriers to discourse, functional, technical and hierarchical, should be minimized (Fairtlough 1994). Something approximating an 'ideal speech situation' (Habermas 1984) becomes the norm, where

> excellent communication is possible within the small compartment where multi-order feedback leads to great creativity. Mutual understanding is high, shared values predominate. There is a common language for communication, there are common criteria for judgement. Strong ties of affection and trust develop between the small number of people involved. They get to know each other well, and share the experience of working together to achieve shared goals. (Fairtlough 1993: 5)

Compartments need order in the creative flux, and to achieve this the manager of the embryonic industry needs to have something akin to the creative genius of a Duke Ellington (without the famous temperament), able to work not only to their own charts but also those of collaborators (like Billy Strayhorn), comprehending the whole and seeing interrelationships, involving people in the ensemble and improvising in harmony with others to maintain the dynamic from the focal point outwards: from the

CEO (McGrath and MacMillan 1993) through a technically sophisticated and involved membership (Senker and Senker 1992).

New Paradigm: Organizational Life-Cycles

If all organizations in embryonic industries must strive to be organic they must do so even more at the initial stages of the life-cycle. In management terms new firms seem to have an advantage relative to established firms the greater the undercutting of existing competences posed by the technology that they use. Abernathy and Clark (1985) have coined the term 'transilience' to describe such innovations. Where both technology and market links are novel there is a process of 'radical innovation' at work. The whole 'architecture' of the firm and the knowledge embedded in it as a coherent set of components require innovation. In new organizations in embryonic industries the comparative advantage of a clean slate enables them to manage transilience better.

At the outset, when dealing with new technologies, new firms can have a competitive edge. This fits the pattern in biotechnology. Start-ups like Celltech and Genetech pioneered the application of novel recombinant-DNA technologies. Bringing such innovation to market is often achieved through 'dynamic complementarity', the pairing of organizationally separate resources and skills. Sometimes, as in Genetech's case, it fails and the innovative firm becomes incorporated within a larger corporate entity like Roche. Technology breakthroughs, once achieved, are accommodated within the established market linkages and subsequent product development of pre-existing large firms.

Below a certain threshold of transilience in innovation it is more probable that organization and management will shift from new organizations in ultra-embryonic industries to more established, knowledge continuous organizations in embryonic industries. Knowledge that undercuts existing competences in both technology and market terms overcomes the threshold. Radical innovation opens up new markets and applications that create great difficulties for established firms (Cooper and Kleinschmidt 1986; Anderson and Tushman 1990; Daft 1982) and opportunities for new firms, particularly the ultra-embryonics.

In the initial phase of a firm in an embryonic industry great hunches and research serendipity may be enough to get started but evidence shows that these cannot sustain the firm in the long term. Reaction has a short shelf life as a strategy for managing sustained innovation. Embryonic maturation requires more intrusive and active interpretation. In contrast, 'prospector' and 'analyser' strategies are the path to managerial excellence for firms in embryonic industries. The more incremental trial and error strategy of the prospector best suits exploratory learning that undercuts existing competences, while competence enhancement and exploitation presuppose an analyser strategy of systems analysis, computation and extensive scanning by the discovering enterprise.

'Radical' innovation always involves an overthrow of existing competences: that is its definition. Less dramatic but as important is 'architectural' innovation, which, while less totally challenging, is difficult to manage. TCG (see Mathews 1993) is a case in point. It works well because it has given explicit consideration to the design of the 'architecture', the organization forms, within which its evolution has occurred. Organizations that want to develop embryonic activities through the management of this form should routinize search for the unexpected, through constant market questioning, surveys and data gathering, as well as through constant organization learning.

Organizational life-cycles have a distinct market-related curve. Typically, technology-based firms start out from a strong consulting and research and development contracting base, and over a few years become more product-oriented firms, with an increased emphasis on sales and marketing, and a diminished technology fixation. The suggestion is that the life-cycle of these firms significantly shifts to a more sales- and marketing-oriented focus, the more so that the firm has not a single- but a multi-founder situation (Roberts 1990). Shanklin and Ryans (1984) note that as the competitive environment stabilizes, often a function of maturity, marketing becomes more important for high-technology companies. Roberts's (1990) research, carried out in 114 technology-based firms within the Greater Boston area of the USA, resonates with the insight that single founders of an embryonic firm, fired by their technological vision, find it difficult to let go – sometimes to the commercial detriment of the firm. Van de Ven (1993: 212) notes that 'entrepreneurs who run in packs will be more successful than those that go it alone to develop their innovations.' Another alternative is to build linkages with large firms. The development of an appropriate infrastructure for entrepreneurship is essential. Successful entrepreneurs are not heroic individualists so much as partners in a collective achievement. Once more, network ideas of governance seem to recommend themselves.

New Paradigm: Core Competences

Innovation in organizations comes from the nurturing and application of 'core competences'. In an influential *Harvard Business Review* article Prahalad and Hamel define core competence in the following way:

> The diversified corporation is a large tree. The trunk and major limbs are core products, the smaller branches are business units; the leaves, flowers, and fruit are end products. The root system that provides nourishment, sustenance and stability is the core competence . . . Core competences are the collective learning in the organization, especially how to co-ordinate diverse production skills and integrate multiple streams of technologies . . . Core competence is communication, involvement, and a deep commitment to working across organization boundaries . . . The tangible link between identified core competences and end products is what we call the core products – the physical embodiments of one or more core competences. Honda's engines for example, are core products, linchpins between design and development skills that ultimately lead to a proliferation of end products. (1990: 82–5)

Goldman and Nagel (1993) suggest that routine 'organizational unlearning' characterizes firms seeking to build on their core competences, particularly those of a strong human resource team. Armed with the wisdom gained through unlearning, whilst preserving their core competences, established firms will be ripe for embryonic industry status, perhaps in temporally specific partnerships with firms in ultra-embryonic industry, in a portfolio of opportunities that is risk-spreading. Paradoxically, new firms in embryonic industries are advantaged by lack of collective memory. Thus they have little to unlearn. However, they lack the collective learning of core competences that Prahalad and Hamel (1990) stress, so they need a specific strategy to resolve the paradox: the resolution is recourse to prospector strategies and network intelligence.

New Paradigm: People

Hayes et al. (1988: 252–3) contrast the command and control paradigm of management with one they call 'continual learning'. The continual learning paradigm makes some fundamental assumptions about people as members of organizations:

- All employees are responsible, thinking adults who inherently want to do their best.
- Human resources are too valuable to waste or to leave untapped.
- Creative talents and skills are widely distributed at all levels of an organization and society.
- Workers will raise important problems and concerns if they feel the organization will respond appropriately.
- Work is more interesting when people are challenged in performing it.
- People take pride in training others.
- Better performance occurs when artificial differences in how people are treated are removed.
- Real responsibility motivates high performance.
- People make better decisions and implement them better, when they work together.

New Paradigm: Knowledge

A vital thread runs through all these discussions. It focuses on the growing importance of highly skilled, highly motivated, knowledge-based workers. Almost every authority mentions this as the critical ingredient for future business success. Drucker (1990: 167) insists 'The social centre of gravity has shifted to the knowledge worker. All developed countries are becoming . . . knowledge societies.' This view has recently received further support in the work of President Clinton's economic adviser, Robert Reich (1992), particularly in his identification of the rise of what he calls the 'symbolic analyst'.

That such pieties might seem a revelation, as Drucker intends, is an ironical indictment of the era of modernist management that Taylor (1911) formally inaugurated with his *Principles of Scientific Management*. Scientific management, it will be recalled, sought to structure and restrict the distribution of knowledge in organizations, redesigning it as a hierarchical rather than convivial tool. The wish was always stronger than the reality. Of necessity, it has always been the case that developed societies were 'knowledge societies'. No complex organization can last long that does not have recourse to, in some ways, the tacit knowledge of its workforce, even where jobs within it have been formally 'deskilled'. Drucker (1992) notes that in contemporary organizations the tendency will be not to 'deskill' but to consciously enhance 'skill formation'. Tacit knowledge will be made more explicit and widely available through the philosophies and techniques of total quality management (TQM). Tom Peters suggests one implication of this for organizations:

> As the service sector grows and the service component of manufacturing comes to dominate, every one of us is in the 'brainware business' . . . Brain based companies have an ethereal character compared to yesterday's . . . outfits. Barking orders is out. Curiosity, initiative and the exercise of imagination are in. (1992: xxxiii)

Stewart (1992: 7–8) suggests that firms capable of innovation display the following:

- leading edge competences
- strategic long term breadth of vision
- diagnostic ability to identify and implement change
- drive based on market and customer
- stress on team membership, vision and values
- commitment to principles not rules
- enabling style
- leadership that is charismatic
- emotional stability
- openness in communication.

These are sufficiently similar to suggestions made by Handy (1991), Clegg (1990), Limerick and Cunnington (1993) and Peters (1992) to convince one that they are key competences for embryonic industry. Many of these have been learnt from Japan. Boam and Sparrow suggest that this shaped a new emphasis upon developing competences:

> The mid-1980s saw a change in the way we thought about human capability. Competitive pressures turned to competitive threat. Workforces were slimmed down. Individual jobs became more self-contained, more skilled and varied, and the reduced levels of supervision that resulted created the need to give individuals more control over their own activities. Giving employees more scope and autonomy meant that organizations had a vested interest in viewing employees as an asset (no longer just a cost). As an asset, people should be invested in, in order to add value to them. (1992: 4)

The emphasis may seem somewhat instrumental in its sentiments, but as Woody Allen once remarked of life, it is better than the alternative. The alternative in this case is organization members who are disempowered, regarded as costs rather than as assets to be valued for their creativity.

How to Cultivate Embryonic Industry

OK – let us assume that the reader is persuaded to this point. Innovation is vital. It can result from either culture or technology. Embryonic industry requires a new paradigm of management. How do we cultivate embryonic industries? Embryonic industries are not immaculate conceptions. Relations tend to produce them. Relationships are rarely random occurrences. There is a context to all relationships. Embryonic industries flourish in an industry complex. Organizations other than innovative firms populate this complex and require analysis. Embryonic industries flourish in and through relationships with other agencies, including mature firms, suppliers and producers, customers and users, government bodies and instruments of public policy, research and development laboratories, markets and occupational interest groups. If this industry complex is not recognized then much of what is important and relevant about embryonic industry can be overlooked.

No enterprise is an island. Interlinked communities of practitioners in and around organizations develop a complex system of interdependence. This links firms, government, and key stakeholders in an industry complex (see Figure 11.3). The firm is at the centre of the embryonic industry complex. In order to innovate firms must manage several processes successfully, as indicated. In addition, firms have various kinds of relationships with other elements in the complex. The industry complex involves more than a collection of autonomous organizations, and, within these, inter-firm relations involve more than price competition. The functioning of the complex has an import upon the organization of individual firms, their strategies, and their collective competitiveness relative to sectors located elsewhere.

Building on work done by van Tulder and Dankbaar (1992), we can conceptualize the context within which firms exist in terms of four distinct nexuses. These delineate the producers and suppliers of human and other resources; the consumers and users of the products, processes and services of firms in the embryonic industry; research and development; and relevant public policies. Figure 11.3 represents the 'embryonic industry complex framework'. Each of these elements in the complex represents an important part of the environment in which any firm in an embryonic industry will operate. If such firms cannot attract human and other resources they will not survive. Once attracted these resources require appropriate and effective management. If consumers and users cannot be recruited, their products will not survive in the marketplace, and, to the extent that the firm is dependent upon these, neither will it. If the firms in an embryonic industry cannot access appropriate or secure research and development that enables them to innovate new products and services then

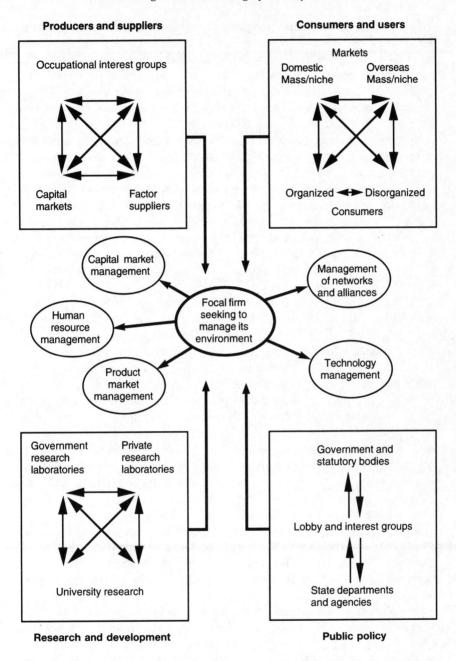

Figure 11.3   *Embryonic industry complex and a focal firm*

they face the prospect of a declining market as others that manage these matters more effectively outflank them. Finally, any government that does not develop appropriate public policies to facilitate these developments will risk erosion and decline of wealth and employment creation opportunities and of its tax base. Hence, public policies for industry development are essential and responsible as supporting conditions that would promote and encourage important leadership and management skills for enterprise productivity, innovation and international competitiveness.

What frames the embryonic industry complex? An industry consists of firms as organizations. Organizations typically seek to cope with the uncertainties of their existence in various ways: they strive for a unifying culture, for standard procedures, for adequate resources and so on. Each of the areas that the organization has to deal with represents a potential zone of uncertainty that may only partially be within its power to control. In striving to exercise this control it will require management of those resources that impinge on its arena of operations. The producers and suppliers of human and other resources; the consumers and users of the products, processes and services of firms in the embryonic industry; research and development; and relevant public policies, all frame the context. The requirements and reality of each organization will differ but, at the minimum, they will need to develop strategies that manage human resources; product and material markets, for both inputs and outputs; capital; technologies; and relationships, often networks and alliances, with other organizations. Some of these other organizations locate within the frame of the complex, as unions, employers' associations, government departments, lobby groups, research laboratories, financial institutions, customers, suppliers. Others will be firms with an interest in their arena: competitors and established firms that might be seeking opportunities for their capital, human resources and product markets, or who might want to tap into those of a firm in an embryonic industry because of perceived symbiotic, competitive or complementary opportunities. Hence, substantively the frame fills rapidly with firms and other organizations in embryonic industries. For reasons of analytical simplicity we display only one such firm, the focal firm, in Figure 11.3.

Zones of uncertainty are not only occasions for organizations to seek to exert control; they can also be opportunities for producers, consumers, users, employees, competitors, unions, finance institutions, etc., to resist. Resistance is rarely random or idiosyncratic, but framed by implicit rules.

Of particular importance in this model is the corner occupied by public policy, because it is from this corner, under conditions of conflict, resistance, lobbying and negotiation, that the 'rules of the game' emerge that frame the understandings of the participants in the complex. All industry develops in a framework of public policy. It should be evident that public policy need not entail 'meddling' by bureaucrats who are risk-averse, nor need it load entrepreneurs with burdensome obligations to government that they can ill afford, despite certain 'populist' misconceptions. Firms are 'embedded' in a socially organized context and involved in

a series of relationships with other organizations w'
patterns that repeat throughout the intricacies of th
constituted. These patterns will have several 'normai
'clusters', 'networks' and 'strategic alliances'. Rather than i
graphically, we will describe them discursively.

Chains

The industry context, conceived of as a set of linkages that connect
disparate organizations, may form a linear chain. Critical linkages can put
virtuous pressure on management to improve innovation. The McKinsey
report into emerging exporters recognizes the importance of these chain
linkages when it urges the construction of supply chains, for which it argues
the Government should provide 'adequate support and resources' (1993:
42). Public policy would thus seek to increase pressure and thus enhance
value in the chain of linkages through competition combined with cooperation, an idea with far-reaching implications. Creative use and shaping of
the market through production linkages might focus, for instance, on
consultative buyer/vendor relations, inter-firm associations and extra-firm
agencies that facilitate continuous improvement in production. Value
enhancement comes through the pressures in the chain. Demands by an
organization that suppliers meet quality standards that it, or an industry
standard, mandates are a common instance of this type of chain functioning as a 'virtuous circle'. Government can have a role to play in the
achievement of this, through defining a public policy framework that is
standard setting (see Marceau and Jureidini 1992).

Clusters

The original idea of firms that can cluster together came from the model of
a Marshallian 'industrial district'. Today it is frequently conceptualized in
terms of many small and medium enterprises integrated at a local level and
specializing in phases that are all part of the same production cycle
(Bianchi 1993: 18). Typically well established with industrial and artisanal
traditions, in some cases the districts may have developed in part as a
consequence of local state interventions, such as the northern Italian
industrial districts that Weiss (1988) has studied, which provided favourable taxation and subsidy policies that encouraged firms to remain small
rather than to grow. In other cases they may be the result of central
government leading the way through a decision to site a key industry in a
particular area. It was such a decision, in the USA that transformed
Huntsville, Alabama, from a sleepy cotton town to a dynamo of the
space race and the spin-off industries that it developed (see Clegg et al.
1994).

In the absence of a leading role for government procurement revolving
around an industry complex such as that of the defence industry, other
strategies must present themselves. One of those that has seen widespread

ɔption is the idea of the 'incubator' as a conscious device for encouraging ɔalized high-technology clustering (Janssen and Topsom 1993). Incuɔators are catalysts for small-business generated developments in a tightly focused geographical area and have a valuable role to play in regional programmes. They play an important role in facilitating the transfer of technology and ideas from large organizations such as universities, government research bodies and large corporations to the marketplace through aiding the development of new business ventures.

The clustering of research excellence, both public and private, and the creation of a 'hot-house' atmosphere in which small organizations can grow in proximity to each other and to established potential commercial partners, are deliberate strategies of clustering.

Networks

Networks are distinct organization and management forms, ones that have a number of advantages, including:

- risk spreading and resource sharing, avoiding costly duplication of independent effort
- enhanced flexibility compared to other forms of integration, such as a takeover or merger, particularly where product life-cycles are short
- increased access to know-how and information through collaborative relations at the pre-formal knowledge stage.

Networks, at their best, link in a loosely coupled cellular structure a chain of value-adding activities that constantly introduce new material and elements. In addition, the velocity and circulation of novelty through the cells add value by virtue of the resulting permeable and linked relations. They represent compartments as described by Fairtlough (1994) and accordingly enhance innovation opportunities. Network organization improves immeasurably the probability that understanding is maximized through learning by doing in the network and through its synergistic strategies. The network is a mechanism for fast organization learning about markets, applications, suppliers – in fact, everything that it would take the competitive stand-alone company far longer to learn. It provides, through organizational form, the solution to a problem. While new, small firms may innovate, they lack the collective memory of past experience that efficiently bureaucratic large organizations have through their files of precedent (Weber 1978). Although large firms have the experience and the precedents they can fail to admit necessary innovation through the patina of tradition that they display as an excess of collective memory, often as a resource for resistance to change by well-entrenched organization members.

Firms that network internationally have a greater access than would be possible through other organization forms to:

- intelligence on competitors
- new technologies
- product sources
- new product applications and new manufacturing processes.

In scanning the business environment, an initiative, modelled in part on a scheme reported by McKinsey (1993: 56), may be useful. Linking technology and innovation in California is the University of California Access Model, an information platform that includes information on technology available for licensing in universities and federally sponsored research programmes in progress and the product lines and capabilities of over 39,000 high-tech corporations. Venture capitalists are able to scan this net site. As is so well known, the relation between venture capital and embryonic industry management is two-way. Venturers have to acquire a sound grasp of the management needs of embryonic organizations striving to innovate in the marketplace. The finance specialism is not a stand-alone set of techniques. Management education needs techniques that allow both venturers and managers of firms in embryonic industries to communicate more effectively.[6]

Such network arrangements allow use to be made of the experience that many firms have available to them through the knowledge of older employees. More use of the skill bases of under-employed and retired strategic managers in contributing to coaching teams is possible. The Canadian Federal Business Development Bank provides training and counselling services at local and regional levels that use such retirees. In Huntsville, Alabama, an important role was played by senior military retirees in building embryonic enterprise. Technology changes and restructuring produce a pool of retired, unemployed or under-employed strategic managers. Educators, firms in embryonic industries, and these managers, would gain by network association. All could learn from the others.

Strategic Alliances

Strategic alliances characterize, in particular, those fast-growing knowledge intensive product sectors which now account for around 42 per cent of the exports from OECD countries. In recent years, given the substantial financial resources necessary for the development of new technology, more firms are entering strategic alliances, often with competitors, to bring innovation to market, while others are turning to their governments to secure support for their technological strategies. Strategic alliances can result in the emergence of networks linking multiple partners, often on an international basis. The importance of networks, between scientists and industrialists, scientists and venture capitalists, venture capitalists and industrialists, is considerable. Venture capital may come from traditional investment companies or it may come from an industrial enterprise that 'ventures'. The brokerage role that a successful venture capitalist plays is crucial. Embryonic firms frequently emerge from brokerage of well-managed networks. Universities can be a locus for this brokerage as well as an opportunity for much organization learning. Strategic alliances are often a significant mechanism for accessing external assets in the commercialization process. The assets include capital, product design and marketing resources. For other partners, establishing alliances with emerging firms offers access to leading edge technical developments in the new field. For emergent firms, those that are ultra-embryonic in particular, alliances may be crucial for bringing an innovation to the marketplace where 'large organizations also play an important role since size and financial muscle are critical for the long pull in an increasingly global economy' (Amara 1990: 145). Other important benefits of such collaborative relationships include shared risks and accelerated technical progress and market entry. A particular form of alliance is 'corporate parenting' or 'mentoring'. Rather than being an opportunistic, project-related alliance this is more permanent: larger and more established firms can play a role in embryonic firm growth through equity participation, providing access to technology, markets, finance, management skills and credibility, and the arrangement also allows the larger firm to maintain control over what may become competition (McKinsey 1993: 60).

One example of a collaborative relationship between a larger and a smaller firm is provided by a biotechnology firm, Invetech, that manufactures laboratory instruments through its subsidiary Australian Biomedical Corporation. To do so it has relied on an alliance with the Swiss multinational Leica. The alliance has provided not only established distributional and marketing channels but also a brand-name recognition that would otherwise be impossible to achieve for small firms in small countries with a small presence in particular industrial sectors. Strategy complementarity refers to the degree to which the strategies of partners are complementary. It reflects the potential offered by an alliance to support the partners' respective strategic initiatives. Established firms often have difficulty in understanding technologies that are different to those they use. Hence, firms in ultra-embryonic industries (where almost everything is uncertain and novel in terms of products, processes, technologies and markets), that most require the complementary services of established firms, may be precisely those to whom they are least likely to be available. The nature of their innovation makes their products differ radically from the knowledge base of existing firms.

Reform of extant management practice to encompass the interests of firms in embryonic industries furthers the interests of established ones as well. It provides managers on both sides of potential alliances with more knowledge about the other party's needs. The BHP guide to successful parenting is an invaluable tool for managing parenting alliances (McKinsey 1993: 61).

Established firms, as well as venture capitalists, that might have asset complementarity with an embryonic firm, through marketing or technology applications, need to broker linkages. Cantley (1986) suggests that:

- well-thought-out technological forecasting
- frequently updated forecasts in the light of current developments
- active search for shared management experience across different projects and for new project opportunities

are the analyser strategies required by established firms or market intelligence with respect to embryonic industry.

As any student of Machiavelli would attest, alliances are risky, however desirable or necessary they may be. What can firms do to minimize the risks associated with strategic alliances? One thing that they can do is to learn from an area of organization life with considerable experience in managing alliances: the management of strategic high-tech cooperative projects in the military (Farr and Fischer 1992). Managers of successful strategic alliances ensure that alliances are project-focused; that project teams have real decision authority and 100 per cent project assignment; that clear goals and deadlines exist; that there are policies for their implementation; and that there is a religious adherence to time-frames for technical, market and other tests. Project teams include key functional representation with authority to act and project leaders chosen by the team with functional representatives reporting to them. Organization careers become strings of projects where each project team is self-sufficient and includes 'outsiders' like user representatives. Teams are not just task-oriented: their celebratory dimension acknowledges team accomplishments and disappointments (Peters 1990: Part 1; Farr and Fischer 1992).

Goals need harmonizing in alliances (as Farr and Fischer 1992: 61 found from their study of successful and failed alliances in European military projects). The success of a project relates closely to keeping the benefits of a project partnership in direct proportion to the relative contribution of each participant. Where project participants had prior experience with relevant technology or previous cooperative programmes, that increased the probability of success in any given project. Project loyalty overrides enterprise loyalty in successful projects. There are important implications of this for any enterprise entering alliances on a project basis. The team commitment has to be greater than for the enterprise interest. Such commitments help successful projects better to handle uncertainties introduced by the politics of the alliance by ensuring fuller goal commitment, irrespective of change.

Farr and Fischer (1992) also have significant comments concerning coping with international differences that are particularly useful for firms for whom many alliances are likely to be international, as in the case of Australia, because of the size and structure of the domestic economy. They note that in the military cases that they studied, 'geographical, cultural, and language barriers appear to be far less of a problem than are differing technical and managerial practices' (1992: 66). One can abstract from Farr and Fischer (1992: 66) some simple, pragmatic but important points that have management implications for alliances that are international, namely that successful strategic alliance managers

- cope with geographical differences by extensive use of confidential e-mail, faxes and couriers, and factor jet-lag entailed by travelling from different time zones into travel plans and meetings
- grasp and factor in cultural differences
- create schedules that allow for different work standards and holidays
- co-locate project teams in a single office
- engage 'culture' consultants
- overcome language differences by specifying an official language in advance and arranging interpreters and translators
- use multilingual teams wherever possible and develop courtesy-level proficiency in the other language(s)
- minimize managerial differences by defining and understanding different contracting policies, procedures, terms and key management processes in advance.

Conclusion

This chapter has ranged widely. Written from Australia it has sought to incorporate insights from around the world. The cases explored exemplify the importance of innovation for organizations, whether based more in culture or in technology, or some fusion of the two. Where, as in the case of Olodum, cultural difference is magnified by distance, the cases are more rather than less useful. It is cultural difference that enables us to think 'outside the box' of what we know already. In this respect, 'The Rhythm of the Saints' fulfils a similar function to discussions elsewhere of 'French bread', 'Italian fashions' and 'East Asian enterprises' (Clegg 1990). It serves to demonstrate through an 'anthropologically strange' case the deep embeddedness of organizational and management action that we take for granted in contexts that are more familiar and close at hand.

Where innovation occurs in embryonic industry, it is suggested, a new paradigm of management may emerge. This new paradigm, in evident affinity with 'postmodern organizations' (Clegg 1990), means innovation not just in knowledge, markets and products but also in management. The implications of this for the politics of management are twofold.

First, the old paradigm of management assumed a certain masculinist, machismo world, one of hierarchies, orders, discipline, rules and control. Most of organization life is still governed in this way. A certain robust style of politics configured this world, one in which orders were given, managerial imperatives were assumed and the right to question these imperatives was deemed hardly legitimate. In such a world individuals frequently would collectively organize for protection. It was a world of 'us' and 'them', a world of industrial relations conflicts fought out through strikes and collective action. It was a world of capital and labour as irrevocably opposed interests. Wins could only ever be at the expense of the losers. Power games were zero-sum.

If the new paradigm is to prevail, much of this older model will change. Organization learning, networks and other features of the new paradigm imply that organizations are places in which it is possible for a diversity of viewpoints, representation of interests and intersecting networks and alliances to coexist creatively. Creative coexistence is not necessarily peaceful: it may just as easily be a state of tension but, if the new paradigm is to prevail, the tension will have to be managed in some new ways. The resolution of tension premised on the dictats of authority is hardly compatible with an organization that seeks to maximize creative contributions from its members. There are traditions to be traduced, old lessons to be unlearnt, past practices to be dismissed. New forms of politics will emerge and as yet, beyond some collectivist foreshadowing, we know hardly at all what these will be. It is a pressing task not only to discover these empirically but also to aid their design where they are emergent.

Second, there are implications for the politics of management knowledge. Much of the past curriculum, its assumptions, organization and design, will require transformation. Here there will be new skills to be cultivated, new lessons to learn and to teach, and some new ways of transmitting them. No more than in the politics of management practice will this be an easy or trouble-free transition. The Herculean nature of the task is most evident at the extreme: it is that faced by academics from what was Eastern Europe who now find that they must learn the liberal ways of the market and unlearn the dogma of the past. A new way of seeing is required in the Western world as well. It may not demand a change as radical as that from Marxist to market economics, but it requires change nonetheless. The novelty involves being attuned less to the corporate world as it exists at present (the focus of most conventional MBA-type activities) and attending more to the emergent world of embryonic industries. The danger to overcome and the risk that must be faced is that management education, in distilling lessons from the corporate world that was, renders itself less able to face the challenges of that embryonic industry which will require tomorrow's managers. Strategically, one of the easiest errors to make is to fight the current war with the knowledge, strategy and skills learnt from the last war, with an adversary unschooled in this way of fighting. The rules of engagement do not stand still as one learns them, in business any more than in war or any other sphere of life.

We make a final point. At one time all industries were embryonic, by definition. As these industries developed and modern organizations grew with them, certain ways of acting became institutionalized, reflecting the world from which they emerged. New times produce new industries in embryo. We are convinced that the management of these, in future, need be no less innovative than was the older paradigm in the past. However, to reiterate one more time: management is irredeemably political. No

necessity attaches to the new paradigm outside of the politics of competitive strategic advantage, shaped by both key managers and organizations.
No illusion should be entertained that, because rust never sleeps, the old
regimes of management and their iron cages will just rot away. Behind the
bars, inside the cage, are people who often know no other way. To clear a
space, even the energy of new, embryonic industry is no guarantee, but it is
a major source of innovation.

Appendix: Embryonic Industries Research Project

The chapter that you are reading grew out of a research project into 'embryonic industries' as
part of The Industry Task Force on Leadership and Management Skills. The original research
was commissioned and funded by the Commonwealth of Australia's Federal Government
Department of Employment, Education and Training to contribute research on the leadership and management needs of Australia for the twenty-first century, chaired by David
Karpin. It was part of a programme of research commissioned to develop policy options for
the Government in developing Australian management. The research team was led by
Stewart Clegg and comprised Larry Dwyer, John Gray, Sharon Kemp, Jane Marceau and
Eddie O'Mara. Thomas Clarke was a consultant to the project. The research relied upon
several methods of data collection and interpretation. The research methodology had to be
able to overcome one fundamental aspect of the research process outside the researcher's
control. The time available to do the work was four months only, from initial conception to
final completion. Within this period familiarity had to be gained with material from a diverse
range of international literature, ranging across industrial economics; organizations and
management; public policy; technology and innovation; science policy and marketing. In
addition, there had to be exposure of the literature to Australian experience.

Out of what was initially a research difficulty, considerable strategic advantage followed.
With more time at our disposal we might have used a survey method, developing questions
based upon the literature, collecting data from a sample of people in and around embryonic
industries. Four months simply did not allow time to develop a questionnaire instrument,
construct a sample, field the instrument, analyse the data, feed back the responses to our
sample and modify the findings accordingly.

To get over the time-frame problem we chose to adopt a focus group method. That is, we
would construct a number of focus groups in different cities, composed of people drawn from
business, academe, government and public policy circles, with whom we would explore our
initial ideas, develop discussion and then modify our views accordingly. The strategic
advantage of this method was major. Had we stuck as close to the literature as a rushed use of
the survey method would have dictated, without the time to extensively pre-test our ideas, we
would have missed the considerable insight that we were to gain from the focus groups.

From the focus groups in their various locations we learnt two recurrent lessons. First,
markets are of key importance to processes of innovation and the development of embryonic
industries. Second, innovation is not simply a technologically based phenomenon. The
insights of the focus groups shifted our conception of technology as the key source of
innovation. Without these insights the focus on the centrality of markets would diminish. In
addition, we would have missed the important role that cultural innovation might play in the
formation of embryonic industries.

The focus groups undoubtedly resolved one problem, that of collecting rich, focused and
qualitative data from a broadly based but relevant constituency of interest in a short period of
time. Yet, another issue remained. Ordinarily, in a substantial research project, which this
proved to be, one would gain further validation of the importance, usefulness and
exhaustiveness of one's findings, through circulating drafts extensively in advance and then
through review responses to the submission of papers to research journals. Again, the time-

frame mitigated against us being able to do this efficiently and still meet the deadline. To address the question of review we designed the 'international hubs'.

The international hubs, conceived as a panel of international experts that would aid us with the research project and who would comment on the draft material that we produced, were a vital part of the design. We realized that well-chosen hubs could achieve much. Not only could they offer academic validation of the material that we were producing, they could also act as convenors of something similar to focus groups in their own countries. Thus, we were able to draw on an international panel of practical as well as theoretical validation, conjecture and refutation of our work. In being the mother of invention, adversity seeded an offspring nurtured through what proved to be a remarkably robust research design.

International hubs were convened in the UK, the USA, Hong Kong and Canada. A logic predicated these choices. In the UK one hub formed around the work of Professor Thomas Clarke as the Academic Director for the Royal Society of Arts Inquiry into 'Tomorrow's Company' and his pivotal role as an adviser to the Institute of Directors. The other formed around Professor David Gann of the Science Policy Research Unit at Sussex University. This enabled access to advice from one of the major centres of science policy research and advice in Europe. The choice of Professor Gordon Redding, the Director of the Hong Kong University Business School, as the locus of another of the international hubs meant exposure to thinking and trends in the dynamic northern economies of East Asia, into whose management practices Professor Redding has conducted considerable research. We were fortunate to be able to tap into insights from his 'Beyond Bureaucracy' project. The United States economy has seen the emergence of a number of well-known cases of high-tech industry complexes, such as Silicon Valley in California. Another case in point is that of Huntsville, Alabama, a spin-off from the United States space programme. Professor Bill Souder, of the University of Alabama, not only formed an international hub in Huntsville that discussed the work of the project, but also contributed a fascinating case study of the Huntsville experience, included as Part 8 of the Appendix to the Full Report. Finally, we asked Professor Urs Gattiker of the University of Lethbridge to form an international hub. We asked him not only because he is a world expert on technology and its management but also because Canada is in so many ways one of the best points of comparison with Australia. They share similar histories, political systems, language, culture and economies. The international hubs shifted our thinking in many substantial and imperceptible ways as well as, what is more important, reinforcing the emergent focus of our research.

Finally, at a late stage of the research we became aware of some points of contact with ideas that were breaking elsewhere in the Task Force's Inquiry, through discussion with the Task Force research team and project mentor. The issue that was emergent was the extent to which embryonic industries required a new paradigm of management. Discussion suggested that it was, in part, subject to characterization as more 'feminine' than the more 'masculinist' practices of convention. The issue had arisen in the Brisbane focus group, and in subsequent discussions that we had with its facilitator, Dr Mary Barrett. As it was clearly an area that was attracting attention in the Inquiry and had already proved salient in this research project, we commissioned Dr Barrett to provide a paper on 'The Feminization of Management', a theme emerging as a key component of the new paradigm of management that we saw developing for embryonic, innovative industries. This explains Mary Barrett's authorship listing in the chapter credits.

Thus, the project had six formal but overlapping stages.

Stage One: Conducting the Literature Analysis

This stage was initial but ongoing and informed much of the opinion and data used in other stages.

Stage Two: Composing the International Hubs

Influential advisers formed around five international hubs in Hong Kong, the United Kingdom, the USA and Canada. We sent them drafts of our deliberations and they responded with advice, corrections, local field experience and case examples. One of these, by Bill Souder and Niles Schoening, on 'Embryos, Gazelles and Derivatives: the Evolution of High-Technology Firms and Industries in Huntsville, Alabama', is part of the Full Report.

Stage Three: Conducting Case Study Interviews

We conducted a number of interviews with people associated with embryonic industries and collected case study data. Part 6 of the Full Report contains these and they are cited extensively in the body of that Report.

Stage Four: Composing the Australian Focus Groups

We adopted a 'focus group' methodology for the project. We chose this methodology, as we advised, because we required rapid and iterative feedback on the academic literature and our emergent findings. Detailed and high-quality feedback requirements were the brief. They came from key figures in embryonic industries and from respondents in and around these industries.

Accessing key figures, exposing ideas, recording responses, drafting and revising after further exposure: this proved to be a most productive methodology for generating insights in a disciplined manner within a tight time-frame.

We formed focus groups in Canberra, Sydney, Brisbane, Wollongong and Melbourne and distributed early draft ideas prior to the focus group meetings. We took extensive notes during and immediately after the meetings. Meetings were tape recorded as a back-up to these notes. We used a common frame of questions for each focus group which we constructed from the main leads found in the literature survey. The focus groups commented upon and refracted the academic literature and emergent findings through the plane of their practical and commercial experience.

The focus group questions were a 'mirror' of the literature that we had consulted. They reflected its concerns faithfully. Yet, rather than doing so as reportage, as practically saying what the literature had to say, we instead formulated the literature's point of view as a series of questions. We turned the literature back upon itself and held it up as a looking-glass for focus group participants. Could they see the relevance or salience of these issues and concerns? In this way we were able to achieve some validation of the literature, and, on occasion, some refutation of its relevance.

How did we comprise the focus groups? Mostly, it was by a snowball effect. The Industry Task Force provided us with some leads while others came through our own contacts. The groups comprised senior representatives from commercial, industrial, governmental, financial, academic and entrepreneurial communities. In this way we were able to gather data rapidly from a wide source as well as check previously gathered data. Questions produced discussion where and when needed; hence, not every group discussed every question.

Stage Five: Cross-Analysis of Data Sources

Throughout the research process data was constantly cross-analysed for harmony or dissonance in themes. Thus lines of inquiry changed as data testing suggested. The penultimate stage of our research involved an orderly review and cross-analysis of all data in the light of research team and mentor discussions.

Stage Six: Exposure of Late Drafts

We exposed drafts to hubs and focus group participants as we neared the end of the project, and at the penultimate stage, to the Task Force research team and the project mentor.

Notes

We would like to thank Renato Orssatto for his comments on 'The Rhythm of the Saints' section of an earlier draft of this chapter. The responsibility for the content remains with the authors, of course. Stewart Clegg wrote most of the chapter, hence his name is first in the list of authors. The order of the other names is alphabetical rather than denoting seniority or authorship. An earlier version of some of these ideas is to be found in Clegg et al. (1996).

1 The term 'postmodern' will be used throughout this chapter not as an index of theoretical debates but as an empirically specific index of forms of life that are 'post', that is distinctly different from and in some sense superseding that which was 'modern'. It need not be the case that they occur, chronologically, after 'modernism'. There is no implicit theory of necessary stages at work in this chapter. Stages may be skipped where reflexivity is developed; stages may merge, seemingly seamlessly, from an earlier to a later stage, as in cases such as 'Italian fashions' that have been addressed elsewhere (Clegg 1990). The nomenclature of 'post-modern' is no more or less than a convenient shorthand for referring to empirical aspects of a world that we constitute through its address.

2 At the University of Western Sydney, for instance, surveys demonstrate that there are eighty-seven different community languages in use in the homes of the current student body: these are not the 'overseas students' but those who are resident, with their families, in Western Sydney. They are the young face of multicultural Australia.

3 The role of Modern Asian Studies in International Business at Brisbane's Griffith University, and of Latin American Studies and Asian Studies in the International MBA at The University of Western Sydney–Macarthur, are cases in point.

4 Although there is some dispute as to the extent of this self-management: see, for instance, Dantas (1994) and the review of this book in *A Tarde* by Antônio Medrado (1994).

5 The term 'post-materialist' first emerges in debates in Germany around new social movements, particularly the Greens (see Brand 1986; Papadakis 1984). It refers to the creation of a space in which values beyond the purely material can develop once material values, for food, shelter and so on, have been met. The basic notion is of a hierarchy of values.

6 Beyond simply putting scientists and technologists together in the same faculties as management academics, the further development of a new paradigm of management requires a shift towards a problem-oriented and project team curriculum that integrates management with other applications, such as science and technology, or design. The specific needs of the successful management of embryonic industries require explicit attention. Firms involved in innovation in embryonic industries look nothing like the corporate bureaucracies that are still the model for much management education, with its stress on functional knowledge and location within a predominantly Anglo-American field of practice.

Many entrepreneurs in new fields are creative artists, technological innovators or scientists. Embryonic industry members that we consulted stated that they did not have time to take on a post-first-degree management qualification. Where they did, they found some of the curriculum irrelevant for their needs. There is an additional issue. Management knowledge is required at an earlier stage of their organizational life-cycle – before, rather than after, having had to struggle to run their embryonic firm. Management education at the post-first-degree level (in honours and above) needs to shift from the education of individuals into the training of project teams. It should move from a disciplinary to a problem focus. The teams should work on projects that require using a range of skills from the team to cooperate with the teachers' design and delivery of the programme and instruct students in cooperating in the teachers' resolution of the problems faced. New project-centred and interdisciplinary technology and science degrees focused on the management of projects may be part of an answer. Such an approach should include industry alliance and permit modular training and education by either ally. The research project noted that the University of Western Sydney–Macarthur was conducting with ANSTO, ICI, and Caltex a technology management programme that had many of these features. Importantly, industry and the University developed the programme as a strategic opportunity. For reasons of economy of effort and targeting of critical consumers, within tertiary education, efforts may focus most effectively on honours and graduate students, rather than the general undergraduate student body.

References

Abernathy, W. and Clark, K. (1985) 'Innovation: Mapping the Winds of Creative Destruction', *Research Policy*, 14: 3–22.

Amara, R. (1990) 'New Directions for Innovation', *Futures*, 22(2): 142–52.

Anderson, B. (1983) *Imagined Communities: Reflections on the Origins and Spread of Nationalism*. London: Verso.

Anderson, P. and Tushman, N.L. (1990) 'Technological Discontinuities and Dominant Designs: a Cyclical Model of Technological Change', *Administrative Science Quarterly*, 35: 604–33.

Argyris, C. and Schon, D.A. (1978) *Organizational Learning: a Theory of Action Perspective*. Reading, MA: Addison-Wesley.

Barrett, M.A. and Sutcliffe, P. (1993) 'Leadership Theories: a Critique and its Implications for Management Education'. Research paper no. 24, Key Centre in Strategic Management, Queensland University of Technology, Brisbane.

Belenky, M.F., Clinchy, B.M., Goldberger, N.R. and Tarule, J.M. (1986) *Women's Ways of Knowing*. New York: Basic Books.

Benack, S. (1982) 'The Coding of Dimensions of Epistemological Thought in Young Men and Women', *Moral Education Forum*, 7(2): 297–309.

Bennis, W. (1993) 'Creative Leadership', *Management*, 10 November: 10–15

Bennis, W. and Nanus, B. (1985) *Leaders*. New York: Harper and Row.

Bianchi, P. (1993) 'The Promotion of Small Firm Clusters and Industrial Districts: European Policy Perspectives', *Journal of Industry Studies*, 1(1): 16–29.

Boam, R. and Sparrow, P. (1992) *Designing and Achieving Competency*. Maidenhead: McGraw-Hill.

Bolman, L.G. and Deal, T.E. (1991) *Reframing Organizations: Artistry, Choice and Leadership*. San Francisco: Jossey-Bass.

Brand, K.W. (1986) 'New Social Movements as a Metapolitical Challenge', *Thesis Eleven*, 15: 60–8.

Bronowski, A. (1992) *The Yellow Lady: Australian Impressions of Asia*. Melbourne: Oxford University Press.

Brown, W.B. and Karagozoglu, N. (1993) 'Leading the Way to Faster New Product Development', *Academy of Management Executive*, 7(1): 36–47.

Bryman, A. (1992) *Charisma and Leadership in Organizations*. London: Sage.

Burns, T. and Stalker, G.M. (1962) *The Management of Innovation*. London: Tavistock.

Cantley, M.F. (1986) 'Long-Term Prospects and Implications of Biotechnology for Europe: Strategic Challenge and Response', *International Journal of Technology Management*, 1(1–2): 209–29.

Chua, W.F. and Clegg, S.R. (1990) 'Professional Closure: the Case of British Nursing', *Theory and Society*, 19: 135–72.

Clegg, S.R. (1989) *Frameworks of Power*. London: Sage.

Clegg, S.R. (1990) *Modern Organizations: Organization Studies in the Postmodern World*. London: Sage.

Clegg, S.R. and Dunkerley, D. (1980) *Organization, Class and Control*. London: Routledge and Kegan Paul.

Clegg, S.R., Dunphy, D. and Redding, S.G. (eds) (1986) *The Enterprise and Management in East Asia*. Hong Kong: University of Hong Kong Press.

Clegg, S.R., Dwyer, L., Gray, J., Kemp, S. and Marceau, J. (1996) 'Managing as if Tomorrow Matters: Embryonic Industries and Management in the Twenty-first Century', in G. Palmer and S.R. Clegg (eds), *Consulting Management*, Berlin: de Gruyter. pp. 267–306.

Clegg, S.R., Dwyer, L., Gray, J., Kemp, S., Marceau, J. and O'Mara, E. (1994) *Leadership and Management needs of Embryonic Industries: A Research Report for Midgley & Company on Behalf of the Industry Task Force on Leadership and Management Skills*. Macarthur: University of Western Sydney.

Clegg, S.R., Higgins, W. and Spybey, T. (1990) 'Post-Confucianism, Social Democracy and Economic Culture', in S.R. Clegg, S.G. Redding and M. Cartner (eds), *Capitalism in Contrasting Cultures*. Berlin: de Gruyter. pp. 31–78.

Connell, R.W. and Irving, T. (1979) *Classes in Australian History*. Melbourne: Cambridge University Press.

Cooper, R. and Kleinschmidt, E. (1986) 'An Investigation into the New Product Process: Steps, Deficiencies and Impact', *Journal of Product Innovation Management*, 3: 71–85.

Daft, R.L. (1982) 'Diffusion of modern software practices: influence of centralisation and formalisation', *Management Science*, 28: 1421–31.

Daft, R.L. and Weick, K.E. (1982) 'Towards a Model of Organizations as Interpretation Systems', *Academy of Management Review*, 9(2): 284–95.

Dantas, M. (1994) *Olodum – de bloco afro a holding cultural*. Salvador: Edições de Olodum.

Dodgson, M. (1993a) 'Organizational Learning: a Review of Some Literatures', *Organization Studies*, 14(3): 375–94.

Dodgson, M. (1993b) 'Learning, Trust, and Technological Collaboration', *Human Relations*, 46(1): 77–95.

Drucker, P.F. (1990) *The New Realities*. London: Mandarin.

Drucker, P.F. (1992) 'The New Society of Organizations', *Harvard Business Review*, September–October: 95–104.

Dwyer, L. and Mellor, R. (1991) 'Organizational Environment, New Product Process Activities and Project Outcomes', *Journal of Product Innovation Management*, 8: 39–48.

Early, P.C. and Stubblebine, P. (1989) 'Intercultural Assessment of Performance Feedback', *Group and Organization Studies*, 14: 161–81.

Eriksson, I.V. (1990) 'Educating End-Users to Make More Effective Use of Information Systems', in U.R. Gattiker and L. Larwood (eds), *End-User Training*. Berlin: de Gruyter. pp. 59–102.

Evans, J. (1986) *Feminism and Political Theory*. London: Sage.

Fairtlough, G. (1993) 'Innovation and Biotechnology'. Talk presented to the Science Policy Research Unit, University of Sussex, 19 February.

Fairtlough, G. (1994) *Creative Compartments: a Design for Future Organisations*. London: Adamantine Press.

Farr, M.C. and Fischer, W.A. (1992) 'Managing International High Technology Co-Operative Projects', *R and D Management*, 22(1): 60–7.

Fischer, T., Dantas, M., Silva, M.F.L. and Mendes, V. (1992) 'Olodum – a arte e o negócio', *Anais de ANPAD*, 16.

Garrat, R. (1987) *The Learning Organization*. London: Fontana/Collins.

Gattiker, U.E. and Nelligan, T. (1988) 'Computerized Offices in Canada and the United States: Investigating Dispositional Similarities and Differences', *Journal of Organizational Behaviour*, 9: 77–96.

Gattiker, U.E. and Willoughby, K. (1993) 'Technological Competence, Ethics, and the Global Village: Cross-National Comparisons for Organization Research', in R.T. Golembiewski (ed.), *Handbook of Organizational Behaviour*. New York: Marcel Dekker. pp. 457–85.

Gilligan, C. (1982) *In a Different Voice*. Cambridge, MA: Harvard University Press.

Goldman, S.L. and Nagel, R.N. (1993) 'Management, Technology and Agility: the Emergence of a New Era in Manufacturing', *International Journal of Technology Management*, 8(1): 18–38.

Goldstone, J.A. (1987) 'Cultural Orthodoxy, Risk, and Innovations: the Divergence of East and West in the Early Modern World', *Sociological Theory*, 5: 119–35.

Gouldner, A. (1954) *Patterns of Industrial Bureaucracy*. New York: Free Press.

Greenpeace Business (1993) 'Greenpeace Plan Helps Win Sydney Olympics Bid', 16: 5.

Habermas, J. (1984) *Reason and the Rationalisation of Society*. London: Heinemann Educational.

Handy, C. (1991) *The Age of Unreason*. London: Business Books.

Hayes, R.H., Wheelwright, S.C. and Clark, K.B. (1988) *Dynamic Manufacturing: Creating the Learning Organization*. New York: Free Press.

Hedberg, B. (1981) 'How Organizations Learn and Unlearn', in P.P. Nystrom and W. Starbuck (eds), *Handbook of Organizational Design*, vol. 1. Oxford: Oxford University Press. pp. 3–27.

Helgesen, S. (1990) *The Female Advantage: Women's Ways of Leadership*. New York: Doubleday.

Hurley, A. (1991) 'Incorporating Feminist Theories into Sociological Theories of Entrepreneurship'. Paper presented at the Annual Academy of Management Meetings, Entrepreneurship Division, Miami, Florida, August.

Janssen, P. and Topsom, R.D. (1993) 'Promoting Regional Economic Development and Technology Transfer through Small Business Incubators'. Paper presented to the Small Enterprise Conference, Melbourne, September.

Kanter, R.M. (1989) 'The New Managerial Work', *Harvard Business Review*, November–December: 85–92.

Lamb, C. (1994) 'United Colors of Pelhourino', in N. Cerqueira (ed.), *Pelhourino Centro Histórico de Salvador – Bahia: A Grande Restaurada*. Salvador: Fundacão Culturaldo Estado da Bahia. pp. 40–6.

Lash, S. and Urry, J. (1994) *Economies of Signs and Space*. London: Sage.

Limerick, D. and Cunnington, B. (1993) *Managing the New Organization*, Chatswood: Business and Professional Publishing.

Littek, W. and Heisig, U. (1991) 'Competence, Control and Work Redesign: *Die Angstellte* in the Federal Republic of Germany', *Work and Occupations*, 18: 4–28.

Loden, M. (1985) *Feminine Leadership or How to Succeed in Business Without Being One of the Boys*. New York: Times Books.

Marceau, J. (ed.) (1992) *Reworking the World: Organizations, Technologies and Cultures in Comparative Perspective*. Berlin: de Gruyter.

Marceau, J. and Jureidini, R. (1992) 'Giants and Dwarves: Changing Technologies and Productive Interlinkages in Australian Manufacturing Industry', in J. Marceau (ed.), *Reworking the World: Organizations, Technologies and Cultures in Comparative Perspective*. Berlin: de Gruyter.

Marley, B. (1977) 'Exodus'. New York: Bob Marley Music/Almo Music Corp. (ASCAP).

Mathews, J. (1993) 'TCG.R and D Networks. The Triangular Strategy', *Journal of Industry Studies*, 1(1): 65–74.

McGrath, R.G. and MacMillan, I.C. (1993) 'Technology and the CEO: Seeking Tomorrow's Edge', *Chief Executive*. no. 82: 64–7.

McKee, D. (1992) 'An Organizational Learning Approach to Product Innovations', *Journal of Product Innovation Management*, 9: 232–45.

McKinsey (1993) *Emerging Exporters: Australia's High Value-Added Manufacturing Exporters*. Final Report of the Study by McKinsey and Co. for the Australian Manufacturing Council, Melbourne.

Medrado, A. (1994) 'Um antes, um depois Olodum', *A Tarde*, 15 de outobro, 11.

Papadakis, E. (1984) *The Green Movement in West Germany*. London: Croom Helm.

Perry, L.T. and Sandholtz, K.W. (1988) 'A "Liberating Form" for Radical Product Innovation', in U.E. Gattiker and L. Larwood (eds), *Studies in Technological Innovation and Human Resources. Vol. 1: Managing Technological Development*. Berlin: de Gruyter. pp. 9–31.

Peters, T. (1990) 'Get Innovative or Get Dead', *California Management Review*, Part 1, 33(1): 9–26, and Part 2, 33(2): 9–23.

Peters, T. (1992) *Liberation management*. New York: Macmillan.

Peters, T. and Waterman, R. (1982) *In Search of Excellence: Lessons from America's Best-Run Companies*. New York: Harper and Row.

Prahalad, C.K. and Hamel, G. (1990) 'The Core Competence of the Corporation', *Harvard Business Review*, May–June: 79–91.

Reich, R. (1992) *The Work of Nations: Preparing Ourselves for the 21st-Century Capitalism*. New York: A.A. Knopf.
Roberts, E.B. (1990) 'Evolving toward Product and Market Orientation: the Early Years of Technology-Based Firms', *Journal of Product Innovation Management*, 7: 274–87.
Rogers, J.L. (1988) 'New Paradigm Leadership: Integrating the Female Ethos', *Initiatives*, 51(Fall): 1–8.
Rothschild-Whitt, J. (1979) 'The Collectivist Organization: an Alternative to Rational-Bureaucratic Models', *American Sociological Review*, 44: 509–27.
Rothschild, J. and Whitt, A. (1986) *The Cooperative Workplace: Potentials and Dilemmas of Organizational Democracy and Participation*. Cambridge: Cambridge University Press.
Rothwell, R. (1992) 'Successful Industrial Innovation: Critical Factors for the 1990s', *R and D Management*, 22(3): 221–39.
Selznick, P. (1957) *Leadership in Administration*. New York: Harper and Row.
Senge, P.M. (1990) *The Fifth Discipline: the Art and Practice of the Learning Organization*. New York: Doubleday.
Senker, Jacqueline and Senker, P. (1992) 'Gaining Competitive Advantage from Information Technology', *Journal of General Management*, 17(3): 31–45.
Shanklin, W.L. and Ryans, J.K. Jr (1984) 'Organizing for High-Tech Marketing', *Harvard Business Review*, November–December: 164–71.
Stewart, V. (1992) 'Human Capital Issues in Organizational Change', *Asia Pacific Journal of Human Resources*, 30(1): 53–64.
Taylor, F.W. (1911) *Principles of Scientific Management*. New York: Harper.
Van de Ven, A. (1993) 'The Development of an Infrastructure for Entrepreneurship', *Journal of Business Venturing*, 8: 211–30.
Van Tulder, R. and Dankbaar, B. (1992) 'The Illusion of a Common Supranational Interest: Democratizing the Standardization Process in Factory Automation', in J. Marceau (ed.), *Reworking the World: Organizations, Technologies and Culture in Comparative Perspective*. Berlin: de Gruyter.
Veloso, C. (1994) 'Cateano Veloso erudito – fragmentos de entrevista coletiva á imprensa para Gideon Rosa', in N. Cerqueira (ed.), *Pelhourino Centro Histórico de Salvador – Bahia: A Grande Restaurada*. Salvador: Fundacão Culturaldo Estado da Bahia. pp. 82–4.
Weber, M. (1978) *Economy and Society*. Berkeley, CA: University of California Press.
Weiss, L. (1988) *Creating Capitalism: the State and Small Business since 1945*. Oxford: Blackwell.
Willoughby, K. (1990) *Technology Choice*, Boulder, CO: Westview Press.
Willoughby, K. (1992) *Biotechnology in New York: a Global Industry in a Global Community*. Stonybrook, NY: Center for Biotechnology, State University of New York.
Womack, J.P., Jones, D.T. and Ross, D. (1990) *The Machine that Changed the World*. New York: Macmillan.

Index

Abernathy, W., 214
academics, salary policy and inequality in Mexican universities, 110–15
Aktouf, O., 130–1
alienation, of middle management, 185–6
AMRAD, 191
Argyris, C., 143
Australia, cultural diversity and innovation in, 197–8
autobiographies of business people, 6–7, 36–7, 175
  decisiveness trait in, 39–40
  intuition trait in, 40–1
  leadership trait in, 37–9
  misunderstanding of reasons for success in, 41–2, 44
  traits as reactions to economic conditions, 42–3
  traits as self-marketing ploy, 44
automation, in car industry, 70

Bamber, G., 181
Barley, S.R., 162
Boam, R., 217
Boisvert, M., 133
Bolman, L.G., 145
boundary rationality, 2
Bourgeois, V.W., 148
branded consumer goods (BCG) companies, cultural image of, 54
Brazil
  cultural innovation in Salvador, 192–6
  and IJVs, 50–1, 52–3, 55
Britain, entrepreneurship movement in, 85, 89, 90, 91, 92
Bronowski, A., 197
bureaucracies
  entrepreneurial governance and reform of public sector, 28, 31–3
  incompatibility with globalization, 21–2, 27
bureaucratic culture
  critique of, 6, 21–2, 23, 24, 27, 28–9
  moral and ethical aspects of, 6, 29–31

rejection of private patronage and corruption, 29–30
  separation of public and private, 23, 30–1
  and social position of management, 176
business people
  autobiographies of see autobiographies of business people
  images of, 36
  popularization of entrepreneurship by, 90–1, 94
  see also entrepreneurs; managers
business re-engineering, 157, 182

Calás, M., 181
car industry
  decline of Fordist model of production, 70–1
  Toyota lean production system, 71–3, 77
  Volvo and Saab production systems, 73–5
carnival, 192–3, 195
chain relationships between organizations, 221
Champy, J., 182
Chanlat, A., 130
Chanlat, J.F., 131–2
Chapman, R.A., 32–3
Child, J., 52
Chinese organizations, in IJVs, 50, 51, 59
Clark, K., 214
cluster relationships between organizations, 221–2
cognitive complexity, 144
Cohen, M., 96
collectivist organizations, 200
commensurability debate of metaphorical analysis, 151
communications, 213–14
consultants, 161, 165–7
consumer sovereignty, in enterprise, 23
content theories of knowledge, 178
contingency theory, 12–13
core competences, 215–16
corporate identities, 54
corruption, and future of middle management, 186